Praise for *The Magi*

"Despite being an integral part of the Christmas story, the journey of the Magi in Matthew's Gospel raises more questions than it answers. For such a bewildering array of traditions, Eric Vanden Eykel's study of the history of interpretation of the Magi story is a reliable and delightful guide to these mysterious strangers who have captivated so many readers."

—Brent Landau, senior lecturer in religious studies,
University of Texas at Austin, and author of *Revelation of the Magi: The Lost Tale of the Wise Men's Journey to Bethlehem*

"This book is lucidly and wittily written, making it accessible to a broad audience while also offering fascinating new avenues for scholars interested in the Gospel of Matthew and in the Magi. Without falling into the trap of repackaging old claims or pursuing novelty for novelty's sake, Vanden Eykel takes us on a cultural journey, allowing us to better understand the Magi in their world, and therefore, to better understand their place in the story of Jesus."

—Shaily Patel, assistant professor of early Christianity,
Virginia Tech

"Eric Vanden Eykel is clearly a consummate teacher—he excels at making difficult concepts and complicated histories comprehensible—but he is also an outstanding researcher, raising all the right questions and digging for the best available answers. *The Magi* is an exceedingly engaging and accessible book that any interested reader will enjoy, but even the specialist will learn something new. Vanden Eykel's expertise in apocryphal Christian literature and tradition is evident on every page."

—Janet Spittler, associate professor of religious studies,
University of Virginia, and coauthor of *Reading Christian Apocrypha: Tradition, Interpretation, Practice*

"Vanden Eykel steps around questions of the historicity of the Magi to focus on tracing their literary journey, from their origin in the Gospel of Matthew through selected ancient and modern transformations and interpretations. With wisdom and whimsy, Vanden Eykel gently guides readers through a detailed scholarly examination of the tale and effectively demonstrates how the brevity of the Magi's story invites other writers to supplement and adapt their search for a king for new audiences and new contexts. It is a thoroughly entertaining introduction not only to the story of the Magi but to ways of reading that can be used for all biblical narratives."

—Tony Burke, professor of early Christianity, York University, and editor of *New Testament Apocrypha: More Noncanonical Scriptures*

"In this fascinating book, Eric Vanden Eykel examines the figures of the Magi from a variety of angles. Full of pertinent scholarship and historical data, *The Magi* also includes vivid descriptions of art as well as anecdotal stories that function as relatable teaching tools. Students, scholars, and congregations will appreciate this book and will never see the Magi in the same light after reading it."

—Christy Cobb, assistant professor of religion, Wingate University, and author of *Slavery, Gender, Truth, and Power in Luke-Acts and Other Ancient Narratives*

THE MAGI

THE
MAGI

Who They Were, How They've
Been Remembered, and Why
They Still Fascinate

ERIC VANDEN EYKEL

FORTRESS PRESS
MINNEAPOLIS

THE MAGI
Who They Were, How They've Been Remembered,
and Why They Still Fascinate

Cover image: Photo © Marie-Lan Nguyen / Wikimedia Commons
Cover design: Kristin Miller

Print ISBN: 978-1-5064-7373-4
eBook ISBN: 978-1-5064-7374-1

Contents

Acknowledgments

THE IDEA FOR THIS BOOK was hatched on a relatively nondescript Monday in March of 2014, in the basement of Memorial Library at Marquette University. I had defended my doctoral dissertation on the *Protevangelium of James* a few days before, and during a celebratory dinner with my committee, I was asked why I didn't talk about the appearance of the Magi in that text. They're not major characters, not by any stretch of the imagination, but they do appear toward the end. So why hadn't I discussed them? The truth is that they didn't really contribute anything to the argument that I was making in the dissertation. With that, my committee agreed. But, I continued, a study of the reception history of the Magi would be a lot of fun. "Sounds like you have an idea for a new book!" my director exclaimed. Having just finished a dissertation, I replied that perhaps an article was a bit more palatable at this point. He huffed and rolled his eyes sarcastically, and with his characteristic grin, remarked, "Well, whatever you do, get started first thing on Monday. But first, be sure to take the weekend to relax!"

Out of sheer force of habit, I went to the library the following Monday. Without a dissertation to write, though, I found myself wandering around a bit like . . . well, a person without a dissertation to write. So I figured why not go ahead and see what sorts of things had been written about the Magi. It couldn't hurt, right? An hour later, I was seated at a large table surrounded by a dozen commentaries on Matthew. As I thumbed through them, I found that they repeated the same talking points about the Magi: who they were, where they were from, why they were interested in Jesus, and so on. Most suggested the same Old Testament passages as possible allusions, and they generally came to the same conclusion about what the larger point of the story was supposed to be. Of course, this wasn't surprising because that is often how it goes with biblical commentaries. A search for journal articles was slightly more fruitful. By far the most "creative" approaches to the Magi came through a simple internet search. A few online queries returned a handful of websites and self-published books on the Knights Templar and other "secret brotherhoods." The claim that the star was a UFO was more common than I expected. My big takeaway from that day was that when you were interested in studying the Magi, you had two options: more of the same or a bit nutty. Works that walked the line between these two poles were apparently few and far between.

Over the next few weeks, I continued to read and think about the Magi. I thought about how Matthew would have wanted his readers to imagine them and why he bothered to even include this odd story in the first place. Because it *is* an odd story, if you've ever stopped and thought about it. But then, during that research, I found myself thinking about other texts that came after Matthew, texts whose authors had obviously read Matthew's story but then retold it and updated a few details in the process. Some of these texts give the Magi a specific homeland. Some give them names. In some of them, the Magi receive gifts back from Mary and Jesus. I also started thinking about the ways in which the Magi had been used for different rhetorical purposes in the first few centuries of early Christianity. How had authors used their story to make and support theological claims? As I continued to explore, I found myself examining a range of other materials, from Renaissance paintings, to early Christian funerary art, to the poetry of T. S. Eliot, and even to the lyrics of a James Taylor song. It finally occurred to me that my director was right: this needs to be a book. So here we are.

I take full responsibility for these words, but I would be a fool to pretend that I wrote any of them by myself. I am supremely thankful for Ryan Hemmer, my editor at Fortress Press and longtime friend from graduate school. From the earliest stages of this book's proposal all the way through the editing of the manuscript, Ryan helped me take years of quite random thoughts about the Magi and turn them into something that people might enjoy reading. He also found creative ways to turn the heat up gently when my writing stalled (which it did). I am also grateful for friends and colleagues who have listened to me talk at length about the Magi for several years now and for those who have asked questions, challenged ideas, read drafts, and given input that has made the project stronger and clearer. Thanks especially to Tony Burke, Christy Cobb, Tim Daniels, Nicole and Mark Greer Golda, Michael Hancock-Parmer, Brandon Hawk, Chanelle and Mat Henderson, Julian Hills, Doug Iverson, Kalpana Jain, Michael Kahn, Brent Landau, Candida Moss, Shaily Patel, Jason Powell, Bradley Rice, Janet Spittler, and Stephen Young. I owe special thanks to my friend and colleague

David "Chopper" Campbell, who read through the prepublication manuscript and offered helpful feedback and some much-needed encouragement in the final stretch of writing. My parents, Cathy and Ike Vanden Eykel, and my in-laws, Louise and Brian Koranda, are consistently among my most enthusiastic supporters, and I hope they like this book more than the last one (which, I will admit, was a bit technical). To Jane, Sidney, and Seth: I am thankful beyond words for frozen yogurt, baseball games, long hikes, school drop-offs and pickups, bedtime routines, and all the ways that you pull me away from work and back into the real world. I love all of you so much more than I will ever be able to express. And to Ellen: in retrospect, choosing to write this book during a pandemic may not have been my brightest idea. It has certainly made our lives even crazier than they normally are. Thank you for pretending to care about this book even when you had more important things on your mind.

This book is dedicated to the memory of my uncle, Stu Spencer, one of the wisest, kindest, and most creative people I have had the pleasure of knowing. When I was about ten, he arrived at our house on Christmas Day with some special gifts that he had made for my mom and grandmother: blue glass vases etched with silhouettes of the Magi and the words "wise men still seek him." I remember being fascinated by these vases, and not only because of the incredible skill that it took to create them. My children's Bible conveyed the story of the Magi as if it were straightforward, a matter of historical fact, something that you just learned about, accepted, and then moved on from. In other words, my children's Bible presented the story of the Magi in the most boring way possible. Uncle Stu's vases prompted me to think in a different way about these familiar and yet mysterious characters from Matthew's Gospel. He brought the Magi into the present and cast them on that blue glass as models for imitation. Models not of faith but of a perpetual and nagging curiosity. Because for Uncle Stu, the thing that "wise" people seek isn't comfort or certainty, or some shiny object at the end of a long and hard journey. The thing that wise people seek is the long and hard journey itself, and all the questions and challenges that come with it. In that journey, there's a certain beauty to be found. Thank you, Uncle Stu.

Introduction

ON THE FOURTH THURSDAY OF November, many residents of the United States celebrate "Thanksgiving," a national holiday during which tables around the country are filled with turkeys, casseroles, and some variety of cranberry relish that simultaneously mystifies and comforts. Intended to celebrate the good fortune of the Puritans who arrived on the eastern shores of North America in the early 1620s, Thanksgiving in the United States also coincides with the start of the Christmas season. And so, in the wake of the Thanksgiving meal, many families begin decorating their homes with lights, trees, and of course, nativities.

A nativity is a miniature representation of the birth of Jesus. Some are small enough to sit atop the mantel of a fireplace, while some are large enough that they do better in the front yard. Details vary, but all nativities share the same basic scene and cast of characters.

Imagine a nativity in your mind. Place yourself within the scene. Where are you? Who is there with you? What are people doing?

If you are at all familiar with the traditional stories of Jesus's birth—whether from reading the New Testament, attending Christmas pageants, or watching the Hallmark Channel during the holidays—you imagined yourself in a small town called Bethlehem. But what about the specifics? Did you find yourself in a stable? If so, where was it? Behind a crowded hotel? Down a dark alley? On the edge of a starlit field? Or perhaps you saw yourself in a house? If so, what sort of house was it? Was it elegant? Was it simple? Or maybe, when you imagined yourself at the birth of Jesus, you imagined yourself in a rugged cave, just outside the city. If that's you, then what sort of cave was it? Was it deep in the side of a mountain? Or was it more of a rocky outcropping?

Next, let's ask the question of who (and what) is there with you. We can start with the obvious cast of characters. Jesus is there (it's his birth, after all!), and you probably imagined Mary, his mother, kneeling nearby. His father Joseph stands somewhere off to the side, perhaps looking a bit disinterested or even confused. But who else was there? Was there an angel? Were there farm animals? A donkey, perhaps? Maybe a few lambs? An ox? What about other humans? Are there shepherds? If so, how many? How are they dressed? What are they doing? Do you see anyone else? Anyone at all?

You also likely saw three older men somewhere in the scene. They were either riding in on camels or kneeling before the newborn Jesus. It is possible that they were dressed in elegant, exotic clothes, vastly different from what others in the scene are wearing. They may have been wearing crowns, and they may have had a darker skin tone than other people in the scene. You probably imagined each of these men holding some sort of elaborately decorated container, and you probably are not surprised that they appeared in your vision. I'm not surprised either. After all, you are currently reading a book about them.

Strangers from the East

The gift-bearing strangers who visit Jesus after his birth are an integral component of the traditional Christmas story, and any nativity would seem incomplete without them. Aside from Jesus, Mary, and a handful of others, there are few characters in the history of Christianity who have exercised a more profound influence on our collective imaginations. Their story has been told and retold for centuries, in many kinds of media and for a variety of purposes. Outside of the New Testament, they appear in several early Christian texts, both as characters and as sermon illustrations. They have captured the attention of artists and inspired thousands of paintings, mosaics, and sculptures. They go by different titles and names. Some people refer to them as "the wise men," while some prefer "kings." Still others may have grown up referring to them as "sages" or "astrologers" or by their traditional names: Caspar, Melchior, and Balthasar. But in the New Testament, they are simply "Magi."[1]

The fact that the Magi feature so prominently in the Christian tradition would seem to suggest that they are major characters in the New Testament. But this is not the case. The story of Jesus's birth appears in two of the four New Testament Gospels—Matthew and Luke—and the Magi appear in only one of them. Luke's Gospel begins with a dedication (Luke 1:1–4), the announcement to Elizabeth and Zechariah of the birth of John the Baptist (Luke 1:5–24), the announcement to Mary of the birth of Jesus (Luke 1:26–38), Mary's visit to Elizabeth (Luke 1:39–56), and the birth of John

---

1 Translations of biblical texts and other ancient sources are my own unless noted otherwise.

the Baptist (Luke 1:57–80). Joseph and Mary then begin their trek from Nazareth to Bethlehem to register in a census, and while they are there, Mary gives birth to Jesus. She uses a feeding trough as a cradle, since "there was no place for them in the inn" (Luke 2:7 NRSV). After this, angels announce the birth to nearby shepherds, and the shepherds travel to Bethlehem to visit (Luke 2:8–20). Luke's account of Jesus's birth ends without even a hint of any Magi coming to visit.

Matthew, by contrast, begins with a lengthy genealogy that traces Jesus's family line back through King David, all the way to Abraham (Matt 1:1–17). The goal of this genealogy is to establish in the reader's mind that Jesus's story is inseparable from the story of Israel and to emphasize that Jesus is a descendant of King David. Matthew then introduces Mary and Joseph. The couple is not yet married, but Mary is pregnant (Matt 1:18). Joseph is troubled by how to handle the situation until an angel comes to him in a dream and tells him, "That which is begotten in her is from the Holy Spirit" (Matt 1:20). Joseph and Mary then wed and Jesus is born shortly thereafter. It is at this point that Matthew tells the story of the Magi.

Matthew's story of the Magi spans twelve short verses, and within those twelve verses, details are sparse. The Magi come to Jerusalem and Bethlehem "from the East" (Matt 2:1). They are led there by a star, and their intention is to honor a king (Matt 2:2). They have a brief run-in with King Herod before they make it to Jesus (Matt 2:3–8), and after they present their gifts of gold, frankincense, and myrrh, they are warned by an angel to go home by a different route (Matt 2:11–12). Neither the Magi nor their gifts are mentioned in the remainder of Matthew's Gospel. If you removed these twelve verses, you would hardly know that they had been there in the first place. Put simply, Matthew's story of the Magi contains a lot less than most readers remember.

So who are the Magi in Matthew? How many are there? Where do they come from? What is the nature of the star that leads them? Why are they interested in Jesus? What made them choose these specific gifts? Why does Matthew bother to tell their story in the first place? What's the point? All these questions are important, yet Matthew doesn't address any of them explicitly. Instead, he leaves it up to his readers to connect the dots. Various attempts to do just this have produced no shortage of reasoned studies and wild speculations, and for nearly two thousand years, the Magi have journeyed through the minds of authors, readers, theologians, biblical scholars, and artists. This is a book about that journey.

History, Faith, Imagination

This is not the first book ever written about the Magi. Far from it, in fact.[2] But my hope is that it is different from other books that you may have encountered on the topic. Many authors who have ventured to write about the Magi have done so with the aim of figuring out who the Magi *actually* were. Where did they *actually* come from? Why were they *actually* interested in Jesus? These studies presume that the Magi were real people who visited Jesus and his family in Bethlehem and that Matthew's account of their visit is, at least for the most part, "historically accurate." When it comes to fantastic and legendary stories in the Bible, questions like this

---

2   A few recent examples include Adrian G. Gilbert, *Magi: The Quest for a Secret Tradition* (London: Bloomsbury, 1996); Richard C. Trexler, *The Journey of the Magi: Meanings in History of a Christian Story* (Princeton, NJ: Princeton University Press, 1997); Michael R. Molnar, *The Star of Bethlehem: The Legacy of the Magi* (New Brunswick, NJ: Rutgers University Press, 1999); and Mark Allan Powell, *Chasing the Eastern Star: Adventures in Biblical Reader-Response Criticism* (Louisville, KY: Westminster John Knox, 2001); see also the essays in Peter Barthel and George van Kooten, eds., *The Star of Bethlehem and the Magi: Interdisciplinary Perspectives from Experts on the Ancient Near East, the Greco-Roman World, and Modern Astronomy* (Leiden: Brill, 2015).

are frequently at the forefront of readers' minds. Did this actually happen? And if not, what *did* happen?

I would like to suggest that while questions about historicity and accuracy can be alluring, they are far from the most important ones that we can ask of Matthew or of biblical texts more broadly. When the pursuit of such questions is coupled with an inability or a refusal to acknowledge when there simply is no compelling evidence for a story's historicity, the studies that result are often an unhelpful mix of boring, fallacious, and even absurd.[3] Most importantly, though, studies that focus on and obsess over questions related to the historical accuracy of the Magi story tend to miss questions that are more important and meaningful.[4] What did this story mean to Matthew? What could it have meant to his earliest audiences? And why has it continued to fascinate readers for nearly two thousand years?

In the pages that follow, my aim is to examine the Magi not as historical figures but as fictional characters in Matthew's narrative. For the purposes of this book, I assume that the Gospel according to Matthew is first and foremost a work of literature and that the

---

3 Dwight Longenecker's recent book on the Magi (*Mystery of the Magi: The Quest to Identify the Three Wise Men* [Washington, DC: Regnery, 2017]) is a case in point. Longenecker assumes that some historical event must undergird Matthew's story, and this assumption leads him to odd places. He argues, for example, that Matthew's Gospel was originally written in Hebrew to Jews who were living in Judea in the first century. None of this is correct. On the basis of a long string of false and idiosyncratic arguments like these, Longenecker concludes not only that the Magi were Nabateans but that Paul the apostle visited them after his "conversion" experience. Here, Longenecker's preoccupation with historicity leads him to a position that is as strange as it is irrelevant to the meaning of the Magi story.

4 Some scholars maintain that there is some historical event behind Matthew's story, but they acknowledge that the question of historicity is secondary. Donald Hagner argues, for example, that while "it need not be denied that a historical tradition underlies the passage, the genre of this pericope continues in the vein of haggadah wherein the historical narrative finds its primary purpose in the conveying of theological truth. The way in which the story is told is calculated to bring the reader to further theological comprehension of the significance of Jesus as well as to anticipate a number of themes or motifs that are to recur repeatedly in the Gospel before the story is over" (*Matthew 1–13* [Dallas: Word Books, 1993], 25). Craig Keener argues similarly, "The story more likely than not preserves a historical core; but with insufficient historical evidence to offer a further judgment, I will focus more primarily on the narrative's theology, which is Matthew's focus in any case" (*The Gospel of Matthew: A Socio-rhetorical Commentary* [Grand Rapids, MI: Eerdmans, 2009], 98).

ultimate source of the Magi story is therefore Matthew's own vivid imagination.[5] If there is even a faint historical memory behind the story of the Magi—that is, if people from the East really did come to visit Jesus in the wake of his birth—then that event is inaccessible to us today, and I remain unconvinced that it is possible to "prove" that the story of the Magi is "true" in the sense of it being "historically accurate." But on the other side of that coin, I am also not sure how one would go about *disproving* the accuracy of a story like this, if that were in fact one's goal. By approaching the Magi as characters in a work of literature, we allow ourselves to focus on the material that *is* accessible to us—namely, the story of the Magi as it is presented to us in the text of Matthew's Gospel and the tradition it inspired.

While I do not consider Matthew's Magi story to be "historical," the approach that I take in this book is not incompatible with the claim that there is some type of historical event lurking beneath the story. I imagine that more than a few readers who acquire this book will do so with a belief that the Magi were actual people who lived two thousand years ago and that they were somehow mysteriously drawn to Jerusalem and Bethlehem after the birth of Jesus. I want to be clear that it is not my intention to discourage or destroy any beliefs about the Magi that readers may bring to this book. Beliefs are, by definition, positions that are maintained in the absence of empirical proof. Once something is "proven" or "disproven," it becomes either fact or falsehood. One does not "believe" something that has been proven to be untrue, for example, but neither does one "believe" something that has been proven true. I do

---

5 There are always assumptions at work in scholarship. This is not something to bemoan, but it is something to be transparent about. It is possible that Matthew inherited the framework of this story from a pre-Matthean source, but that is another conversation for another time. Regardless of where the story comes from, it is in its present form a thoroughly Matthean episode.

not "believe" that the earth is flat because its roundness is a matter of observation for those who have traveled to space and a matter of evidence for those who have not. I also do not "believe" that my youngest daughter enjoys the taste of Nutella; I know for a fact that she likes it because she requests it every morning for breakfast.

As a scholar of early Christian literature, my goal in this book is to examine the story of the Magi as it exists in Matthew and to understand its literary and theological significance in that context. And questions about the literary and theological significance of the Magi are not tied to the question of whether they actually existed. Any reader should therefore be able to find something of value in this book, regardless of their stance on the story's historicity or lack thereof.

Plotting Our Journey

Our exploration of the Magi proceeds over the course of seven chapters. In chapter 1, I set some methodological parameters related to the question of "meaning." In this chapter, I argue that a reader's perceived familiarity with a story can sometimes get in the way of understanding it and that an integral step to studying any ancient text is to examine that text in its ancient context. I suggest that this requires our attention to not only what an author may have meant when they wrote it but also how their readers would have understood what they were reading. In chapter 2, the question shifts to translation. In this chapter, I examine a few Greek words in the Magi story in order to come to a better understanding of what these words may have meant to Matthew and his earliest readers. I close this chapter with my own translation of the Magi story.

Chapter 3 explores the complicated nature of the word *magoi* in Matthew's first-century context. A survey of ancient literature reveals that this word doesn't have a single meaning or connotation.

It is used with reference to respected and highly trained religious professionals, for example, but also as a synonym for *charlatan*. Is it possible to tell what meaning Matthew may have intended? The focus of chapter 4 is the Magi story as we find it in Matthew. I begin by examining the immediate literary context of the Magi story and by taking a closer look at several facets of the story, including the star that leads them, the words they speak to Herod, and the gifts they bring to Jesus. In this chapter, I highlight the story's "political" nature, which I argue is meant to portray Jesus as the rightful king of the Judeans.

In chapter 5, we transition to a body of narrative texts commonly called "noncanonical" or "apocryphal" Christian literature. These texts present the story of the Magi in ways that are often quite different from Matthew. By examining their differences, we discover what sorts of questions their authors had about the Magi as well as what they found valuable about their story. These texts also evidence the rich diversity that characterizes early Christianity, and they serve as important reminders that even the earliest readers of the Magi story didn't always agree on how to understand it.

The focus of chapter 6 is on patristic understandings of the Magi story. In this chapter, we examine letters, hymns, sermons, and commentaries that use the Magi to bolster various theological claims. One of the striking things that emerges in the course of this chapter is the frequency with which the story of the Magi has been used toward nefarious ends, including the fostering of anti-Jewish attitudes among Christians. In chapter 7, we fast forward quite a few years and examine some more recent literary appropriations of the Magi. These include two short stories, a novel, and a recent children's book. In this final chapter, we discover new readings of the story, but ones that are nonetheless characterized by familiar themes.

1

Authors, Readers, and Meanings

IN 1915, THE METHODIST EPISCOPAL minister Jesse Lyman Hurlbut (1843–1930) published what would become an instant and enduring classic: *Hurlbut's Life of Christ for Young and Old: A Complete Life of Christ Written in Simple Language, Based on the Gospel Narrative.* As the title and subtitle suggest, his goal was to present the life and ministry of Jesus in a way that would be accessible to readers of all ages and reading levels. The book is in many ways a combination children's Bible and biblical commentary, with stories and exposition woven together seamlessly.

Hurlbut's *Life of Christ* is also a prime example of a Gospel harmony, an attempt to reconcile the often disparate narratives and chronologies of Matthew, Mark, Luke, and John and to produce one smooth and consistent story. Hurlbut is far from the first to attempt such a monumental task; even as early as the second century CE, a Syrian theologian named Tatian (ca. 120–80 CE) used the four canonical Gospels to construct a single, master story. His work is commonly called the *Diatessaron*, which in Greek means "out of four." The *Diatessaron* survives in only fragmentary form today, but it was enormously influential in Syria during the earliest centuries of the Christian movement. Hurlbut's *Life of Christ* has likewise been a huge success, and even a hundred or so years after its initial publication, it remains standard reading in many contexts.

In a brief preface, Hurlbut outlines his aims for the book: "to tell the story of Jesus Christ in a manner that will be attractive to both young and old" and "to adapt the narrative to the understanding of a child of ten years, so that he will not need to ask the meaning of a sentence or a word" (3).[1] The most striking part of this preface, however, is where Hurlbut specifies that he has taken great caution to avoid adding anything to the biblical stories: "In order that this book may not lead its younger readers or listeners away from the Bible, but directly toward it, no imaginary scenes or conversations have been introduced. The design has been to write the biography of Jesus, not a romance founded upon his life" (3). On the surface, this claim seems innocuous enough, but it becomes curious when one considers that Hurlbut's *Life of Christ* weighs in at approximately five hundred pages, making it significantly longer than the four New Testament Gospels combined. As we will see, part of the issue is precisely the amount of material that Hurlbut ends up adding to the stories.

---

1 Page numbers in this section correspond with Jesse Lyman Hurlbut, *Hurlbut's Life of Christ for Young and Old: A Complete Life of Christ Written in Simple Language, Based on the Gospel Narrative* (Philadelphia: John C. Winston, 1915).

Delusions of Objectivity

Hurlbut tells his story of the Magi in chapters 9 and 10 of his *Life of Christ*. He begins with the assumption that they are gentiles (non-Jews) who come from Parthia, which in the first century CE was located in present-day Iran/Persia. He writes that the Parthians were "like the Jews" in their distaste for human-made images and that they were monotheists who "worshipped the One God of all the earth" (66). The Magi who come to Bethlehem, he argues, were Parthian astrologers who had committed their lives to the study of the stars. Their journey is recounted in dramatic terms. They travel through a barren wasteland for an entire year, crossing both the rivers Tigris and Euphrates and riding most of the way on camels. All the while, their gazes are fixed faithfully on the star that dangles in front of them, leading them westward (68).

When they arrive in Jerusalem, they inquire of every person they meet, "Can you tell us where is to be found the little child who is born to be the King of the Jews? We have seen his star in the east, and we have come to do him honor" (66). They make their way to King Herod, who is alarmed by the visitors' questions and vows secretly to murder Jesus when he finds him to secure his kingdom from any attempted overthrow (69). As the Magi depart Jerusalem for Bethlehem, they are elated when the star reappears in the sky. "Look," they say. "There is the star once more! See it in the sky just before us!" (70). The star leads them to the house where Jesus is, and they enter and bow before him, presenting their gifts (70–71). Hurlbut's account of the Magi ends at the start of chapter 10, when the Magi are warned in a dream, "Do not go to meet king Herod again. He is no friend to this princely child. Return to your own land by some other way, and do not let Herod know it" (73).

Chapter 9 ends with a Judeophobic aside from Hurlbut: "While in [Jesus's] own land only a few people showed their gladness at the coming of their king, the strangers from a distant country came to pay him homage. We would have thought that some of the learned Jews, who could tell King Herod where the King was born, might have come with the Wise Men to see him. But these great scholars really cared very little about Jesus. They stayed home and soon forgot the men of the east, their journey, and their question" (71).[2]

While Hurlbut claims in the preface that his *Life of Christ* presents stories about Jesus just as we find them in the New Testament, even a cursory skim of the volume reveals that this is not accurate. The book is replete with examples of modifications, expansions, and redactions of the biblical stories. To be sure, many of these are relatively innocent and not of much consequence. In his retelling of the Magi story, for example, when the star reappears south of Jerusalem, he has the Magi remark to one another, "There is the star once more! See it in the sky just before us!" (70). Matthew, by contrast, doesn't specify what they said, if they said anything at all. He simply notes that "they celebrated with a joy that was exceedingly great" (Matt 2:10). What Hurlbut has done in this example is imagine what the joy of the Magi would sound like if it were vocalized. And one could make the argument that an expansion like this serves to clarify Matthew's story, not modify it. It doesn't affect much about how readers understand the story in Matthew.

---

2 For the purposes of this book, *Judeophobia* is an umbrella term that encompasses a range of prejudicial and discriminatory attitudes toward Jews and Judaism, including anti-Judaism, anti-Semitism, supersessionism, and so on. I agree with Peter Schäfer's assessment that *Judeophobia* is an appropriate term for anti-Jewish attitudes because it reflects the fact that these attitudes are driven by both "hatred and fear" (*Judeophobia: Attitudes toward the Jews in the Ancient World* [Cambridge, MA: Harvard University Press, 1997], 11). For a more recent defense of the term, see Jonathan Judaken, introduction to "Rethinking Anti-Semitism," *American Historical Review* 123, no. 4 (October 2018): 1133.

There are other instances, however, where Hurlbut's modifications and commentary have enormous implications for how readers understand the story. His characterization of King Herod as a paranoid and feeble ruler who is determined from the beginning to murder Jesus is one possible way of reading Matthew's story. But it is not the only way to read it, and in fact, it is not even necessarily the most natural reading. Moreover, Hurlbut's presumption that the Magi were gentiles recasts Matthew's story as one that is about Jewish rejection of Jesus from the moment of his birth. Hurlbut's Judeophobic conclusion at the end of chapter 9 makes clear that this is the interpretation that he has in mind. Is it possible that this was Matthew's underlying message? Yes, without question. But there are far more interesting ways to read and make sense of the Magi story.

Hurlbut's *Life of Christ* is no anomaly, and one can see similar harmonization, expansion, and commentary in many other children's Bibles and Gospel harmonies. Hurlbut likely believed every word that he wrote in the preface. My sense is that he saw his retellings of Gospel narratives as sticking quite closely to the texts themselves and that he considered his commentary as clarifying details that were already present in some form on the page. Yet as we have seen, his story of the Magi is filled with details that are nowhere to be found in Matthew's Gospel.

Familiarity Breeds Unfamiliarity

I do not want anyone to think that I am attempting to bully Hurlbut or that I am suggesting that his motivations were sinister. I begin with Hurlbut because he is a prominent example of a reader who by every estimation is both earnest and sincere but whose familiarity with something has blinded them to what's there and what isn't.

This does not make Hurlbut unique, however; to the contrary, it makes him quite normal.

The more familiar we become with something, or at least the more familiar we *think* we are with something, the easier it is for us to lose sight of that something's finer details. I don't tend to notice how quickly my children grow, for example, because I see them every day, and so I don't perceive that they're just a little taller every morning. But their grandparents do notice because they see them less frequently, and so the changes from visit to visit are more dramatic. Familiarity breeds unfamiliarity.

This phenomenon is well known to anyone who has ever taught or taken a biblical studies course. Every semester, my students will swear up and down that Adam and Eve take a bite of an apple in Genesis, that Moses's mother floats him down the Nile River in Exodus, and that Saul's name is changed to Paul when Jesus appears to him on the road and knocks him off his donkey. They are often astonished to find that none of these details are present in the biblical texts; all of them are fabrications. If you don't believe me, you can check for yourself. The fruit in Genesis 3:6 is just "fruit." In Exodus 2:3, Moses's mother places him and his basket on the shore of the river, among the reeds. There is no donkey in Acts 9, and Saul's name is still Saul even after he is baptized in Damascus. His name doesn't change to Paul until several chapters later, in Acts 13:9, and there it happens without any real significance or commentary.

Artistic representations are often to blame for such misreadings; painters, sculptors, and filmmakers who deal with biblical narratives and themes routinely introduce foreign elements into their productions, sometimes by accident and other times on purpose. These elements are then incorporated into the popular imaginations of readers and then read back into the stories as if they were there all along. Nearly every Hollywood version of the Moses story, for example, has Moses's mother floating him down the Nile River in a basket.[3] When I ask my students to read Exodus 2 and then narrate that story from memory, they often import this foreign detail without realizing it. Something similar happens when we discuss the birth of Jesus according to Luke. Many insist that in Luke, Jesus is born in a stable, when in fact, Luke never mentions a stable. He only says that Jesus sleeps in a feeding trough (or manger) and that there was no room for Joseph and Mary in the place that they tried initially.[4] Readers supply the detail of the stable because this is what they've seen in nativity scenes and because, on some level, the stable helps them make sense of why there would have been a feeding trough available for Jesus to sleep in.

This is simply how reading works. *All* stories are read in light of what a reader brings to the text. This includes their own sense of familiarity with that text, their perceptions and experiences of the world, as well as their knowledge of other stories and media. Every reader brings a certain amount of interpretive baggage to the task of interpretation. Our perspectives always affect how we make sense of what we read. This dynamic only becomes a problem when it is not acknowledged, when a reader is piled over with baggage but doesn't believe that they have any. Interpretive problems arise not because we have baggage but because we pretend that we don't.

So if objectivity is an illusion, and if readers are unable to completely escape whatever baggage they bring to the task of interpretation, how then are we going to read Matthew's story of the Magi?

---

3 See the classic film *The Ten Commandments*, directed by Cecil B. DeMille (1956; Hollywood, CA: Paramount Pictures) as well as *The Prince of Egypt*, directed by Brenda Chapman, Steve Hickner, and Simon Wells (1998; Universal City, CA: DreamWorks) as two examples.

4 Stephen Carlson notes that the Greek word often translated as "inn" (*kataluma*) is far more ambiguous. He suggests translating it as "place to stay," as a reference to "a cramped marital chamber attached to [Joseph's] father's or other relative's village house" ("The Accommodations of Joseph and Mary in Bethlehem: Κατάλυμα in Luke 2.7," *New Testament Studies* 56, no. 3 [2010]: 342).

My suggestion is that we aim to read this story as readers with baggage, but with first-century baggage.

Reading Matthew with First-Century Eyes

Biblical scholars read and study ancient texts from a range of interpretive approaches. And there are frequent debates within the scholarly community about these approaches and their merits (or lack thereof). Yet much modern biblical scholarship is united over a concern for what is usually labeled "authorial intent," or what an author meant to convey to their readers when they put pen to paper. But while authorial intent is in many ways a sort of unifying force, not everyone agrees on how best to address it.

Many conceive of authorial intent as *the* critical question that should drive all scholarly inquiry into biblical literature. From this perspective, the question of how Matthew understood his story of the Magi is the primary one; all others are peripheral and interesting only to the extent that they shed light on Matthew's own understanding. On the other hand, some consider the question of Matthew's intended meaning to be both unanswerable and irrelevant; we don't have access to Matthew's mind, but we do have access to how readers, both contemporary and historical, have understood his Gospel.

I imagine that most biblical scholars would likely locate their own methodologies somewhere between these two poles. The question of the author's intended meaning is important, but the same is true for the question of how texts have been understood by readers. I do not wish to outline or engage in the ongoing debate between author- and reader-centric approaches to biblical literature. Instead, here are a few "guiding principles" that will be helpful as we continue to set the stage for our study of Matthew's Magi.

First, with any ancient text (biblical or otherwise), we must keep in mind that we are always dealing with authors who cannot confirm for us whether our interpretations of their texts are "good" or "bad." In the case of a text like Matthew's Gospel, we are dealing with a piece of literature whose goal is not to explain every contour of every narrative episode in detail but rather to invite readers into the theological world that its author is attempting to create for them. There are some instances in Matthew's story where he does explain why he is including certain details. The so-called fulfillment formulae fall into this category. After the angel has visited Joseph to inform him of the nature of Mary's pregnancy, for example, Matthew adds that "this happened in order to fulfill what the Lord had said through the prophet: 'Look, the virgin will conceive and bear a son, and they will name him Emmanuel, which means God is with us'" (Matt 1:22–23). Similar citations occur ten times in Matthew's Gospel,[5] and they leave little doubt in the reader's mind regarding the author's intention. In all these cases, the author is effectively saying, "This is the reason why I've just told you this story."

But there are also plenty of instances—like the story of the Magi—where there are no fulfillment formulae and where Matthew's meaning is less than clear. In these instances, we can only hypothesize about what Matthew may have meant. We then test these hypotheses, refine them, and start again. If the object of our search is "what Matthew meant when he wrote his Magi story," then our search is never-ending because we can never be certain that we've reached the author's purpose. In the absence of Matthew's agreement or disagreement with our reading, we can never know whether we have captured and articulated his intended meaning accurately. Any claim to have discovered "what an author meant"

---

5 In Matt 1:23; 2:15, 18, 23; 4:15–16; 8:17; 12:18–21; 13:35; 21:5; 27:9–10.

should therefore always be framed in terms of what is "plausible" or "likely" rather than what is "definite."

Second, when we restrict our search for a text's "meaning" to the question of what its author meant when they wrote it, we ignore a crucial piece of the interpretive puzzle: the person reading the text. All texts are media of communication between authors and readers, and this is as true for Matthew's Gospel as it is for grocery lists, love letters, short stories, graffiti, and phone books. Texts communicate things. Perhaps this is most obvious when we are reading letters (or emails or tweets) that are addressed to us or to other people. We read these messages as intending to convey something, regardless of whether what they're trying to convey is clear or obscure. And with these messages, we have an almost instinctual awareness that what the author of the message *intended* to say actually does matter.

Yet words may sometimes be understood in ways that an author did *not* intend, and these unintended meanings are not insignificant. A poorly chosen word or phrase in an email may offend a reader, regardless of whether the author of that email meant to offend. What an author means to convey by telling a story remains an important question, even if we cannot answer it with certainty. This preliminary step helps us ground our interpretation in something, lest we fall into the trap of making someone else's words convey whatever we want them to.

If my spouse asks me whether it feels cold in the living room, there are several ways that I could interpret her intended meaning. She may want me to go and turn the heat up, grab her a blanket, or put another log on the fire. She may also want me to call a technician to come and inspect our furnace and make sure it is functioning properly. Regardless of what she means, all of these interpretations are legitimate, potential meanings of "Does it feel cold in here to you?" It is unlikely that she would ask me a question like this and intend for me to go to the kitchen and clean the floor or make her a sandwich. In all acts of communication, whether spoken or written, contemporary or ancient, we must first ask what an author means by the words that they are using. But we must also acknowledge that the question of how readers interpreted and understood those words is an essential piece of the puzzle.

Finally, because of what we know about how texts are written and understood, questions about what an author meant to convey in a particular text and how a reader may understand that text are not mutually exclusive. When an author writes something, they do so by incorporating various elements of their own experiences and knowledge of other stories and texts. Similarly, readers interpret and understand what they read in light of their own experiences and in the context of their own knowledge of other stories and texts. The Italian literary critic and novelist Umberto Eco used the concept of the "cultural encyclopedia" to explain this phenomenon. Eco conceived of the cultural encyclopedia as a vast, labyrinthine framework within which literary texts make sense.[6] When authors write, they draw from and allude to parts of the encyclopedia that they are familiar with. If we imagine the encyclopedia as a type of labyrinth, the author's text then becomes a map or guide through it. Readers who are familiar with the same parts of the labyrinth that an author draws from will follow along easily, whereas those who are less familiar may have a more difficult time and will sometimes even get lost.

---

6   See Umberto Eco, *Semiotics and the Philosophy of Language*, Advances in Semiotics (Bloomington: Indiana University Press, 1984), 81. New Testament scholar Werner Kelber describes the concept of "tradition" in similar terms: "Tradition . . . is a circumambient contextuality or *biosphere* in which speaker and hearers live. It includes texts and experiences transmitted through or derived from texts. . . . Tradition in this broadest sense is largely an ascertainable and invisible nexus of references and identities from which people draw sustenance, in which they live, and in relation to which they make sense of their lives. This invisible biosphere is at once the most elusive and foundational feature of tradition" ("Jesus and Tradition: Words in Time, Words in Space," in *Imprints, Voiceprints, and Footprints of Memory: Collected Essays of Werner Kelber*, Resources for Biblical Study 74 [Atlanta: Society of Biblical Literature, 2013], 127).

When I am in the classroom, I'm tasked with leading my students through a cultural encyclopedia that we share (although it is usually quite clear that we are familiar with different parts of it). Our cultural encyclopedia includes whatever materials I have assigned for class on a given day, but it also includes other texts, movies, music, television shows, and so on. When I communicate with students through lectures and discussions these days, a reference to Michael Scott is far more likely to make my students chuckle than, say, a reference to Cosmo Kramer. And the explanation for this is simple: *The Office* is part of the cultural encyclopedia that we share, while *Seinfeld* is not. The most effective communication happens when I can draw from those parts of my encyclopedia that are also familiar to my students.

The same is true for Matthew and his readers. Matthew is a first-century author writing in Greek, and we know some details about his knowledge of his own cultural encyclopedia based on the texts that he refers to explicitly. The fulfillment citations noted earlier are one example of this, but there are also instances where he quotes directly from other ancient sources. In Matthew's telling of the Sermon on the Mount, for example, Jesus refers to the so-called Law of Retribution with a direct quote from the Greek translation of Exodus: "An eye for an eye and a tooth for a tooth" (Matt 5:38 NRSV, quoting Exod 21:24). From this and other quotations of Exodus, we can draw the reasonable conclusion that Matthew is familiar with this text. There is also plenty that we *don't* know for certain about Matthew's cultural encyclopedia, and there may be places in his narrative where he alludes to material that we no longer have access to. Because texts in the ancient world were only preserved through a process of hand copying, texts that were not deemed useful enough to copy generally did not survive.

Matthew's earliest audience was composed primarily of first- and second-century Greek readers. There are many ways of speaking about this audience, whether it was part of Matthew's own Christian community, or a network of elite Roman authors, or some combination of the two.[7] It is also worth noting that the literacy rate in the first-century Roman Empire was low—probably hovering around 10 percent—and one did not simply walk into a bookstore in the first century and purchase a copy of Matthew (or any text, for that matter).[8] As such, it is helpful to think of Matthew's audience not only as people "reading" Matthew. Many would have "read" it by hearing it read or performed in a more public setting. When we think about the question of "readers" in a study like this, we are always thinking in terms of "hypothetical readers" that are constructed for the purposes of our analysis. Later in this book, we will discuss several examples of *actual* readers of Matthew whose interpretations we still have access to today. But when we think about readers in terms of Matthew's earliest audience and the sorts of things they brought to their understandings of the text, we are making, testing, and refining hypotheses. This procedure is simply part of the process of reading and interpreting ancient texts.

One of the primary challenges of reading ancient texts like Matthew is that we are far removed from the cultural encyclopedias of their authors and their earliest readers; what was both obvious

---

7 Biblical scholars often conceive of the Gospels as texts that reflect the beliefs and dispositions of small, primitive communities as passers on of oral traditions about Jesus. Robyn Walsh (*The Origins of Early Christian Literature: Contextualizing the New Testament within Greco-Roman Literary Culture* [Cambridge: Cambridge University Press, 2021]) cautions against this, arguing instead that the Gospels are best understood as texts conversant with broader Greco-Roman literary culture.

8 See William Harris, *Ancient Literacy* (Cambridge, MA: Harvard University Press, 1989), 141, 272, 323–32. Kim Haines-Eitzen complicates the notion of "literacy" in the ancient world by noting the example of Petaus, the village scribe of Ptolemais Hormou, who was apparently not able to understand his own writing (*Guardians of Letters: Literacy, Power, and the Transmitters of Early Christian Literature* [Oxford: Oxford University Press, 2000], 27).

and familiar to them is neither for us. So when we read these texts, we must be mindful that we are visitors to a strange and unfamiliar territory. If we ignore this basic fact, then we risk interpreting these texts through our own categories, and when we do, we are almost guaranteed to misinterpret them. But when we approach the questions of the author's intended meaning and the reader's understood meaning as two interrelated and inseparable sides of the same coin, they have the capacity to inform each other in interesting and illuminating ways that can help us chart a course through the literary labyrinth.

Setting Forth

Now that we have established some of the methodological parameters of our study, it's time to turn to Matthew's Gospel, to read the story of the Magi afresh, as if we had never read it before and as if we don't already have answers to what may seem like simple questions. Yet as we saw with the example of Rev. Jesse Hurlbut, this is easier said than done.

At the start of every semester, I walk my Bible survey students through the subject matter of the course. I encourage them to approach biblical texts as if they have never heard of the Bible before. For the purposes of our course, it is a collection of ancient documents that has only just been discovered, and none of us knows what's in it or what it's about. I don't think I have ever had a student in class who has never heard of the Bible, but I have had plenty of students who have never read any of it before, and for a variety of reasons. Many of my students are not particularly religious, and some identify with non-Jewish and non-Christian religious traditions. Some have just never bothered. For these, the task of assuming unfamiliarity is relatively easy because it is their reality; they don't have to approach these stories as if they've never read them because, in fact, they never have.

The issue is significantly more complex for students who *are* familiar with the biblical texts, or who at least think that they are. Some may find themselves in the same position as Rev. Hurlbut. They read their Bibles often and are so familiar with the material that they have reached the point of unfamiliarity. For these students, I borrow a Latin phrase popularized by the nineteenth-century Danish philosopher Søren Kierkegaard: *de omnibus dubitandum est*.[9] In English: "Everything is to be doubted." I urge students who are familiar with the biblical texts to internalize this phrase over the course of the semester and to question everything that they encounter. I encourage them to question what they find in the assigned texts, but I also encourage them to question *me*, the one whose job it is to help them learn how to think about the subject matter in new and interesting ways.

Readers of this book will undoubtedly be approaching its subject matter from varying levels of familiarity. For some, this may be just the most recent addition to a library well stocked with works of biblical scholarship. For others, this may be the first book you've ever read related to biblical scholarship. I offer all readers the same advice that I offer my students: Question everything. Question those things that are familiar as well as those things that are unfamiliar. Never assume that you know a thing for certain. Always assume that you don't. And if you are convinced that you *do* know a thing, then ask yourself *how* you know it and *why*. Never take something at face value. Everything is to be doubted. Everything is to be questioned.

---

9   This phrase is the title of Kierkegaard's treatise on Cartesian skepticism, which was published after his death.

Some may argue that an approach like this is risky, perhaps even irreverent. After all, we are dealing with the Bible, right? You're not supposed to question the Bible, are you? Isn't that some kind of sin? Certain theological traditions might maintain that it is, but I would suggest that such a claim is misguided. The Bible is revered around the world as a collection of sacred texts, but this does not change the fact that its contents were written by people. These authors wrote out of their own experiences and struggles, but more importantly, they wrote from and to their own historical and social contexts. Reading biblical texts as the literary products of human authors does not negate the belief that they are in some way "sacred," or at least it shouldn't do so out of necessity.

The goal of this approach is not to cheapen the biblical texts or somehow lessen their importance but to come to a deeper and more complex understanding of them. We might think of our questions as akin to knocking holes in the walls of an old house. An activity like this is driven by an impulse to explore. Knocking a hole in the wall of an old house enables one to look inside and see what's there. And anyone who has ever worked on an old house can attest to the fact that you never quite know what you are going to find behind old walls. Antiquated wiring, used razor blades, or perhaps some sort of mummified rodent. We learn by exploring, and so the desire to see what's there is valid in and of itself. But for many, knocking a hole in the wall of an old house is driven not solely by the desire to understand what's behind the walls but also by an impulse to improve the old house and ensure that it remains standing.

If the old house in this analogy is the Bible, then the primary function of the present study is to help you knock holes in some of the walls and see what's behind them. What you do with that knowledge once you have it is ultimately up to you. Some readers may choose to just leave the holes there. Perhaps they will move to other rooms of the house and start knocking holes in those walls as well. Others may choose to patch up the holes with plaster and drywall and pretend that there were never any holes to begin with. Others still may see what's behind the wall and choose to bring the whole thing down and perhaps build another in its place. The thing about "true" exploration is that you never quite know what you will find, or how you will react when you find it.

2

Magicians, Wise Guys, and Translators

LIKE THE REST OF THE New Testament, Matthew's Gospel was written entirely in an ancient style of Greek. And just as scholars of French literature are expected to read French texts in French, scholars of the New Testament are expected to be able to read and understand the New Testament in the language in which it was written. Translations of the New Testament exist so that those not trained to read Greek can still make sense of these texts. Translations are wonderful for this reason. But they are also tricky things, because translators do not always agree on what specific words or phrases mean. The Bible has been translated more times and into more languages than any other collection of writings in human history, and anyone who has spent time comparing translations can attest to just how different many of them are from one another.

Sometimes they even disagree on which verses should and should not be included![1]

The Greek text of the Magi story in Matthew is not complicated, but there are a few terms in it that can give translators problems. So as part of our process of reading Matthew with new eyes, we must first wrestle with a few questions related to translation. What does the word *magoi* mean? Astrologers? Wise men? Something else? Who and what precisely are Matthew's visitors looking for? The king of the Jews? The king of the Judeans? What's the difference? And finally, what are they seeking with respect to Jesus? Do they want to worship him? Or do they want to bow before him as a sign of honor? The question of translation is far more complicated than What do these words mean in English (or any other language)? Questions like this can take us only so far in terms of deepening our understanding of the Magi story because the translation of any language into another is an art, not a decoding exercise. All languages have certain nuances, and the task of the translator goes far beyond looking in a dictionary for the "right answer."

This chapter seeks to complicate the story of the Magi by interrogating how we translate and understand certain key words and phrases. We begin with a quick overview of the types of decisions that inform the translation process and then examine how various English translators through the years have dealt with the word *magoi* in Matthew's Gospel.[2] The remainder of the chapter addresses

---

1 There are around twenty "contested verses" in modern translations of the New Testament. These are passages that, for a variety of reasons, many biblical scholars argue were not part of the "original" texts of the New Testament. In Matthew's Gospel alone, readers will find 17:21, 18:11, and 23:14 missing from their modern English translations. One of the more well-known examples of this is the "woman caught in adultery" story in the Gospel of John (in John 7:53–8:11). Most modern translations will include this story in brackets, with a footnote indicating that it was likely added to John's Gospel at a later date.

2 I restrict my analysis here to English translations because these are likely to be the most relevant to readers of this book.

the object of the Magi's search—whether that is the king of the *Jews* or the king of the *Judeans*—and, finally, the verb that is usually translated either as "worship" or "pay homage to." At the end of the chapter, I incorporate these observations into my own translation of the Magi story, and this translation will serve as our base text for the remainder of the book.

What's in a Name?

When Matthew penned his story of the unusual visitors from the East, he had a few decisions to make. What level of detail should I include? Should I give them names? Should I say how many there are? Should I indicate the point of the story? Ultimately, Matthew chose the path of simplicity. His visitors are unnamed and unnumbered. While the nativity in your living room likely has *three* Magi in it, Matthew never says that there are three. He says there are three types of *gifts*, not that there were three *gift givers*. Twenty people could attend a baby shower, and all of them could show up bearing diapers, wipes, and toys. We aren't told anything about the star that they follow, and we aren't told why they are interested in Jesus in the first place. Our first clue as to who Matthew believes them to be is a solitary Greek word: *magoi*. But what does this word mean? The answer is more complicated than most realize.

The Greek word *magoi* is the plural form of the singular *magos*. Strictly speaking, *magos* is an adjective, which means that its primary function is to say something about whatever noun (a person, place, thing, or idea) it is attached to. If we were to speak about "the good dog, the bad dog, and the ugly dog," then *good*, *bad*, and *ugly* are adjectives that are used to describe three different dogs. In English, it is also perfectly acceptable to use adjectives as stand-alone nouns. It would not be even a little incorrect for someone to write about "the good, the bad, and the ugly," for example, even though *good*, *bad*, and *ugly* are all technically adjectives. They function in this example as nouns because of the nouns that they imply: "the good [dog], the bad [dog], and the ugly [dog]." Without context, you are left with "the good [thing], the bad [thing], and the ugly [thing]." And you are left guessing about the identity of the "thing." You know that it's good (or bad or ugly), but what is *it*?

Adjectives in Greek are similar in this way to adjectives in English. Their primary function is to modify nouns, but they are also routinely used in place of nouns. This is how the word *magoi* operates in Matthew's story; it describes the visitors who come to Jerusalem in search of a king. When trying to understand what the word *magoi* means in Matthew's Gospel, our problem is not identifying the noun that it implies, because this is relatively clear: *magoi* describes the *people* who visit Jesus. The real challenge is determining how best to understand the meaning of the adjective *magos*. What *sort* of people are these? How does Matthew want his readers to understand them?

The English words *magic*, *magical*, and *magician* are all derivatives of the Greek *magos*. So if our goal was to pick an English word that would make translation easy, the adjective *magical* may be an obvious choice. Rereading Matthew's story in this light, we would be left with "Magical people from the East came to Jerusalem" (Matt 2:1). While this would be an easy choice, it is far from the best in terms of arriving at a meaningful translation. After all, the word *magical* can be used in several ways and can send several different messages. One could have a *magical* experience at a theme park but also have a friend from high school who sells essential oils that skeptics describe as *magical*. The former is positive, while the latter is sardonic. The word *magical* becomes even more problematic in contexts where *magic* might be considered *sinister* or even *evil*. What's the difference between a *magician* and a *sorcerer*, for example? Might we translate Matthew 2:1 as *"sorcerers* from the East came to Jerusalem"? Perhaps. But this would be about as helpful as calling them *magical people* or even *magicians.*

Translators in the past have dealt with the word *magoi* in a few ways. Two of the earliest and most influential English translations of Matthew's Gospel are in William Tyndale's New Testament (1526) and the King James Version (1611). Both translate the word *magoi* as "wise men." Many of the major twentieth-century English translations have followed this convention. The American Standard Version (1901) and its successor, the Revised Standard Version (1952), for example, both translate *magoi* as "wise men," and the same is true for the New Revised Standard Version (1990). The Amplified Bible (1965) and the Revised English Bible (1989) depart from this traditional rendering and instead translate *magoi* as "astrologers."

"Wise men" is perhaps a more neutral translation than "astrologers," but it is also unusual. Matthew doesn't seem to show much interest in the "wisdom" of these characters. They are curious and knowledgeable, but this is not the same as being "wise." The "wise men" translation may reflect the use of *magoi* in other Greek texts, in which they are mentioned as advisory figures. And in some later retellings of Matthew's story, these visitors *do* become sages who offer philosophical reflections on the nature of things. We will address these possibilities in subsequent chapters. Translating *magoi* as "astrologers" instead of "wise men" attempts to account for the fact that they are concerned with the stars and appear to have discerned some type of significance from the one that has prompted them to journey to Jerusalem. The term *astrologers* may also be intended to cast these characters in a sort of exotic, mysterious, or "foreign" light.

The New American Standard Bible (1971) and the New International Version (1978) take a different approach to *magoi.* They avoid the problem of translation by not translating it. In both versions, the visitors are not "wise men" or "astrologers" but simply "Magi."[3] In what is commonly called a "loan translation" or "calque," these translators have taken the Greek word and anglicized it. The *magoi* become the Magi. This approach to translation could be frowned upon because it defeats the purpose of translating a text in the first place. If the aim of a translation is to make a certain text accessible to a broader audience by putting it into their language(s), then what is the benefit of leaving some words untranslated? Such criticism is well founded, at least in some instances. But I would like to suggest that in the case of Matthew's *magoi*, *Magi* may in fact be the best option. In what follows, I use *Magi* with reference to the characters in Matthew and *magoi* when speaking about the word itself and with reference to characters in other Greek literature. I have followed the NIV's decision to capitalize *Magi* because in Matthew it functions as a proper noun.

The other translations of *magoi* are not necessarily "bad," and it would be a mistake to say that any of them are "inaccurate." It is probably the case that all of them capture some aspect of how Matthew understands these characters. The danger comes when we choose one translation to the exclusion of the others. Whether "wise men" or "astrologers" or "magicians" or "sorcerers," all of these have the disadvantage of priming readers to understand the *magoi* too narrowly. All these translations put Matthew's visitors into tidy categories that are familiar to contemporary readers. And in doing so they remove the strangeness and complexity of the story. By referring to them as "Magi," we continue our process of defamiliarizing Matthew's story and removing at least some of our preconceived notions about who and what these visitors are supposed

---

3   This is also the approach taken by the Latin Vulgate, which renders the Greek *magoi* as *magi*.

to be. "Magi" reminds us that these characters are ultimately mysterious. And as we will see in the next chapter, highlighting their mystery and intrigue may in fact be one of Matthew's goals.

King of the Whos?

When the Magi arrive in Jerusalem, they indicate that they are looking for a king. But *whose* king are they looking for? The phrase in question is "basileus tōn Ioudaiōn," and all major English translations address it in the same way: the Magi are in search of the "king of the Jews" (Matt 2:2). But is this the best translation? The specific word of interest here is *Ioudaioi* (the plural form of the singular *Ioudaios*). Unlike *magos*, the word *Ioudaioi* is quite common in the New Testament, appearing nearly two hundred times. It derives from the Greek word *Ioudas*, which refers to the geographical territory of Judea.[4] For much of the history of biblical scholarship, translating *Ioudaioi* as "Jews" has been the default practice. But more recently, there has been an ongoing and sometimes heated debate among scholars over whether this is the best and most accurate way to understand the word *Ioudaioi*. Why not translate it as "Judeans," since this is what it seems to mean, at least at face value?

Historian Steve Mason provides one of the more sustained and well-known arguments for translating *Ioudaioi* as "Judeans" rather than "Jews." He notes that in contemporary parlance, the term *Jew* has explicitly—and perhaps predominantly—religious connotations that are tied to a modern understanding of religion that did not exist in the ancient world. As Mason puts it, "The concept of *religion*, which is fundamental to our outlook and our historical

---

4   *Judea* is the Latinized form of the Hebrew *Judah*, and for our purposes, they are largely interchangeable. In what follows, I use *Judea* when the subject is the geographical territory and *Judah* when the subject is the son of Leah and Jacob (see Gen 29:35).

research, [lacks] a taxonomical counterpart in antiquity."[5] Brent Nongbri echoes this sentiment, writing, "In the ancient world the gods were involved in all aspects of life. That is not to say . . . that all ancient people were somehow uniformly 'religious'; rather, the act of distinguishing between 'religious' and 'secular' is a recent development. Ancient people simply did not carve up the world in that way."[6] In the ancient world, "religion" is inseparable from other facets of life, including geography, ethnicity, or even work. The notion that modern readers conceive of things like "religion" and "religious identity" in ways that are foreign to ancient sensibilities has become standard currency in the study of the ancient world. The question is the extent to which it should encourage us to read *Ioudaioi* as "Judeans" rather than "Jews." If "religion" as a concept does not exist in antiquity, is not the latter designation an anachronism?

The study of the ancient world is inherently anachronistic. When we explore the lives, thoughts, and writings of individuals and groups who lived thousands of years ago, we are always doing so as outsiders and through our own lenses and categories. Scholars of antiquity regularly use terminology like *religion* and *religious* to understand a variety of practices, beliefs, and dispositions in the ancient world. And they can do this while simultaneously acknowledging that these specific categories would not have made much sense to ancient people. One can find several books on "Roman religion," for example, even though the Romans themselves wouldn't have understood the concept. "Religion" is a heuristic device that helps us make sense of various ancient phenomena in ways that we are able to understand. And there is value in that. Yet there is also

---

5 Steve Mason, "Jews, Judaeans, Judaizing, Judaism: Problems of Categorization in Ancient History," *Journal for the Study of Judaism* 38, nos. 4–5 (2007): 480.

6 Brent Nongbri, *Before Religion: A History of a Modern Concept* (New Haven, CT: Yale University Press, 2013), 3.

a keen sense among scholars that when we study the ancient world, one of our primary goals should always be to understand the people who inhabited that world on *their* own terms.

This leads us to two critical and interrelated questions. First, is it the case that the people called *Ioudaioi* would have understood this designation as primarily a "religious" one, at least as we define that category today? And second, when an ancient author like Matthew used the word *Ioudaioi*, would they have understood it as a reference to a group's "religious identity"? Mason's answer to both questions is an unequivocal *no*.

Mason argues that *Ioudaioi* is best understood not as a religious group but as an *ethnos*, "a people comparable and contrastable with other *ethnē*."[7] In the ancient world, Mason argues, the "distinctive nature or character" of an *ethnos* would be defined by a few factors, including "ancestral traditions" as well as "charter stories [*mythoi*], customs, norms, conventions, mores, laws [*nomoi, ethē, nomima*], and political arrangements or constitution."[8] Certain of these markers may have "religious" dimensions, but all of them depend on and exist inseparably from one another. An indispensable part of one's *ethnos* is their ancestral homeland. Mason observes that "if one asked where a Babylonian or Egyptian or Syrian or Parthian was from, in what laws or customs they had been educated, the answer was apparent in their ethnic label." The same is true, he suggests, for the category *Ioudaioi*. It is used to identify people who are, in terms of *ethnos*, "of Judea." And because the English designation *Jew* does not capture the full complexity of this, he argues that in all ancient texts, *Ioudaioi* should be translated not as "Jews," but "Judeans."[9]

---

7 Mason, "Jews, Judaeans," 489.
8 Mason, 484.
9 Mason, 489.

Mason's argument is compelling, but many disagree with it, including New Testament scholar Adele Reinhartz. She agrees that "[*Ioudaios*] was a complex term that carried ethnic, political, cultic, and many other dimensions, even if the jury is still out on the existence or non-existence of religion in antiquity."[10] But she cautions against allowing this fact to dictate that all instances of *Ioudaios/Ioudaioi* be translated without question as "Judean/Judeans." Reinhartz maintains that "Jews" is in fact a legitimate translation of *Ioudaioi*, and that *Jew* is not an indicator of one's "religion" in most cases. She notes that the category *Jew* today includes many of the components that Mason emphasizes as part of ancient Judean identity, including the "ethnic, political, cultural, genealogical, and, yes, geographical."[11] Reinhartz's concern is that moving away from translating *Ioudaioi* as "Jews" has promoted and will continue to promote the "growing invisibility of Jews and Judaism in English translations of ancient texts and scholarship about them."[12] Translating *Ioudaioi* as "Jews" rather than "Judeans" serves as a persistent reminder, Reinhartz argues, that Jews today are not dispassionate and disconnected observers of the *Ioudaioi* but rather connected to them through the very identity markers that Mason and others outline.[13]

In an era when anti-Semitism and Judeophobia run rampant, Reinhartz's concerns about how best to translate *Ioudaioi* are important. And they stand as a reminder that decisions about the translation of texts (biblical or otherwise) are seldom "neutral." Something is always at stake. It may also be the case that context should be the determining factor. *Ioudaioi* need not *always* mean

---

10 Adele Reinhartz, "The Vanishing Jews of Antiquity," in *Marginalia Ioudaios Forum*, ed. Timothy Michael Law and Charles Halton (Los Angeles: Marginalia Review of Books, 2014), 8.

11 Reinhartz, 8.

12 Reinhartz, 6.

13 Reinhartz, 10.

"Judeans" or *always* mean "Jews." As we saw with the preceding analysis of the term *magoi*, there must be room within translation for the creative choices of the translator.

It has not been my intention here to resolve this debate. I have presented this small portion of it here as part of the effort to further defamiliarize the story of Matthew's Magi. And with that, we return to the question What king are the Magi looking for?

For reasons that will become clearer in the following chapters, I have opted to translate *basileus tōn Ioudaiōn* not as most translators do—as "king of the Jews"—but as Mason recommends: "king of the Judeans." In chapter 4, I discuss some of the ways in which Herod's kingship was fraught with tension because of his own *ethnos*. Herod himself was not a Judean but rather an Idumean. And I will suggest that when the Magi arrive in Jerusalem inquiring about the *basileus tōn Ioudaiōn*, this is Matthew's way of evoking the sorts of ethno-political markers that both Mason and Reinhartz discuss. I opt to translate *Ioudaioi* as "Judeans" for the simple reason that, in this instance, this more ancient category better captures that ethno-political tension.

To Worship or Not to Worship?

A final question concerns what the Magi are seeking to do when they come to visit the newborn Jesus. Some translations of Matthew 2:2 read, "We . . . have come to pay him homage" (NRSV), while others read, "We . . . have come to worship him" (NIV). The question is important because it affects our understanding of how the Magi view this one who has been born "king of the Judeans." Do they understand him as a deity to be worshipped? Or is he merely a new ruler that they wish to bow down before as a sign of honor and respect? Or is there even a difference between bowing before someone and worshipping them? Most importantly, how would Matthew have understood this action?

The way that one answers these questions depends on how one understands a single Greek verb in Matthew's Magi story: *proskuneō*. The verb itself is idiomatic, and idioms are notoriously tricky to translate. *Proskuneō* translates literally as something like "to direct one's face to the ground," and it occurs a total of sixty times in the New Testament. Thirteen of those occurrences (a full 20 percent of the total) are in Matthew's Gospel, and three of these are in the Magi story (Matt 2:2, 8, 11). For the sake of simplicity and consistency, I translate it as "to bow" in the following analysis, although at the end, I will suggest a slightly more nuanced approach as we move to translate the verb in the Magi story.

One way to determine how Matthew understands *proskuneō* in his story of the Magi is to examine how he uses it elsewhere in his Gospel. And if we look at the other ten instances in Matthew, we find that it is used in a variety of ways. At four points in Matthew, *proskuneō* is used in stories about people who come to Jesus to ask for something for themselves or for someone else (Matt 8:2; 9:18; 15:25; 20:20). In all these cases, the verb suggests the simple act of kneeling or bowing. The people who come to Jesus to make a request for healing or something else begin by humbling themselves physically. It is used another time in a similar sense, in Jesus's parable of the unforgiving slave (Matt 18:21–35). Here the slave bows (*prosekunei*) before his master and begs for more time to pay off his debt (Matt 18:26). In none of these instances is the act of "bowing" equated with "worship." In fact, in some cases translating *proskuneō* as "worship" would be quite strange. The slave in Matthew 18:21–35 isn't understood to be "worshipping" his enslaver. It is tempting to interpret the other instances noted here as indicative of worship, since the people who are bowing are doing so toward Jesus. But this interpretation does not fit the context of any of these stories.

Yet there are other instances in Matthew where the use of *proskuneō* seems to suggest something more than just the physical act of bowing or kneeling. In these cases, there is a sense that the one doing the bowing is also adopting an emotional or even "spiritual" posture, perhaps one that could be called "worship." When Jesus is tempted after his baptism, for example, Satan promises him all the kingdoms of the world if he agrees to bow (*proskunēsēs*) before him. When Jesus responds to this temptation, he uses the same verb, but with reference to the god of Israel: "Bow [*proskunēseis*] to the Lord your God, and serve only him" (Matt 4:9–10). Later in Matthew's Gospel, the verb appears again in the story of Jesus walking on water. When he gets in the boat, "those in the boat bowed [*prosekunēsan*] before him, saying, 'You truly are the son of God!'" (Matt 14:33). This usage is notable because it pairs the physical act (bowing) with an articulation of Jesus's divine status ("You are the son of God").

The verb appears twice more in Matthew, and both occurrences are in the context of Jesus's postresurrection appearances. In the first, Jesus greets the women as they are leaving his empty tomb. When they saw him, "they grabbed his feet and bowed [*prosekunēsan*] to him" (Matt 28:9). Here the verb that we have been translating as "bow" is paired with another physical act—namely, grabbing Jesus's feet. And if *proskuneō* here just means "bow," then the sentence is redundant, and the actions are out of sequence. Why would Matthew say that the women grabbed his feet and then bowed before him? This usage suggests that Matthew's understanding of *proskuneō* can involve more than the physical act of bowing.

In the second, the disciples gather on a mountaintop in Galilee, and Jesus appears to them. The narrator comments, "Seeing him, they bowed [*prosekunēsan*], but some doubted" (Matt 28:17). Like the previous example, this one is instructive because of the pairing of *proskuneō* with another verb: *distazō*, meaning "to doubt." *Distazō* is used only one other time in Matthew, in reference to Peter. When Jesus is walking on the water, Peter steps out of the boat and begins to walk toward him before he falters and then begins to sink under the waves. Jesus catches him by the hand and says to him, "You of little faith, why did you doubt [*ti edistasas*]?" (Matt 14:31). Here "doubt" is used as a negative characteristic of "one who has little faith." It would not be unreasonable to conclude, then, that when Matthew pairs *proskuneō* with *distazō* in chapter 28, he invites readers to understand them in light of each other, as opposing dispositions.

How, then, are we to understand *proskuneō* in the story of the Magi? Do the Magi wish to worship Jesus? Or do they wish to bow to him as a sign of respect? Or is it the case that this dichotomy exists for modern readers but not necessarily for Matthew? The plurality of ways in which Matthew employs *proskuneō* in his Gospel suggests that the third option is probably the best. In fact, out of the thirteen times that Matthew uses this word, there is only one instance where *proskuneō* clearly does *not* indicate worship (the parable of the unforgiving servant in Matt 18:23–35).

In my translation, I render *proskuneō* as "honor" for a few reasons. First, in the broader context of Matthew's Gospel, "honor" reflects the various uses of *proskuneō* that we find outside of the Magi story; "honoring" someone may involve "worship," but this is not necessarily the case. Second, translating *proskuneō* as "honor" acknowledges those instances where it is paired with other verbs suggesting a type of physical posture. Returning to the example of the women who encounter the resurrected Jesus in the garden, here Matthew pairs the grabbing of Jesus's feet with *proskuneō*, and in this case, it is repetitive to translate *proskuneō* as "bow." But "they grabbed his feet and honored him" (Matt 28:9) makes good sense. A similar pairing occurs in the Magi story when the Magi reach Bethlehem. Here Matthew pairs *proskuneō* with another physical act: "falling down" (*piptō*). And finally, translating *proskuneō* as "honor" highlights the political nature of this story. This translation reminds readers that Matthew's Magi are not searching for a deity. They are searching for the rightful king of the Judeans, and their goal is not to worship him but to honor him as the heir to the throne.

Translating the Magi Story

In order to establish a common base for understanding, I suggest the following translation of Matthew 2:1–12 for the purposes of this book. For this translation, I have used one of the standard critical editions of the Greek New Testament.[14]

> After Jesus was born in Bethlehem of Judea, in the days of Herod the King, behold Magi from the East came to Jerusalem,[15] saying, "Where is the one who has been born king of the Judeans? For we saw his star at its rising and have come to honor him." King Herod panicked when he heard this, and all of Jerusalem panicked with him. He gathered together all the chief priests and scribes of the people, and asked them

---

14 Barbara Aland et al., eds., *Novum Testamentum Graece*, 28th ed. (Stuttgart, Germany: Deutsche Bibelgesellschaft, 2012).

15 "From the East" is a standard translation of *apo anatolōn*. The noun *anatolōn* is the plural form of *anatolē*, which means "dawn" or "rising." So *apo anatolōn* in this case might be understood as something along the lines of "from the place of the risings," a reference to the risings of the sun. Hence "from the East." *Anatolē* appears again in the following verse when the Magi speak of the star's rising. Here it is in the singular, signifying an event rather than a series of events.

where the anointed one is to be born.[16] They said to him, "In Bethlehem of Judea, for thus it has been written by the prophet: 'And you, O Bethlehem, in the land of Judah, are by no means least among the leaders of Judah. For from you will come a leader who will guide my people, Israel.'"[17] Then Herod summoned the Magi in secret, and he interrogated them regarding the time of the star's appearing. As he sent them to Bethlehem, he said, "Go and investigate carefully concerning the child. As soon as you find him, report back to me, so that I too may go and honor him." They heard the king and then set out, and behold: the star that they saw at its rising went on ahead of them, until it came and stopped over where the child was. When they saw the star they celebrated with a joy that was exceedingly great. They entered the house and saw the child with Mary his mother, and falling down, they honored him. They opened their chests and offered him gifts: gold, incense, and myrrh.[18] Having been warned in a dream not to return to Herod, they returned to their own land by another route.

With the question of translation addressed, we are now ready to begin a more intensive and thorough exploration of the Magi story and to determine what this story may have meant to Matthew and

---

16 "Anointed one" is here translating the Greek *christos*, which is a title that in New Testament texts refers exclusively to Jesus. It is nearly always translated as "Christ." Here the reader of Matthew is meant to understand this as a reference to Jesus, but on the lips of Herod, it is meant as a reference to a Davidic monarch. I explore this point more fully in chapter 4.

17 This is not a quotation of any one prophetic text but rather a hybrid paraphrase of the Greek translation of Mic 5:2 and 2 Sam 5:2.

18 The second gift of the Magi (*libanos*) is usually translated as "frankincense." This translation is not inaccurate per se, but it is not terribly precise. Strictly speaking, *libanos* is what is made from the dried resin (*libanōtos*) of the frankincense tree that grows in the Arabian Peninsula. I translate it as "incense" to capture that distinction.

his earliest readers. But we have one final stop to make before we get to Matthew. In the next chapter, we examine how other ancient authors thought about *magoi* as a designation for certain people. How was this title used? Was it a positive attribute? Or negative? What sorts of people were called *magoi* in the ancient world? Answers to these questions will vary depending on the author, which further contributes to the mysterious nature of Matthew's visitors.

3

Frescoes, Funny Hats,
and Faraway Places

WANDERING THE STREETS OF ROME is a wonderful experience. The smells of espresso and gelato greet you after every few steps, and around each corner, there seems to be another historical or architectural wonder just waiting for you. But for all the amazing things visitors see, countless more treasures lie buried beneath their feet. Rome is an ancient city, and like all ancient cities, it is a city of layers.

One of the many hidden wonders of Rome, tucked far beneath the sidewalks and noisy cabs, is the collection of vast and labyrinthine cemeteries known as catacombs. Archaeologists have identified more than forty separate catacomb networks in and around Rome today, and among these, the Catacomb of Priscilla is one of the more well known. Located north of the city, on the Via Salaria, the Catacomb of Priscilla contains some of the earliest and most well-preserved examples of ancient Christian art and iconography. It was discovered during the sixteenth century, and by the mid-eighteenth century, excavators were hard at work exploring and cataloging the ancient burial ground.[1] It was there that two of the earliest depictions of Matthew's Magi were discovered.

The first image is located in one of the more colorful locations within the Catacomb of Priscilla: the Cappella Greca (Greek Chapel), a small chamber adorned with vivid frescoes of early Christian symbols and biblical scenes, some of which date from as early as the third century CE. These include Noah and his ark (Gen 8–9), the annunciation of Jesus's birth to Mary (Luke 1:26–35), and Jesus's healing of a paralyzed man (Mark 2:1–12; Luke 5:17–26; John 5:5–9), among others.[2] The Magi make their appearance on the first ceiling arch beyond the chapel's entrance.[3] The scene is simple, nondescript, and yet immediately recognizable. Mary is seated to the right, holding Jesus in her lap, while the Magi approach from the left. None of the figures appear in any level of detail—at least not in their current state—but one can see quite clearly from the Magi's silhouettes that they are moving toward the infant and his mother with their arms outstretched, gifts in hand. Each of the Magi is painted in a different color: yellow, red, and green, from left to right. They also seem to be wearing hats. We will return to this detail in a moment.

The second image is carved onto a rectangular slab of Italian white marble that functioned as a seal for one of the catacomb's

---

1 Early archaeological excavations left much to be desired in terms of methodology and record keeping, and by the time a "proper" study of the catacombs was underway, many had already been ransacked and looted by treasure hunters.

2 Images of the Capella Greca and its frescoes are readily available online.

3 Robin Jensen estimates that the Magi fresco was painted either at the end of the third century or at the start of the fourth (*Understanding Early Christian Art* [London: Routledge, 2000], 95).

niche tombs (called *loculi*).[4] On the left side of the slab is a hauntingly beautiful portrait of a person named Severa, whose burial niche the slab would have guarded. With her left hand she clutches a scroll, and with her right she offers a blessing. Next to her is a short Latin epitaph: *Severa in Deo vivas*, or "Severa, may you live in God." The slab is small—only one foot high by about three feet wide—which has led some to conclude that Severa was probably a child when she died. The Magi scene stands to the right (Severa's left), and it occupies more than half of the slab's face. There are two primary details present on the slab that are missing in the Capella Magi fresco: a six-pointed star hangs between Jesus and the Magi, and an unidentified man behind Mary gestures toward it.[5] But otherwise, it is similar to what we find in the Capella Greca: Mary sits on a high-backed chair with her infant perched precariously on her lap. Jesus reaches out to three Magi, who approach from the left and hold out their gifts as they draw near.

The Magi from Severa's slab and the Capella fresco belong to the same era and to similar artistic traditions. When they are examined together, they complement one another. In contrast to the nondescript silhouettes that we find in the Capella fresco, for example, the Magi on Severa's slab appear in sharp detail. They are wearing knee-length tunics and capes, and each is wearing a distinctive style of hat called a *pileus*, more commonly referred to as a "Phrygian cap."[6]

---

4 This slab was removed from the catacomb after its discovery in 1751 and was taken to the Basilica di Santa Maria in Trastevere, where it remained for around one hundred years. It now resides in the Vatican Museums (Lapidario Cristiano, Inv. 28594). Images of it are available online.

5 It is difficult to determine the identity of this figure with any certainty. The two most likely options seem to be Joseph or, as some have suggested, Balaam, a prophetic figure from Num 24:11 who prophesies about the rising of a star from Israel (see Engelbert Kirschbaum, "Der Prophet Balaam und die Anbetung der Weisen," *Römische Quartalschrift für christliche Altertumskunde und Kirchengeschichte* 49, no. 3/4 [1954]: 144–64).

6 The Phrygian cap is a common feature in artistic representations of the Magi. Another example in Rome is found in the fifth-century CE mosaics in the Basilica di Santa Maria Maggiore, where the Magi wear Phrygian caps while appearing both to Herod and Mary. Strabo mentions distinctive headwear when describing *magoi* in *Geogr.* 15.15, 19.

Looking back at the Magi in the Capella fresco, one can reasonably conclude from their painted silhouettes that these figures are dressed in much the same way. In Roman art, the Phrygian cap was a popular way of indicating that a subject was from somewhere in the eastern Mediterranean, whether that be Phrygia or as far east as Persia.[7] In this context, the Magi's distinctive hats send a strong and clear message: these visitors aren't from around here.

Why "Magi"?

Like the Phrygian caps in the Catacomb of Priscilla, Matthew's use of *magoi* as a designation for his visitors highlights, among other things, that they are from a foreign and faraway place. Ancient sources quite often associate *magoi* with Persia or other "Eastern" locales.[8] But *magoi* in the ancient world is used in a variety of ways that sometimes have little to do with geography. The term comes with an enormous amount of ideological baggage as well as, occasionally, some negative connotations.[9] Hippocrates (ca. 460–370 BCE), for example, believed that *magoi* were part of the group responsible for promoting misunderstandings about

---

7 These hats were also used by Romans to identify enslaved persons who had been freed. They were later adopted by artists in France and the United States (where they are often dubbed "liberty caps"). In his *Apotheosis of Washington*, which adorns the eye of the rotunda in the US Capitol, for example, Italian-born painter Constantino Brumidi (1805–80) painted the personification of liberty—who is seated to Washington's right—wearing a red *pileus*.

8 Authors who connect *magoi* with Persia include Chariton, *Chaer.* 5.9.4; Dio Chrysostom, *Or.* 36.41; Diogenes Laertius, *Liv.* 1.1; (Pseudo-)Lucian, *Oct.* 4; Philo, *Prob.* 74; *Spec.* 3.18; Plutarch, *Inv. od.* 537; and Strabo, *Geogr.* 15.13–14; 16.2.39.

9 It is not the case that *magoi* are always understood negatively by authors. As Gábor Betegh notes, and as the sources surveyed in this chapter will illustrate, "[*magos*] could refer either to a specific Persian priestly caste, experts on religious matters, or to people who were supposed to be able to perform some kind of wizardry or black magic" (*The Derveni Papyrus: Cosmology, Theology and Interpretation* [Cambridge: Cambridge University Press, 2004], 78–79). For a helpful overview of the origins and development of *magoi* terminology—including its positive uses and how those influenced and gave rise to negative ones—see Jan N. Bremmer, *Greek Religion and Culture, the Bible and the Ancient Near East*, Jerusalem Studies in Religion and Culture 8 (Leiden: Brill, 2008), 235–47.

epilepsy (*Morb. sacr.* 2). Plato (ca. 423–347 BCE) used *magoi* as an insult for people who knowingly deceive the young (*Resp.* 9.2). Aeschines (ca. 389–314 BCE) likewise spoke of *magoi* alongside traitors and other people who couldn't be trusted (*Ctes.* 135). These are only a few examples.

There are plenty of other ways to refer to visitors from the East that do not involve calling them *magoi*, and yet this is the word that Matthew chose. Why not just call them "people"? Matthew doesn't elaborate, and the reason behind his silence is probably simple: he doesn't explain his use of *magoi* because he assumes that his readers won't need an explanation. Why say what you mean when your audience already knows? If everyone laughs at a joke, there's no need to say why it's funny. This may have been a safe assumption for many of his earliest readers because of their shared cultural encyclopedia. While these readers would not have necessarily understood the word *magoi* in the same way that Matthew did, they would have had an intuition for details like this that surpasses what most modern readers bring to the text. But as readers of this Gospel have moved further away from its first-century context, that collective understanding has faded.

One way to approach the issue of how Matthew and his readers may have understood the identity of these visitors is to examine how other authors in the ancient world understood the people that they referred to as *magoi*. Is the term descriptive? An insult? An accolade? A combination of these? We begin our exploration in what may seem an unlikely place—the New Testament Acts of the Apostles—where we will look at two other *magoi* named Simon and Bar-Jesus. Next, we examine the Greek translation of the Old Testament book of Daniel, which we know from several direct citations is a text that Matthew was familiar with. The remainder of the chapter will be spent looking at *magoi* in other ancient Greek literature, with a special focus on stories of *magoi* in the widely read and highly influential works of the Greek historian Herodotus (ca. 484–425 BCE). We address the *magoi* in these texts from three angles: their proximity to positions of power, their role as advisers and dream interpreters, and the various rituals and "religious" phenomena that they are often associated with.

Two caveats are in order before we begin. First, I do not intend for the following exploration to be exhaustive. My aim is to provide snapshots of various points in ancient literature where authors speak of individuals and groups as *magoi* and to understand how that terminology functions within those snapshots. Second, I am not suggesting that Matthew is alluding to or attempting to allude to any of the sources analyzed in this chapter, and I am also not arguing that they are texts that Matthew's earliest audience would have been intimately familiar with. The snapshots presented here are meant to paint a complex picture of the various ways that the category *magoi* functions in the literature of the ancient world. By looking at how other ancient authors use this word, and by reading Matthew's story against this backdrop, we move toward a better understanding of why Matthew may have chosen this term to describe his visitors from the East.

The Wicked *Magoi* of Acts

Outside of Matthew's Gospel, *magoi* appear in only one other New Testament text: the Acts of the Apostles. Acts is a collection of stories about some of Jesus's earliest followers, who travel throughout the Mediterranean world preaching, healing, and partaking in various sorts of adventures. Because of similarities in style, vocabulary, and themes between Acts and the Gospel of Luke, the scholarly consensus is that Acts was written as a "sequel" to Luke's Gospel, either by the same person or by someone who was able to imitate Luke's style and vocabulary.[10] Most scholars maintain that Acts is a late first-century text written around the same time as Matthew's Gospel. Because they were all copied by hand, texts in the ancient world took time to circulate, so it is unlikely that a text written around the same time as Matthew would have been known to Matthew while he was writing his own Gospel. Some have even suggested that Acts was written several decades *after* Matthew, possibly as late as the early second century.[11] In either case, it is unlikely that this text is serving as one of Matthew's literary influences.

I begin with Acts, not to uncover overlooked literary dependencies or parallels, but because doing so provides a helpful introduction to the complex nature of the designation *magoi* during the time that Matthew was writing. Matthew's story of the Magi gives readers no indication that these visitors arrive with ill intentions. In the words of New Testament scholar Raymond E. Brown, "They are wholly admirable."[12] Mysterious, yes, but not nefarious. In Acts, by contrast, the two *magoi* mentioned by the author are paragons of manipulation and wickedness. Acts is therefore a good example of how the same terminology can be used toward drastically different ends by authors writing with similar audiences and aims in mind.

---

10   Acts is styled as a sequel to Luke. In the preface, the author makes note of "the first book" and also addresses it to the same person, "Theophilus" (Acts 1:1).

11   Shelly Matthews argues that a later date for Acts (ca. 125 CE) makes more sense in light of the text's attitude toward "Jews" as well as the story's reflection of "emerging intra-Christian debates" (*The Acts of the Apostles: An Introduction and Study Guide: Taming the Tongues of Fire* [London: T&T Clark, 2017], 22–23). An overview of issues related to the dating of Acts, including arguments for earlier and later dates, can be found in Joseph B. Tyson, *Marcion and Luke-Acts: A Defining Struggle* (Columbia: University of South Carolina Press, 2006), 1–23.

12   Raymond E. Brown, *The Birth of the Messiah: A Commentary on the Infancy Narratives in the Gospels of Matthew and Luke*, Anchor Bible Reference Library (New York: Doubleday, 1993), 168.

Simon

The first *magos* that we encounter in Acts is a man named Simon.[13] After the violent stoning of Stephen in Acts 7, Jesus's disciple Philip travels to Samaria to preach. There he meets Simon, whom the author of Acts describes as having "previously practiced magic [*mageuōn*] in the city" (Acts 8:9 NRSV). In this story, we do not find the specific adjective *magos* but rather a closely related verb: *mageuō*. English translations often render this occurrence of *mageuō* as "to practice magic" or "to practice sorcery" as a way of highlighting the fact that Simon's former life is viewed negatively by the author of Acts. Calling to mind our discussion about translation in chapter 2, I would suggest that a more neutral translation of the verb as "to be or act like a *magos*" is perhaps more fitting. This translation highlights the fact that while the author of Acts does not directly label Simon a *magos*, he does suggest this identity for him by specifying what sorts of things Simon has done in the past.

The author of Acts characterizes Simon as a self-promoter (and an effective one at that). Those who hear him speak marvel at him and refer to him as "the power of God that is called Great" (Acts 8:10 NRSV). The people are interested in him first and foremost not because of his words but "because for a long time he had amazed them with his magic [*mageiais*]" (Acts 8:11 NRSV). But then Philip arrives on the scene, and when Simon and the people of Samaria hear him preach, they are so taken by his message that they are all baptized (Acts 8:12). At this point, Simon becomes a companion to Philip, and the author notes that he was "amazed when he saw the signs [*sēmeia*] and great miracles [*dunameis megalas*] that took

---

13 Simon is known in later traditions as "Simon Magus." He appears in the apocryphal *Acts Pet.* as one of Peter's archnemeses. In this text, Simon is able to fly (3:2) and is referred to as "the angel of the devil" (3:13).

place" (Acts 8:13 NRSV).[14] This comment sets the stage for the drama that will begin to unfold when Peter and John arrive. Simon watches as the apostles go about laying hands on various people so "that they might receive the Holy Spirit" (Acts 8:15 NRSV). Awestruck by this show of power, Simon offers them money in hopes that they will give him the ability as well (Acts 8:18–19). Peter rebukes and scolds him for thinking that such things can be purchased. He accuses Simon of being motivated by the wrong intentions and orders him to repent (Acts 8:20–23). Hearing all of this, Simon is frightened and perhaps even a bit remorseful. He asks Peter to pray that no harm may come to him (Acts 8:24). At this point, he disappears from the narrative of Acts. The Simon episode performs several important functions in the context of Acts, including emphasizing for readers the possibility of conversion and the danger and allure of money. But for our purposes, it illustrates some of the complexity that surrounds the idea of the *magos* in the first century. Of course, we don't know precisely what "being a *magos*" entails for the author of Acts, but in the case of Simon, it is meant as a negative character trait.

The author of Acts also makes clear that Simon's identity as one who "previously practiced magic" is still part of him in some ways. The fact that he is amazed by the powerful signs of Philip, John, and Peter, and that he desires these abilities for himself, suggests that he retains vestiges of his previous life that was built on impressing the crowds with acts of power. The author's message is clear: once a *magos*, always a *magos*. And for the author of Acts, this message is one of woe.

---

14 The author of Acts here makes a clear distinction between Simon's "magic [*mageiais*]" in 8:11 and Philip's "signs [*sēmeia*]" and "great miracles [*dunameis megalas*]" in 8:13. The aim is to clarify that while both of these people are powerful, their displays of power do not exist in the same category.

The second *magos* mentioned in Acts appears several chapters after Simon, when Paul and Barnabas travel to the island of Cyprus. When they arrive, they begin traveling from town to town, preaching in synagogues (Acts 13:5). After a short while, they encounter a man named Bar-Jesus, whom the author of Acts describes both as a *magos* and as a "Jewish false prophet" (Acts 13:6 NRSV).[15] Bar-Jesus's story is shorter and less detailed than Simon's, and as a character, he differs from Simon in at least two ways. First, Simon is described as a former *magos* (see Acts 8:9), but the author of Acts describes Bar-Jesus as a current and active *magos*. Second, Simon was interested in the powers of the apostles, and even if for the wrong reasons, he is initially receptive to them and their preaching. Bar-Jesus, by contrast, is from the beginning opposed to the apostles, and he works actively to ensure their failure.

After the author of Acts introduces Bar-Jesus, he notes that he is with the proconsul of Cyprus, an "intelligent" man by the name of Sergius Paulus (Acts 13:7). The proconsul summons Paul and Barnabas because he is interested in hearing them preach, but Bar-Jesus doesn't want this to happen for reasons that he doesn't specify. Not only does he try to keep the proconsul from having an audience with Paul and Barnabas, but, the author of Acts indicates, he actively tries "to turn the proconsul away from the faith" (Acts 13:8 NRSV). When Paul discovers this, he lashes out at Bar-Jesus: "You son of the devil, you enemy of all righteousness, full of all deceit and villainy, will you not stop making crooked the straight paths of the Lord? And now listen—the hand of the Lord is against you, and you will be blind for a while, unable to see the sun" (Acts 13:10–11

---

15 Bar-Jesus is a Hebrew name, and in the same story, the author of Acts refers to him by the Greek name Elymas. These names are not etymologically related.

NRSV). Bar-Jesus loses his sight immediately. Groping his way out of the narrative, he searches for someone to help him find his way. The story ends with an ironic turn: Sergius Paulus comes to believe the teaching of Paul and Barnabas precisely because of what Paul had done to Bar-Jesus. The blinding of the *magos* who tried to keep him from the faith is what ultimately leads him to the faith.

Both Bar-Jesus and Simon are negative characters in the narrative of Acts, but for different reasons. Simon is driven by greed, a lust for supernatural powers. It is unclear what drives Bar-Jesus, who at points in the story almost seems to be animated by forces that are beyond his control. But the message of Acts could not be clearer: *magoi* are not good people. At best, they are driven by selfish ambition. And at worst, they are opposed to the preaching of the gospel. The case of Simon, however, indicates that the *magoi* in Acts are not hopeless figures inseparably chained to their wickedness. Simon's conversion from a *magos* to something else was ultimately incomplete, but the fact that it ever got started suggests a capacity for change.

How then do these portraits of *magoi* in Acts affect how we understand Matthew's visitors? After all, Matthew does not indicate that Magi are false teachers or power-hungry charlatans. The *magoi* in Acts serve as a reminder that there is no easy definition for these characters in the first century.

Daniel and the *Magoi*

The Greek translation of the Hebrew Bible is commonly called the Septuagint. The word *Septuagint*—which I will refer to with its standard abbreviation, LXX—comes from the Latin word *septuaginta*, meaning "seventy." The legend behind its creation comes from a second-century BCE text called the *Letter of Aristeas*. In this text, the Egyptian pharaoh Ptolemy the Great commissions a Greek translation of the Hebrew Bible for the Library of Alexandria. At the pharaoh's request, the high priest in Jerusalem sends six representatives from each of the twelve tribes of Israel to Egypt to serve as translators. These seventy-two translators work for seventy-two days, and the resulting translation is—at least according to *Aristeas*—perfect and without any need for amendment. This story of the LXX's creation is likely no more than legend, and most scholars agree that this collection is the result of a much lengthier and far more complicated process.[16]

Unlike Acts, the LXX is part of Matthew's cultural encyclopedia. When he describes the circumstances leading up to Jesus's birth, for example, he recounts a conversation between Joseph and an angel. Joseph has discovered that Mary is pregnant, and he ponders whether "to dismiss her quietly" (Matt 1:19 NRSV). But the angel reassures him: "Do not be afraid to take Mary as your wife, for the child conceived in her is from the Holy Spirit. She will bear a son, and you are to name him Jesus, for he will save his people from their sins" (Matt 1:20–21 NRSV). Immediately after this, Matthew comments, "All this took place to fulfill what had been spoken by the Lord through the prophet: 'Look, the virgin shall conceive and bear a son, and they shall name him Emmanuel,' which means, 'God is with us'" (Matt 1:22–23 NRSV). The quotation in this passage ("Look, the virgin . . .") is from LXX Isaiah 7:14. And if you compare Matthew's quotation with what we find in the LXX, they

---

16 On this process, see Timothy Michael Law, *When God Spoke Greek: The Septuagint and the Making of the Christian Bible* (Oxford: Oxford University Press, 2013). The function of the story in the *Letter of Aristeas* is to convince and assure Greek-speaking Jews that when they are reading Hebrew texts that have been translated into Greek, they are reading a translation that is not only *reliable* but also somehow guided by a process of divine intervention. This is a message that would have resonated with some early Christians as well. The LXX also includes works that were originally written in Greek, including *1–4 Maccabees*, the *Wisdom of Solomon*, and *Tobit*.

are nearly identical.[17] With this short aside, Matthew frames the birth of Jesus as an event of great consequence that was foretold by "the prophet." But he also alerts readers to his familiarity with this portion of the LXX.[18]

Magoi is not a common term in the LXX. In fact, the only place where it is used with reference to people is the book of Daniel.[19] The plot of Daniel is set in Babylon, in the wake of the destruction of the first temple in Jerusalem and the Babylonian exile that followed it.[20] Daniel is one of the main characters in the story, and he is presented as a visionary who is at the center of numerous controversies.[21]

Matthew demonstrates familiarity with a Greek version of Daniel at numerous points in his Gospel. Near the end, for example, Jesus warns his disciples, "So when you see the desolating sacrilege

---

17 The only difference between them is a verb toward the end of the quotation. In Isaiah, these words are directed toward the prophet himself: "*You shall call* his name . . ." In Matthew, these words are directed toward a broader audience: "*They shall call* his name . . ." The verb (*kaleō*) is the same in both passages. The difference is that Matthew changes the *form* of the verb to fit better within his story. But even with this change, it is clear that Matthew's source is the LXX version of Isaiah.

18 That Matthew feels the need to draw attention to this passage ("All this took place to fulfill . . .") highlights its importance for the story he is trying to tell; he wants his readers to see the story of Jesus as a continuation of the story of Israel as well as a "fulfillment" of certain bits of prophecy. It may also suggest that he was not confident in his readers' ability to make these connections on their own. Matthew's earliest readers would no doubt have been familiar with Isaiah and the body of literature attributed to him, but it is uncertain whether their knowledge of this literature would have been so extensive and exhaustive that they would be able to detect unmarked references to it.

19 A related word, *magikos*, appears in the *Wisdom of Solomon*. Here it is used with reference not to people but to "the craft of magic" (Wis 17:7).

20 In the following analysis, I follow the Rahlfs-Hanhart critical edition of the LXX (*Septuaginta*, 2nd ed. [Stuttgart, Germany: Deutsche Bibelgesellschaft, 2007]). The textual history of LXX Daniel is far from simple, to the point where it would be inaccurate to speak of *the* LXX version of Daniel. Readers interested in some of these textual issues should consult Timothy R. McLay, *The OG and Th Versions of Daniel*, Society of Biblical Literature Septuagint and Cognate Studies Series 43 (Atlanta: Scholars, 1996); and McLay, "The Old Greek Translation of Daniel IV–VI and the Formation of the Book of Daniel," *Vetus Testamentum* 55, no. 3 (2005): 304–23. My thanks to Robert Ward for pointing me toward these sources.

21 Perhaps one of the most memorable among those is when Daniel is thrown into a den of lions for disobeying a royal edict against praying to anyone who isn't the king of Babylon. When he survives the ordeal, it is interpreted as a sign that he is favored by the god of Israel, so much so that the king issues another edict proclaiming that Daniel's god "is the living God, enduring forever" (Dan 6:26). In short, Daniel in this story is a powerful character who can influence people in unexpected ways.

[*to bdelugma tēs erēmōseōs*] standing in the holy place, as was spoken of by the prophet Daniel . . . then those in Judea must flee to the mountains" (Matt 24:15–16 NRSV). Here, Matthew not only credits Daniel as the source of this warning; the phrase "desolating sacrilege" is taken almost verbatim from LXX Daniel: "They . . . will give instead a desolating sacrilege [*bdelugma erēmōseōs*]" (11:31). Elsewhere, Matthew seems to allude to the episode in Daniel where King Nebuchadnezzar sets up a golden statue and indicates that anyone who doesn't worship it will be hurled into a blazing furnace (Dan 3:6; Matt 13:42, 50). Finally, at two different points, Matthew draws explicitly from the famous "son of man" scene in Daniel 7. The first is when Jesus speaks with his disciples before his arrest, and he warns of coming hardships: "Then the sign of the Son of Man will appear in heaven, and then all the tribes of the earth will mourn, and they will see 'the Son of Man coming on the clouds of heaven' with power and great glory" (Matt 24:30 NRSV). The second is when Jesus speaks with the high priest after his arrest. When asked whether he is the son of God, Jesus responds, "You have said so. But I tell you, From now on you will see the Son of Man seated at the right hand of Power and coming on the clouds of heaven" (Matt 26:64 NRSV). In both instances, Matthew is drawing from a series of visions in LXX Daniel. In one of these visions, Daniel sees "one like a son of man coming on the clouds of heaven" (Dan 7:13 LXX). All of this is to say that LXX Daniel is a text with which Matthew is undoubtedly familiar.

Magoi terminology is not prominent in LXX Daniel. In fact, it appears only twice. Daniel himself is not described explicitly as a *magos*, but a story at the start of the book invites readers to interpret his character in light of others who are. The book begins with the siege of Jerusalem in the early sixth century BCE, when the king of Babylon conquers Joachim, the king of the Judeans. The Babylonians take a cohort of Israelite elites into exile, and Daniel is among them. When they arrive in Babylon, Daniel and the others are educated in the ways of the Chaldeans.[22] The narrator indicates that any knowledge or insight that they acquire during this process comes from the god of Israel, not from the gods of Babylon. Daniel is singled out as one who was given the ability to interpret dreams and visions (Dan 1:17). When the king speaks with Daniel and the others, he finds that they surpass all others in wisdom, and so he places them in positions of authority in his kingdom (Dan 1:20).

Not long after this, the king of Babylon is plagued by dreams that keep him from sleeping. Eager to know what they mean, he summons a crowd of advisers from among the Chaldeans: *epaoidoi* (enchanters), *pharmakoi* (sorcerers), and *magoi* (Dan 2:2). Narratively speaking, there is no reason to understand these groups as excluding the exiled Israelites who are described in the previous chapter as being trained in the ways of the Chaldeans. The king instructs them to recount the exact details of his dream before they give an interpretation. If they are unable to do so, he says, he will make examples of them, and all that they have will be taken away. But if they can tell him not only *what* he dreamed but also what the dream *means*, the king promises that they will receive "gifts of every kind" (Dan 2:6).

The advisers plead with the king to tell them the details of the dream so that they can interpret it for him, but the king refuses. He becomes increasingly frustrated and insists that they must be able to provide those details themselves. If they cannot, the king says, they will be executed (Dan 2:9). "No one on earth," they remark, "is able to tell the king what he has seen in the way that you are asking.

---

22 In the LXX, *Chaldean* is frequently used as a synonym for *Babylonian*. Here it is meant to specify some type of a sage or advisory figure, as we will see.

And no king or ruler has asked such a thing from any wise person [*sophon*] or *magos* or Chaldean" (Dan 2:10).

Daniel is not among those who are summoned, although his absence is only brought to the reader's attention later. But while he may not be *physically* present, Daniel as a character clearly *is* considered part of this group. For when the king loses his patience, he decrees that "all of the wise people [*sophous*] of Babylonia" be executed. This includes Daniel, as well as "all those with him" (Dan 2:12–13). Daniel indicates his absence when he asks one of the king's servants why the king is having the *sophoi* executed; he doesn't know because he wasn't there. Daniel fasts and prays, at which point the details of the king's dream are revealed to him by the god of Israel (Dan 2:19). Daniel is then brought before the king and presented as one who is wise (*sophos*). He too tells the king that what he asks for is not possible for any person, regardless of their wisdom, training, or status. But, Daniel says, the god of Israel is both able and willing to disclose these things. Daniel proceeds to tell the king all the details of his dream and then interpret them for him (Dan 2:31–35). The king is elated, and he appoints Daniel head of all the wise people (*sophistai*) of Babylon (Dan 2:48). This story has two primary aims: first, to establish Daniel as one who enjoys a privileged and possibly unique relationship with Israel's god, and second, to depict Daniel not only as a wise person but as "the wisest of the wise."

We can infer a few things about LXX Daniel's *magoi* from this story. The first is that in this story, *magoi* are a subcategory within a larger population of *sophoi*, or "wise people." At a few points, these categories become conflated, which suggests that for the author (or translator), the boundaries between the two were sometimes not clear. Second, the *magoi* and other advisers in Daniel are only "effective" to the extent that Israel's god enables and allows them to be. Finally, in contrast to the explicitly negative depiction of the *magoi* that we encountered in Acts, Daniel's *magoi* occupy a gray area. Yet even when they are unable to perform the tasks that the king demands, their association with Daniel casts them in a favorable light.[23]

Assuming this story in Daniel is part of the cultural encyclopedia of Matthew and his earliest readers—and there is no reason to suggest that it isn't—there are a few things worth highlighting that could affect our understanding of Matthew's visitors. First, the *magoi* in Daniel are individuals who possess unique wisdom and insight, not because of who they *are*, but because of how they have been *trained*. Daniel's story of the *magoi* prompts readers to see these individuals as "professionals," in a sense, almost like skilled craftsmen. Second, it is worth noting that Daniel in this story is the only one able to do what the king asks—namely, recount *and* interpret his dream. But he is only able to do this because the god of Israel has given him the ability to do so (Dan 1:17) and because this god reveals those details to him (Dan 2:19).

Courtiers and Kings

The *magoi* examined thus far are different from one another in a few ways. Simon is intrigued by Peter, John, and Philip because he is interested in their special abilities, which he understands as a type of "magic" that he could potentially procure for himself. Bar-Jesus, on the other hand, wants nothing to do with Paul and Barnabas, and he attempts to keep them away from the proconsul of Cyprus. And both characters are meant to be read as negative. The *magoi* in Daniel, by contrast, are advisers to the king of Babylon, and while they

---

23 In Josephus's expanded retelling of this story, before Daniel reveals the interpretation of the king's dream, he pleads with the king to not understand him as somehow wiser or more than the Chaldeans and *magoi* just because he was able to understand the dream and they were not. His ability to complete this task, he argues, is because of his god, not because of any special abilities that he possesses (*Ant.* 10.195–204).

are unable to perform their function to the king's satisfaction in this instance, there's no indication they are negative characters like Simon and Bar-Jesus. What all these *magoi* share, however, is an attraction to people in positions of power. Simon is drawn to the apostles, Bar-Jesus is introduced alongside the proconsul of Cyprus, and the *magoi* in Daniel are members of the king's court.

We see similar dynamics at play in other ancient texts about *magoi*. In his influential *Histories*, the Greek historian Herodotus recounts a story about two *magoi* who attain political power through deception and trickery. The story is set in Egypt and begins with a man named Cambyses, the son of the Persian king Cyrus the Great (3.30).[24] Cambyses has a dream in which he sees his brother, Smerdis, sitting exalted on a throne, his head reaching up into the heavens. Cambyses is terrified by the thought of having to compete with his brother for power, so he exiles Smerdis to Persia. Then, just to make sure he is out of the picture, he sends his servant Prexaspes to murder him (3.30). One of the *magoi* in this story—named Patizeithes—works as a steward in Cambyses's house. Patizeithes's brother is also a *magos* and not only resembles Cambyses's murdered brother but also shares his name. Seeing an opportunity to grasp control, Patizeithes seats his brother, Smerdis, upon the throne and announces to the troops in Egypt that this is Smerdis, son of Cyrus, and that they are to obey him, not Cambyses (3.61). Cambyses is surprised and agitated when he hears this news, but initially, he does not suspect that the *magoi* are behind it. Rather, he assumes that Prexaspes lied about having killed Smerdis (3.62).

When Cambyses learns that one of the *magoi* is named Smerdis, he begins to suspect that they are attempting a coup. But he also remembers his dream (in 3.30), and he realizes that he misinterpreted

---

24 This story of Cambyses and the *magoi* appears in abbreviated form in Strabo, *Geogr.* 15.3.24.

what he saw; it wasn't his brother Smerdis on the throne but Smerdis the *magos*. Cambyses weeps, but then he determines to wage war on the *magoi*. As he is mounting his horse, he slips and is stabbed in the thigh by his own sword (3.64). He summons the Persians and tells them the whole story—how he had ordered his brother to be murdered and how the person on the throne is not Smerdis, son of Cyrus, but Smerdis the *magos* (3.65). Cambyses succumbs to his injury, but the Persians conclude that he was trying to manipulate them into a war. They choose to believe that Smerdis the *magos is* the son of Cyrus and, therefore, the heir to the throne. Prexaspes aids the ruse by now denying that he had killed Cambyses's brother in the first place.

Smerdis the *magos* rules as king for seven months, and at least according to Herodotus's commentary, he does a good job (3.67). When his true identity finally comes to light, a small group of Persians make plans to retake the throne (3.68–73). Unbeknown to them, however, the *magoi* have befriended Prexaspes, and they ask him to reaffirm publicly that Smerdis the *magos* is the son of Cyrus and therefore the true and rightful king (3.74). Prexaspes agrees. He climbs a high tower to give his speech, but at the last minute, he chooses to reveal instead that he had murdered the son of Cyrus and that the Persians were currently being ruled by *magoi*. He then leaps off the tower and plummets to his death (3.75). The Persians are enraged, and they storm the palace of the *magoi*. The *magoi* are decapitated, and their heads are paraded around for all to see. The Persians then resolve to murder every *magos* that they can find. Herodotus writes that these events are commemorated on a holy day known as "the slaughter of the *magoi*" and that it is one of the holiest days in Persia (3.79).[25]

---

25 Josephus likewise mentions this story and the ensuing slaughter of the *magoi* in *Ant.* 11.31.

We find references to *magoi* in proximity to kings in other ancient sources as well. In Philo of Alexandria's (ca. 20 BCE–50 CE) retelling of the Exodus scene where Moses and Aaron turn a staff into a serpent, Philo refers to Pharaoh's court officials as *sophistai* (wise men) and *magoi*.[26] Here, as in Exodus, this group counters Moses's miraculous power by showing that they too can make their staffs become serpents (*Mos.* 1.92; cf. Exod 7:8–13). In this instance, Philo portrays the *magoi* not only as powerful but also as people in close proximity to a powerful ruler—the pharaoh. By speaking of *magoi* as among the opponents of Moses and Aaron, Philo reveals his negative view of the *magoi*. Elsewhere, Philo speaks of *magoi* in a Persian context, and he says that it is apparently not possible for one to even become a king without first learning the ways of the *magoi* (*Spec.* 3.18). A similar tradition is reflected in the works of the Greek geographer Strabo (ca. 64 BCE–24 CE), who references a council of the Parthians, which includes wise people (*sophoi*) and *magoi*. According to Strabo, kings are appointed only from within these groups (*Geogr.* 11.3). Strabo also speaks of *magoi* in the context of deceased kings, indicating that *magoi* were responsible for standing guard at the tomb of Cyrus. Although Strabo also suggests that they aren't particularly good at their job, for just before he mentions the *magoi*, he notes that Cyrus's tomb had recently been robbed (*Geogr.* 15.7).

Diviners and Dreamers

In ancient literature, *magoi* are often advisory figures who can interpret dreams and other phenomena. This ability earns them

---

26   In the LXX translation of Exod 7:11, by contrast, they are called *sophistai* (wise people) and *pharmakoi* (sorcerers).

proximity to power, as was the case with the *magoi* in LXX Daniel. Another story from Herodotus illustrates this same function. In this story, Herodotus tells of the birth and childhood of Cyrus the Great. The *magoi* appear at several points in the story, and their advice and dream interpretation drive the narrative.

Herodotus introduces the *magoi* early in *Histories* as one of the six tribes of the Medes that were unified under the rule of Deioces (1.101). Deioces's son, Phraortes, inherited the throne when his father died, and he set to work conquering Persia and much of the Asian subcontinent before being defeated by the Assyrians (1.102). Phraortes's son, Cyaxares, picks up where his father left off and, after a few defeats, succeeds in conquering the Assyrians (1.105–6). The *magoi* enter the scene after Cyaxares's death, when his son, Astyages, has an unusual dream of water gushing from his daughter and filling the city and surrounding country (1.107). Astyages summons the *magoi* to interpret this dream. Herodotus doesn't say what their interpretation was, but he does say how Astyages reacts to it. Instead of choosing another Mede for his daughter, Mandane, to marry, he instructs her to marry a Persian whom he considered to be of lower status than a Mede (1.107).[27] This doesn't solve his problem, however, and after they are married and Mandane becomes pregnant, Astyages has another dream that terrifies him even more than the first: a vine comes out of his daughter and blankets all of Asia. He again calls the *magoi*, and they interpret this dream as signaling that Mandane's child will replace Astyages on the throne, so Astyages instructs his servant Harpagus to kill the child after he is born and dispose of his body. Mandane gives birth to a boy and names him Cyrus (1.108).

---

27 The Persian's name is Cambyses, who is related to the eponymous character discussed earlier, but is here a distinct character.

Harpagus is hesitant to kill Cyrus, so he enlists a cowherd to do it for him. The cowherd is no more enthusiastic about this task than Harpagus, so he and his wife decide to keep Cyrus and raise him as their own child (1.109–13). The *magoi* appear again when Cyrus is ten. After playing a bit too roughly with some boys in the village, he is brought before his grandfather Astyages, who is somehow able to recognize Cyrus, and almost immediately. Harpagus comes clean to Astyages and is punished for his failure to follow orders and kill the boy when he was first born (1.118–19).[28] Astyages then summons the *magoi* for council, and they offer him some truly unusual advice. As it turns out, when Cyrus was playing with the boys in the village, they proclaimed him king over them as part of their game. As they continued to play, Cyrus treated them as if he were actually their king, and they were his subjects. The *magoi* conclude that this must have been the meaning of Astyages's dream about the vine a decade before. Certainly, Cyrus will not become king a *second* time (1.120).

Following the advice of the *magoi*, Astyages sends Cyrus to Persia, where he grows to adulthood. But then, prompted by Harpagus, Cyrus rallies the Persians and attacks the Medes, scattering their armies (1.126–28). Astyages is furious with the *magoi* for misleading him, and he has them impaled (1.128). Cyrus is in the end victorious, and although he defeats Astyages, he permits him to live out his life in peace, in his own home (1.130). This is one of the lengthier stories where *magoi* serve as advisers and dream interpreters, but there are other stories in which they also perform this function.

---

28 Astyages's punishment of Harpagus is brutal. He invites Harpagus's thirteen-year-old son to the palace and then kills and dismembers him. He has the pieces of his body prepared for dinner and then feeds them to an unknowing Harpagus. At the end of the meal, the child's head, hands, and feet are delivered to Harpagus, at which point he realizes who and what he has just eaten. He departs to his house to bury what is left of his son (1.118–19).

Philo defines *magoi* as people who have the special ability to find truth and meaning in things like visions (*Prob.* 74). Elsewhere in Herodotus, *magoi* interpret the dreams of King Xerxes as an indication that he should go out and conquer (7.19). According to Plutarch (ca. 46 CE–119), *magoi* witnessed the destruction of the temple to Artemis in Ephesus and interpreted this as a sign of impending doom (*Alex.* 3.7). Plutarch says that *magoi* served as advisers and dream interpreters for King Darius, although he also indicates that these *magoi* are deceptive; they interpret one of the king's terrifying dreams in a positive light so that he won't be worried about it (*Alex.* 18.6). Diodorus of Sicily (ca. 90–30 BCE) describes a Syrian slave named Eunus—leader in the slave rebellion in the First Servile War—as a *magos* because of his ability to do things like shoot fire from his mouth, see the future, and interpret dreams (*Bib. hist.* 34/35.5–6). According to Diodorus, Eunus made a habit of telling his fellow slaves and even his enslaver that a Syrian goddess told him he would be king (*Bib. hist.* 34/35.7–8), which at the end of the slave rebellion is precisely what happened (*Bib. hist.* 34/35.14).

Josephus likewise describes *magoi* as diviners in his retelling of the mysterious writing on the wall (in Dan 5 LXX). In Daniel's version of this story, mysterious words appear on the wall of a dinner party thrown by King Belshazzar. As was the case with the earlier account of a different king's dream, specialists are called in to interpret the omen. LXX Daniel does not list *magoi* as being among them, but Josephus does. *Magoi* are summoned along with the Chaldeans and others, but they are not able to interpret the words that appear on the wall (*Ant.* 10.234). The king offers a valuable reward to anyone able to read the words, at which point more *magoi* begin pouring into the building. Still, no one can read the words (*Ant.* 10.235–36). It is at this point that someone recommends Daniel as someone who is "wise [*sophos*]" and who will likely be able to tell the king what these words mean (*Ant.* 10.237). Daniel arrives and succeeds (again) where the *magoi* failed, delivering to the king a message of impending doom for his kingdom (*Ant.* 10.239–44).

Priests and Sacrificers

No discussion of *magoi* in ancient literature would be complete without attention to the ways that they are described in relation to ritual, sacrifice, and other "religious" phenomena. Many ancient authors identify *magoi* as followers of a teacher named Zarathustra, who is known more commonly by the Greek version of his name, Zoroaster.[29] Scholars are unsure of when Zoroaster lived, but estimates hover around 1000 BCE. Plutarch refers to Zoroaster himself as a *magos* who taught a form of dualism—namely, that there are two divine beings: one responsible for good and the other responsible for evil.[30] The former is characterized by light and the latter by darkness. The *magoi*, he says, structure their worldview around what sorts of animals and plants belong to each power, but they offer sacrifices to both (*Is. Os.* 46). Diogenes Laertius (ca. 180–240 CE), likewise, says that Zoroaster was the first of the *magoi* (*Liv.* 1.2) and that *magoi* are known for being devoted to their gods through prayer and sacrifice. He says that they live simply—wearing only white and sleeping on the ground—and that they are diviners who can see the future (*Liv.* 1.6–7). Although quite different in many respects from what is described here, Zoroastrianism still exists

---

29 Authors who identify *magoi* as Zoroastrians include Dio Chrysostom, *Or.* 36.40; Plutarch, *Quaest. conv.* 4.5.2; *Def. orac.* 10; and Lucian, *Men.* 6.

30 Plutarch says that Zoroaster considered the "good" divine being to be a god (*theos*) and the "evil" divine being to be a demon (*daimonos*), although it is unclear whether Plutarch considers the difference to be meaningful in this case (*Is. Os.* 46).

today and is better known to its adherents as "Mazdayasna," or "the praise of wisdom."[31]

As we will later see, some early Christian authors interpret Matthew's Magi as Zoroastrians.[32] In chapter 7, we will see that this characterization persists until the present. There are a few possible explanations for this. Perhaps the most obvious is the clear connection of *magoi* with Persia, where Zoroaster was born and where his teachings originated and thrived. It is also possible that the dualistic nature of Zoroaster's philosophy of "good versus evil" may have been interpreted by some as compatible with or adjacent to certain forms of early Christianity. Even the name *Zoroaster* may have had something to do with it. Translated roughly as "pure star," the potential parallel with Matthew's celestial guide is undeniably alluring. It is possible that Matthew imagines the religious identity of his visitors in such specific terms, but regardless of whether that is the case, the connection of *magoi* in ancient literature with ritual and sacrifice more broadly is undeniable.

In Herodotus, the *magoi* are frequently depicted as presiding over and performing sacrifices. The *magoi*, he says, are present to chant over the offering, and without them, sacrifices are not possible (*Hist.* 1.132). Later in Herodotus, when King Xerxes comes to Troy, he sacrifices one thousand cows to Athena while *magoi* pour out drink offerings for those who have died (*Hist.* 7.43). Later, when Xerxes arrives at the Struma River, the *magoi* slaughter white horses on the riverbank as a sacrificial offering (*Hist.* 7.113). When Persian

---

31 For an accessible introduction to Zoroastrianism, readers should consult Jenny Rose, *Zoroastrianism: A Guide for the Perplexed* (London: Continuum, 2011). For a more in-depth analysis of Zoroastrianism in ancient literature, see Albert de Jong, *Traditions of the Magi: Zoroastrianism in Greek and Latin Literature*, Religions in the Graeco-Roman World 133 (Leiden: Brill, 1997).

32 The author of the *Arabic Gospel of the Infancy*, for example, says that Zoroaster (here Zeraduscht) himself predicted the birth of Jesus (*[Arab.] Gos. Inf.* 7). Clement of Alexandria likewise suggests a Zoroastrian background (in *Strom.* 1.15; 6.5).

ships are caught in a horrible storm, *magoi* cause the storm to still by sacrificing to Thetis and the other Greek sea nymphs (*Hist.* 7.191).

Xenophon (ca. 430–355 BCE) recounts a speech by Cyrus in which he instructs his men to obey the *magoi* in all things related to sacrifice because the *magoi* alone can discern the will of the gods (*Cyr.* 4.5.51).[33] Later, Xenophon speaks about a formal "college" of *magoi* that was established to direct proper worship of the gods (*Cyr.* 8.1.23). The fragmentary Derveni papyrus (fourth century BCE) also portrays *magoi* as religious experts and practitioners. In column 6 of this text, *magoi* are described as appeasing spirits and souls through their chanting and sacrificial offerings.[34] Shaily Patel notes that, in contrast to some of the more negative portrayals of *magoi* in Greek literature, the *magoi* in the Derveni papyrus are understood positively, "as those who can placate *daimones* with sacrifices so that souls may travel unhindered."[35]

Strabo likewise notes that *magoi* were charged with the directing of all sacrifices (*Geogr.* 15.13), but he then goes on to describe various rituals in great detail. Sometimes, he says, the sacrifices of the *magoi* are directed toward specific deities (Zeus, Aphrodite, Mithras, etc.), but that *magoi* are most known for sacrificing to fire and water (*Geogr.* 15.13–14). Strabo says this involved killing a victim near a body of water and then ensuring that none of the blood mixes with it. They then pour oil, honey, and milk on the ground, all the while speaking incantations over the victim (*Geogr.* 15.14). The *magoi*'s slaughter of white horses at the Struma River is a clear

---

33 Similar statements are found in Xenophon *Cyr.* 4.6.11; 7.3.1; 7.5.57; 8.3.12; 8.3.24.

34 The Derveni papyrus was discovered in 1962 in the detritus of a funeral pyre in the Derveni necropolis. Details about the text and its discovery are available in Betegh, *Derveni Papyrus*, 56–73. Betegh and others have argued that the *magoi* in this text are best understood as Greek religious professionals. Amir Ahmadi, by contrast (in "The *Magoi* and *Daimones* in Column VI of the Derveni Papyrus," *Numen* 61 [2014]: 484–508), maintains that they are best understood in an Iranian context.

35 Shaily Shashikant Patel, "Magical Practices and Discourses of Magic in Early Christian Traditions: Jesus, Peter, and Paul" (PhD diss., University of North Carolina at Chapel Hill, 2017), 70–71.

example of such a practice.[36] Strabo speaks of a fire that is kept perpetually burning, which *magoi* attend to and make offerings before (*Geogr.* 15.15). According to Strabo, the unique rituals of the *magoi* follow them even into their deaths. Rather than be buried like "normal" Persians, Strabo says that the *magoi* see to it that their bodies are left exposed so that they can be eaten by birds (*Geogr.* 15.20).

Who, Then, Are the Magi?

Why did Matthew choose to refer to his visitors as *magoi*? What was he trying to convey with this label? What sort of people does he understand them to be? There are no simple answers to these questions. *Magoi* in ancient literature are complex characters who play a variety of roles. Does Matthew understand his Magi to be Zoroastrians? It's possible. Are they meant to be construed as priestly figures? Also possible. Or are they meant to be seen as Diaspora Jews, descendants of Daniel and the others who were brought to Babylon and trained in the ways of the Chaldeans?[37] This too is possible. In the absence of additional clues from Matthew, it is important to be honest about the level of certainty that can be attained. But there are a few details we can more confidently assert.

Matthew's use of *magoi* has clear geographic connotations. These are further highlighted by the prepositional phrase "from the East" (Matt 2:1). At least part of his interest in the term *magoi* seems to be casting his visitors as exotic, from a distant land. But the significance of the designation *magoi* should not be limited to geography.

---

36 Strabo notes that there is a particular sect of *magoi* in Cappadocia that prefers to beat their victims to death with clubs instead of killing them with a blade (*Geogr.* 15.15).

37 This fascinating interpretation was explored by W. K. Lowther Clarke (in *Divine Humanity: Doctrinal Essays on New Testament Problems* [London: Society for Promoting Christian Knowledge, 1936]) and revisited briefly by C. S. Mann (in "Epiphany—Wise Men or Charlatans?," *Theology* 61, no. 462 [1958]: 495–500).

In texts that associate *magoi* with Persians, for example, the terms are not synonymous. Even if it were the case that all *magoi* were Persian, it is not the case that all Persians were *magoi*. Matthew's use of this terminology, then, indicates not just someone from the East—whether that be Persia or elsewhere—but rather a special type of person from the East. It is reasonable to assume that Matthew imagines his Magi to be people with a certain set of abilities and dispositions that are not characteristic of "normal" people. Matthew's Magi are able to interpret stars and find significance in them.[38] Like the *magoi* in other ancient literature, Matthew's Magi are depicted as having a particular interest in positions of power. In this case, the king of the Judeans. Unlike the *magoi* in Herodotus's story of Cambyses, however, Matthew gives no indication that his Magi are interested in usurping Jesus's kingship for themselves. Rather, they and their journey seem to be one of Matthew's ways of validating Jesus's own claim to the throne.

Of all the identity markers of the *magoi* outlined in this survey, the one that Matthew doesn't address is their association with ritual practice, specifically sacrifice. Because of how prevalent this association is in ancient literature, it is unlikely that Matthew is ignorant of it. The same is probably true for his earliest audiences. There are at least two possible explanations for why this trait doesn't appear in Matthew. One is that it doesn't add anything of value to the point that Matthew is trying to make. His story of the Magi is short and efficient, and as we will see in the following chapter, nearly every detail is there for a specific purpose. The other explanation—which

---

38 It is tempting to see their dream at the end of the episode (in Matt 2:12) as another example of their divination skills, but in Matthew, the ability to understand dreams is not limited to the Magi. Joseph, for example, has four distinct dreams in Matthew's Gospel: one before the birth of Jesus (Matt 1:20), one in which he is told to take Jesus and Mary to Egypt (Matt 2:13), one where he is told to return from Egypt (Matt 2:19–20), and one where he is warned about Herod's son Archelaus (Matt 2:22). The wife of Pontius Pilate also has a dream about Jesus toward the end of the Gospel (Matt 27:19).

to my mind is the more compelling one—is that the association of the *magoi* with ritual and sacrifice is already present within the designation "*magoi*," and so the thought of highlighting it further would never have occurred to Matthew. As I suggested at the start of this chapter, this is the same reason why Matthew does not explain why he calls his visitors *magoi* in the first place; he assumes that no explanation is necessary.

What, then, can we know about Matthew's Magi? Aside from what is highlighted here, probably little. But perhaps this is the point, even for the ancient reader. The various texts surveyed in this chapter coincide in a few places regarding the various people called *magoi*. Yet these texts are far from univocal in their respective portraits. As it turns out, there is no widespread agreement in the ancient world on who and what *magoi* were and how they should be understood. They are powerful and mysterious, and as a category, they are separate from what is considered "normal" or "mainstream." Their presence in Matthew may well be intended as a bit of a surprise to readers—a suggestion that the story they are reading may not be the story that they were expecting.

4

Sages, a Star, and the Search for the True King

NEAR THE COAST OF THE Adriatic Sea in Northern Italy stands the historic and picturesque city of Ravenna. It is the final resting place of the Florentine poet Dante Alighieri (ca. 1265–1321), and it served as the capital of the Western Roman Empire during the fifth century CE. Archaeological evidence suggests that the area has been inhabited for around 3,500 years. According to the Roman historian Suetonius, Julius Caesar camped in Ravenna before marching his troops south to the Rubicon River, where in defiance of the Roman Senate, he crossed into Italy while uttering his infamous *Iacta alea est*, "the die is cast" (*Jul.* 30–32). Today, tourists flock to the city to marvel at the "Early Christian Monuments of Ravenna," a UNESCO World Heritage Site composed of eight Christian buildings from the fifth and sixth centuries CE. One of these structures, the Basilica of Sant'Apollinare Nuovo, is known for its beautiful sixth-century mosaics, including one featuring the Magi.

When entering this basilica through the main doors, visitors walk down the nave toward the apse and altar. High up on the right is a lengthy procession of twenty-six martyrs, all of them male. They march from the palace of the Ostrogoth king Theodoric toward an enthroned, adult Jesus, who is flanked by two angels on each side. On the opposite wall of the nave, visitors find another long procession of martyrs, twenty-two in total, and all of them female. They process from the nearby port town of Classe, just south of Ravenna. Their destination is an enthroned Mary and Jesus, who are also flanked by two angels on each side. Leading this procession of female martyrs are none other than the Magi.

As in the scenes in the Catacomb of Priscilla, the figures in this one are immediately recognizable. They are three in number, the star goes on ahead of them, and they come with arms outstretched, bearing gifts. They even have their characteristic Phrygian caps. But here in Ravenna, what is particularly striking about this image of the Magi is that they are also named: Balthassar, Melchior, and Gaspar.[1] Like all the martyrs who process behind them and those on the other side of the nave, the Magi in the Ravenna mosaic have also been given the special designation of *Sanctus*, or "holy."[2] No longer anonymous visitors from the East, these Magi have been given both names and sainthood.

Those who grew up with the story of the Magi may recognize these traditional names because of how prominent they have become. The desire for them to have names also apparently arose quite early. New Testament scholar Bruce Metzger notes that the earliest literary

---

1 Variations in spelling for these names are common. *Balthassar* is often spelled with only one *s*, and *Gaspar* is sometimes written as *Caspar*.
2 Here abbreviated "SCS."

reference to the names of the Magi is in a sixth-century text known to scholars as the *Excerpta Latina Barbari*.[3] The fact that they also appear in this sixth-century mosaic in Ravenna, however, may suggest that they had already been in use for some time. The sainthood of the Magi is likewise not a detail that will surprise many modern readers who may have grown up celebrating their arrival to Bethlehem on Epiphany (also known as Three Kings' Day), a day that has been recognized by various Christian groups since at least the fourth century CE.

So much of what we think we know about these characters—like their names and sainthood—comes to us through the lenses of later tradition. Many of these lenses will be discussed in the final chapter of this book, and all of them contribute to the rich and complex portrait of the Magi that has been so influential throughout the centuries. Our goal in the present chapter, however, is to strip away as many of these lenses as possible, with the aim of rediscovering Matthew's Magi in their first-century context.

We start a full chapter before the Magi arrive in Jerusalem, with the very first lines of Matthew's Gospel. This relatively neglected section of text will serve to contextualize the Magi's journey as well as its function in the broader narrative. We then transition to the Magi's arrival and the question that they pose to Herod about the king of the Judeans. This question, I argue, is meant to cast doubt upon the legitimacy of Herod's kingship. Next, we examine the star in greater depth. I outline some well-known efforts to connect the star with known astronomical events around the time Jesus was born and then discuss some of the ways that the star is meant to intensify the polemic that the original question of the Magi sets up. Lastly, we examine the Magi's gifts to see what significance, if any, they might hold for Matthew.

---

3 Bruce M. Metzger, "Names for the Nameless in the New Testament: A Study in the Growth of Christian Tradition," in *Kyriakon: Festschrift Johannes Quasten*, ed. Patrick Granfield and Joseph A. Jungmann (Münster, Germany: Aschendorff, 1970), 80.

My argument is that Matthew imagines Jesus as the rightful Judean king and that the function of the Magi is to clarify and bolster this claim. And yet, by the end of the Gospel, it becomes clear that his "kingship" will not be business as usual. I therefore conclude with a few thoughts on the nature of Jesus's kingship in Matthew's Gospel.

In the Beginning . . .

When you meet a new person and ask them about their life, you can expect them to lead with their line of work, the sorts of things they do for fun, and maybe even where they live. It would be more than a bit odd if they chose instead to answer your question with the names of their great-great-grandparents. Details like this are a component of who we are as people, but we usually don't think about them as a place to begin an introduction. Yet this is precisely how Matthew begins his story about Jesus: with a lengthy genealogy that stretches back centuries (Matt 1:1–17).

By today's standards, it is difficult to imagine a more tedious way to begin a story than with a list of who begat whom. When I teach the first few chapters of Matthew, I often begin by asking students to raise their hands if they skipped over this part, and every semester, nearly every hand in the classroom goes up. I can't say that I blame my students for this decision; a list of names can read like a dictionary or phone directory. But Matthew has an essential point to make by beginning his Gospel this way, and to sidestep that point is to miss the significance of the Magi story entirely.

Matthew's genealogy of Jesus starts with Abraham and traces Jesus's lineage all the way to Joseph.[4] It is divided neatly into

---

4 Readers are often struck by Matthew's choice to trace Jesus's lineage through Joseph while also specifying that Mary's conception of Jesus was by the Holy Spirit (see Matt 1:18) and not through human sexual intercourse. Joseph is not, in modern terms, the "biological father" of Jesus. This

three sections. Several notable characters from the Hebrew Bible appear in the first section, including Jacob, Tamar, Ruth, Jesse, and David. With David, the genealogy shifts for a time to kings who are descended from David and who ruled after him. The Davidic dynasty in this section of Matthew's genealogy ends with Jechoniah, whose defeat by the Babylonians preceded the destruction of the temple in Jerusalem in 587 BCE and the Babylonian exile that ended in or around 536 BCE. The third section of the genealogy is composed of mostly unknown, minor characters.

Matthew's presentation of this genealogy and who he chooses to include are significant.[5] At the end, in fact, he highlights for his readers exactly how he has structured things: "Therefore all the generations from Abraham up until David, fourteen generations; and from David until the Babylonian captivity, fourteen generations; and from the Babylonian captivity up until the anointed one [*christos*], fourteen generations" (Matt 1:17). Three distinct sections, according to Matthew, each made up of fourteen generations.[6] There are several interesting observations that could be made about this genealogy and the path that Matthew has chosen for Jesus's lineage. For our purposes, I emphasize two, both of which have to do with David and his dynasty.

---

likely reflects the "patrilineal principle," by which one's status as a Jew is determined not by their mother but by their father (in this case, whether adopted or biological). Shaye J. D. Cohen describes this principle in more depth, noting also the sudden shift to a "matrilineal principle" in the aftermath of the Second Temple period (in *The Beginnings of Jewishness: Boundaries, Varieties, Uncertainties* [Berkeley: University of California Press, 1999], 263–307).

5   Compare Luke's genealogy (in Luke 3:23–38), which starts in a different location and includes a different cast of characters. Those wishing to harmonize these disparate family trees sometimes suggest that in Luke we find Jesus's genealogy on Mary's side, but there is no actual evidence for this.

6   There are only thirteen generations in the first and final sections of Matthew's genealogy. Brown (in *Birth*, 81–82) suggests that in the first section, Matthew may expect his readers to remember that Abraham had to have been begotten by someone. This "unmentioned generation," according to Brown, is meant to count as the fourteenth. The lack of a fourteenth generation in the final section remains mysterious.

First, it is no coincidence that the middle grouping is exclusively Davidic kings. David and his royal descendants constitute a full two-thirds of Jesus's family tree in Matthew, and they make up the backbone of Jesus's lineage; everything leads up to and then proceeds from this sequence of Davidic monarchs. The second point, related to the first, involves the number fourteen. To many or most contemporary readers, this may seem to be an arbitrary number without much significance. But many ancient readers would have understood fourteen as the numerical value of David's name, which drives home the point that this entire genealogy is built around King David and his descendants.

Such numerology may seem at first glance reminiscent of a bad History Channel documentary, but a closer look reveals simplicity and significance for ancient readers. In Hebrew, there are no characters that are used specifically and uniquely for numbers; there are only characters for letters. The same is true for the Roman alphabet (A, B, C, D, etc.). Before the adoption of the Arabic numerals (1, 2, 3, 4, etc.) that are widely accepted today, authors working with Roman characters had to use the letters to signify various numerical values (I, II, III, IV, etc.). In Hebrew, too, numbers are represented by letters; *aleph* (the first letter) equals one, *bet* (the second letter) equals two, and so on. Because every letter in Hebrew matches up with its own number, every word has a numerical value that can be calculated by simply adding the values of the individual characters in that word. The shorthand for this practice is *gematria*, and within this system, names are particularly meaningful.[7]

---

7 One of the best examples of gematria from the New Testament is the number 666 in *Revelation*, which biblical scholars generally argue is a coded reference to the Roman emperor Nero. On this and other examples of gematria from the ancient world, see chap. 6, "Calculating Numbers with Wisdom: Inscriptions and Exegetical Impasses," in D. Clint Burnett, *Studying the New Testament through Inscriptions: An Introduction* (Peabody, MA: Hendrickson, 2020).

David's name in Hebrew is spelled with three Hebrew characters: *dalet*, *vav*, and *dalet*.[8] *Dalet* is the fourth letter of the Hebrew alphabet, and *vav* is the sixth, so these letters carry the values four and six, respectively. Add all of them together, and the numerical value of David's name is fourteen. David is also the fourteenth person listed in Matthew's genealogy. Matthew's invocation of this number is not coincidental, and it is unlikely that its significance would have been lost on his earliest readers. David is the glue that holds Matthew's lineage of Jesus together. He is even present in the opening lines of Matthew's Gospel: "An account of the lineage of Jesus Christ, son of David" (Matt 1:1). The broader point that Matthew is trying to make by structuring things in this way could not be clearer: Jesus is descended from kings and is part of the Davidic lineage that was disrupted by the Babylonian exile of the sixth century BCE.

At the close of his genealogy, Matthew transitions to the backstory of Jesus's birth. Here he focuses almost exclusively on Joseph and his perspective. Mary is a relatively minor character.[9] The couple is introduced by scandal: they are engaged to be wed, and Mary is found to be pregnant, but Joseph knows he isn't the father because they haven't yet had sex (Matt 1:18). While attempting to find a solution to the problem that would spare Mary public disgrace or embarrassment, Joseph is visited by an angel in a dream who assures him that no infidelity has occurred. Mary's child is of

---

8 It is sometimes claimed that there are no vowels in Hebrew, but this is not exactly true. There are vowels in Hebrew (as there are in all languages), but in the most ancient copies of Hebrew texts, they are not written out. Beginning in the early medieval period, Hebrew vowels are written as small "diacritical" marks that accompany the consonantal characters. These vowels are not characters, though, and so they are not included when calculating the numerical value of words.

9 Matthew's account here stands in stark contrast with Luke's, wherein the author's focus is on Mary, not Joseph. In Luke, Mary is an active character who speaks with the angel who visits to announce the birth of Jesus (Luke 1:26–38) and utters a lengthy prophetic poem commonly referred to as her "Magnificat" (1:46–56).

"the Holy Spirit," and not from another man (Matt 1:20). Matthew uses one of his famous "fulfillment citations" to connect this story of Jesus's virginal conception with the Greek text of Isaiah 7:14: "Look, the virgin [*parthenos*] will conceive and give birth to a son, and you will name him Emmanuel."[10]

The birth of Jesus occurs at the end of Matthew's first chapter, and without any fanfare. In fact, the birth itself occurs "off-screen" and is mentioned only in passing. Joseph and Mary are wed, and Joseph "did not know [Mary] until she had given birth to a son; and he named him Jesus" (Matt 1:25). This is the extent of Matthew's commentary on Jesus's birth. But even so brief an account prepares the way for the introduction of the Magi, whose role in the story emphasizes the political message of the genealogy, a message that grows more explicit once the Magi arrive in Jerusalem.

Take Us to Your Leader

Matthew introduces the Magi with another brief reference to the birth of Jesus: "After Jesus was born in Bethlehem of Judea, in the days of Herod the King, behold Magi from the East came to Jerusalem, saying 'Where is the one who has been born king of the Judeans? For we saw his star at its rising and have come to honor him'" (Matt 2:1–2). This short introduction situates the birth of Jesus both geographically ("in Bethlehem") and chronologically ("in the days of Herod the King"). These details help Matthew build upon and intensify the political significance of Jesus's birth that he established in the genealogy. The Magi are looking for a king, and because Matthew has already indicated that Jesus has

---

10 The Hebrew text of Isa 7:14 reads "young woman [*almah*]," which the Greek version renders as "virgin [*parthenos*]." In the literary context of Isaiah, "Emmanuel" is the name of Isaiah's second son. The young woman is presumably his spouse.

a royal lineage, readers have already been primed to see that Jesus fits that bill.

Both Matthew and Luke emphasize that Jesus was born in Bethlehem. They must reconcile this detail with another seemingly contradictory fact about his childhood: that he is from Nazareth. How is it that a person can be from Nazareth but born in Bethlehem?[11] Each author answers this question in a different way. In Luke's story, Jesus's parents are from Nazareth, and they travel to Bethlehem in order to register in a census.[12] Mary goes into labor while they are there (Luke 2:1–6). After Jesus is born, the family travels back to Nazareth, and this is where Jesus grows up and begins his public ministry (Luke 2:39–40; 4:14–15).

In Matthew, by contrast, Jesus is born in Bethlehem because this is where Joseph and Mary live. He comes to reside in Nazareth because he and his family move to Egypt after his birth to escape Herod's wrath, which erupts once he realizes that the Magi are not coming back to Jerusalem as instructed (Matt 2:16). Once Herod dies, an angel tells Joseph that it is safe to return from Egypt, but when they do, they opt for Nazareth instead of Bethlehem because Herod's son Archelaus is ruling in Jerusalem (Matt 2:13–15, 19–22). This move allows Matthew the chance to introduce another fulfillment citation: "There he made his home in a town called Nazareth,

---

11 These cities still exist and are about seventy miles from each other as the crow flies. In our present age of relatively easy mobility, it is not uncommon for someone to be born in one city but then grow up in another city. Moves such as this were not unheard of in the ancient world, but in the case of Jesus, it seems more likely that the Bethlehem tradition arose out of a desire to facilitate the connection with David.

12 The census is a plot device that Luke creates in order to move Joseph and Mary from Nazareth to Bethlehem and then back to Nazareth. There are records of censuses having occurred in the Roman world, but this particular one makes little sense outside of Luke's Gospel. The goal of a census is to determine how many people are living in a specific area for the purposes of taxing them. As such, no census would have one return to an ancestral home in order to be registered.

so that what had been spoken through the prophets might be fulfilled, 'He will be called a Nazorean'" (Matt 2:23).[13]

Bethlehem is one of the few points of contact between the disparate birth narratives of Matthew and Luke. Both authors want Jesus to be born in Bethlehem, and for the same reason: Bethlehem is where King David is said to have been from. The city is mentioned a few times in the Hebrew Bible, but it features prominently in the book of Ruth, in which two widows—Naomi and Ruth—move to Bethlehem in search of security. Ruth marries a man named Boaz, and they have a child named Obed, who has a child named Jesse, the father of David (Ruth 4:17; also 1 Sam 16). Ruth, then, is David's great-grandmother, a lineage articulated in Luke's genealogy (Luke 3:31–32) as well as Matthew's (Matt 1:5). As we saw from our earlier analysis of his genealogy, Matthew has a particular interest in framing the story of Jesus's origins in Davidic terms, and Bethlehem is part of that broader strategy; Jesus is a descendant of David (see Matt 1:6), but even more than this, they were also born in the same city. Matthew articulates this explicitly with his hybrid paraphrase of Micah and 2 Samuel: "And you, O Bethlehem, in the land of Judea, are by no means least among the leaders of Judea. For from you will come a leader who will guide my people, Israel" (Matt 2:6, drawing from Mic 5:2 and 2 Sam 5:2). The latter portion of this paraphrase—"a leader who will guide my people, Israel"—are words spoken to David in 2 Samuel, again highlighting Matthew's Davidic intentions.[14] Jesus, accord-

---

13 "He will be called a Nazorean" does not occur in the Hebrew Bible or in any other extant texts, so biblical scholars aren't sure what source Matthew is citing. It is likely that he uses the prophetic designation here in order to establish Nazareth as a city with the same level of significance as Bethlehem.

14 See W. D. Davies and D. C. Allison, *Matthew 1–7*, International Critical Commentary (London: T&T Clark, 2004), 243.

ing to Matthew, is not merely a distant relative of King David; he is a new King David.

The Herod that Matthew references is Herod the Great (born ca. 72 BCE), who ruled in Judea from circa 37 BCE until his death in 4 BCE. Outside of this story in Matthew, Herod the Great is mentioned only once more in the New Testament, at the start of Luke's Gospel (in 1:5). When the name *Herod* appears elsewhere in the New Testament, it is in reference to one of Herod's sons—either Herod Antipas or Herod Archelaus—who ruled in the wake of his death.[15] Matthew portrays Herod as a villain who is responsible for the massacre of children in Bethlehem (Matt 2:16), and while it is true that the historical Herod had a reputation for authoritarian and sometimes violent rule, there is no evidence outside of Matthew to corroborate the charge that Herod instigated a slaughter like this. The episode was likely created by Matthew to evoke comparisons between Herod and the Egyptian pharaoh in Exodus, a character who likewise orchestrates the murder of children in order to maintain power (Exod 1:15–22). The effects of Herod the Great's reign are still visible today in the ruins of his numerous building projects. These include the Western Wall in Jerusalem—which is what remains of Herod's vast expansion of the temple complex—as well as the ruins of the coastal town of Caesarea Maritima and the desert fortress of Masada.[16]

Historians often portray Herod the Great as a "puppet king." When he came to power around 37 BCE, the region of Judea had been under Roman occupation since the famous general Pompey's

---

15 References in Matt 14:1, 3, 5–6; Mark 6:14, 16–18, 20–22; 8:15; Luke 3:1, 19; 9:7, 9; 13:31; 23:7–8, 11–12, 15; and Acts 4:27; 12:1, 6, 11, 19–21; 13:1.

16 A more comprehensive catalog of Herod's building projects (with photos) is available in Eric M. Meyers and Mark A. Chancey, *Alexander to Constantine: Archaeology and the Land of the Bible*, Anchor Yale Bible Reference Library 3 (New Haven, CT: Yale University Press, 2012), 50–82; and Géza Vermes, *The True Herod* (London: T&T Clark, 2014), 109–46.

conquest more than two decades earlier. The first-century Jewish historian Josephus (ca. 37–100 CE) is one of our most important sources for understanding Herod and his reign as well as daily life and politics in Judea during this period. Josephus describes Herod's kingship as built upon the legacy of his father, Antipater I (ca. 114–43 BCE), whom Julius Caesar had appointed as the first steward (*epitropos*) of Judea (*Ant.* 14.143). After his father died, Herod met with Caesar's adopted son Octavian on the island of Rhodes and assumed power not long after (*J.W.* 1.386–92; *Ant.* 15.187–201). Josephus tells us that not long after he was put in control of Judea, the Roman Senate bestowed upon him the more prestigious title "king of the Judeans" (*J.W.* 1.282). A crucial ingredient in the positions of both Antipater and Herod is precarity, and it is essential to keep this in mind when discussing their respective rules. Any authority that either possessed was given to them by Rome, and it was given with the understanding that it could be taken away if they fell out of favor.

Antipater and Herod were controversial choices. While they were charged with overseeing the people and affairs of Judea, neither of them was Judean. Antipater was from a region south of Judea and the Dead Sea called Edom, which the Romans referred to with the Greek designation *Idumea*. Written and archaeological records show that Judea in the first century was far from a homogenous territory; Judeans lived alongside a variety of people who weren't, strictly speaking, "Judeans." This included Idumeans. The Greek historian Strabo (ca. 64 BCE–24 CE) claims that Idumeans not only lived among Judeans but also adopted Judean religion and customs (*Geogr.* 16.2.34). Josephus echoes this claim when discussing Antipater and Herod. While he often notes their Idumean heritage (e.g., in *Ant.* 14.8), he also speaks of them as "native" Judeans. He goes so far as to describe Antipater as being "of the same tribe [*homophulon*]" as Judeans living in Egypt (in *Ant.* 14.131), for example, and at one point he refers to Herod as "a Judean by birth [*to genos Ioudaion*]" (*Ant.* 20.173).

Josephus has plenty of negative things to say about both Antipater and Herod (particularly in his *Antiquities*), but in terms of their being Idumeans, he sometimes goes out of his way to downplay it. The fact that he feels inclined to offer such commentary in the first place suggests that this may have been more than slightly problematic for some of his readers. Queen Gertrude's famous line from Shakespeare's *Hamlet* is perhaps instructive here: "The lady doth protest too much methinks."[17] The fact that Josephus feels the need to comment on Antipater and Herod's acceptance by Judeans may suggest that such an acceptance was neither easy nor universally shared. Josephus recounts the accusation of Antigonus the Hasmonean (d. 37 BCE), who described Herod both as "an idiot and an Idumean, that is, a 'half-Judean' [*hēmiioudaiō*]" (*Ant.* 16.292). All of this is to say that when we approach the topic of Herod's kingship, we would do well to remember that while Herod was technically a king, his kingship was for many reasons unstable.[18]

In this light, a few details from Matthew's story come into focus. First, we note that the Magi travel first to Jerusalem, not Bethlehem. And they do so with no indication from Matthew that they are lost or in need of directions. Jerusalem is their destination. When they arrive, they begin asking about the whereabouts of the king they are seeking because they assume that Jerusalem is the city in which they will find him. In the first century CE, Jerusalem is most recognizable as the location of the temple (at least before

---

17 *Hamlet, Prince of Denmark*, ed. Philip Edwards (Cambridge: Cambridge University Press, 1985), 3.2.211.
18 Richard Horsley gives a helpful overview of Herod's kingship and the tyranny that characterized much of it in *The Liberation of Christmas: The Infancy Narratives in Social Context* (Eugene, OR: Wipf & Stock, 2006), 39–49.

it is destroyed by the Romans in 70 CE), and as such, it was the center of Judean religious practice. But Jerusalem is also the center of the Judean government and, since the days of King David, is where the king of the Judeans lived. So if the Magi are searching for "the one born king of the Judeans," then Jerusalem would be the obvious destination. But when the Magi begin to ask about this king's whereabouts, they discover that their actual destination is somewhere else entirely.

A King or a Christ?

Matthew 2:2 is the only time in the narrative where the Magi speak. Their opening question—"Where is the one born king of the Judeans?"—is often mistakenly interpreted as the Magi asking about an infant. "The *newly born* king of the Judeans," if you will.[19] But this is not what they are asking, and framing the question in this way makes little sense in Matthew's narrative. The Magi are looking for a king, and the question they pose is politically subversive. Herod's title was his by vote of the Roman Senate, not by Davidic lineage. The Magi's question reflects his kingship's contingency. "Where is the one *born* king of the Judeans?" could be rephrased as "We are looking for the *legitimate* king of the Judeans, not one who received his title from the Romans." Herod's response to the Magi indicates that he interprets their inquiry as a challenge to his legitimacy.

When Herod hears the Magi's question, Matthew writes that "he gathered together all the chief priests and scribes of the people and asked them where the anointed one is to be born" (Matt 2:4).

---

19 Raymond Brown suggests, for example, that a better read of "the one born king of the Jews/Judeans" might be "the one who has been born, namely, the king of the Jews [or Judeans]" (*Birth*, 70). But this translation is based in little more than wishful thinking.

There is a rather unsubtle shift in terminology in this line of questioning that may appear odd at first glance; the Magi arrive in Jerusalem asking about a king, and Herod in turn asks about the birthplace of "the anointed one." Why the change? This shift indicates that Herod understands that the Magi are looking not only for a king but for a specific type of king. Moreover, his question suggests that he is self-aware enough to realize that they aren't looking for him or any of his heirs.[20]

The Greek noun translated here as "anointed one" is *christos*. Its Hebrew equivalent is *maschiach*, which is often rendered in English as "messiah." Both terms are idiomatic and could be translated woodenly as "someone who has had oil poured onto them." While the ritualistic pouring of oil is part of being an anointed one (at least in some cases), the chief function of this category has little to do with oil and everything to do with having been chosen and set apart for a particular task. In the New Testament, the designation *christos* is used exclusively as a title for Jesus, and it is almost always translated as either "Christ" or "Messiah."[21] But being "anointed" or even "an anointed one" takes on a few different meanings when we look at how the language is used outside the New Testament. In the Septuagint (LXX), for example, the concept of anointing is used to describe priests (e.g., in Exod 29:7; Lev 4:3; and 2 Macc 2:10), prophets (e.g., in Isa 61:1), and even sacred objects (e.g., in

---

20 As Richard Horsley puts it, "The fact that Herod had to inquire of the chief priests and scribes where 'the anointed one' was to be born indicates that he himself was definitely not the divinely anointed king of the Jews" (*Liberation of Christmas*, 40). Of course, this observation applies to Herod the Great as a literary character in Matthew's Gospel. How the historical Herod may have felt about the legitimacy of his own kingship is a question that is not relevant for the purposes of this study.

21 There are over five hundred occurrences of the word *christos* in the New Testament, so I refrain from listing all of them here. The vast majority of these are in the letters of Paul, although *christos* is also a popular designation for Jesus in the Gospels. The only instance in the New Testament in which someone other than Jesus is connected with the concept of anointing is 1 Cor 1:21, in which Paul refers to himself and his fellow missionaries as having been anointed by God.

Exod 29:36; Lev 8:11–12; and Num 6:15).[22] But by far the most common application of anointing language in the LXX is with reference to kings.

Some uses of "anointed one" refer to kings in a generic, almost conceptual sense. Near the start of 1 Samuel, for example, when Hannah commits her son Samuel to the service of her god, she recites a lengthy poem (1 Sam 2:1–10). Her words foreshadow the future establishment of the monarchy: "[the Lord] will judge the ends of the earth. He gives strength to our kings, and he will exalt the army of his anointed one [*christou*]" (1 Sam 2:10). We find a similar use of *christos* shortly after, when a prophetic figure speaks to Eli: "I will raise for myself a faithful priest . . . he will go on before my anointed one [*christou*] all the days" (1 Sam 2:35). Once Samuel anoints Saul as king over Israel (in 1 Sam 10:1 and then again in 1 Sam 11:15), the language of anointing shifts to refer more specifically to kingship (in 1 Sam 12:3, 5; 15:1, 17). Throughout the rest of the LXX, one encounters numerous other references to kings as "anointed ones."[23] Most are kings of Israel, but *christos* is even used to refer to the Persian king Cyrus the Great (in Isa 45:1). We can surmise that when Herod asks the chief priests and scribes about where "the anointed one" is to be born, he is asking about a kingly figure.

When coupled with the references to Bethlehem in Matt 2:5–6, however, it is clear that the anointed one is not only a kingly figure but a specifically *Davidic* one. And among those kings in the LXX

---

22 Additional examples of anointing in relation to priests in Exod 28:41; 29:29; 30:30; 40:13; Lev 4:5, 16; 6:13, 15; 7:36; 16:32; 21:10, 12; Num 7:88; 35:25; 1 Chr 29:22. Additional examples of anointing in relation to sacred objects in Exod 30:26; 40:9; Num 7:1, 10, 84. Readers interested in a more thorough analysis of these and other sources should consult Matthew V. Novenson, *The Grammar of Messianism: An Ancient Jewish Political Idiom and Its Users* (New York: Oxford University Press, 2017).

23 See 1 Chr 16:22; Pss 2:2; 19:7; 27:8; 83:10; 104:15; Sir 46:19; Song 17:32; 18:5, 7; Hab 3:13; Lam 4:20; Dan 9:26.

who are described as "anointed," David is among the most prominent and recognizable. Like Saul before him, David is said to have been anointed by Samuel, although this takes place in secret because at the time of David's anointing, Saul is still king (1 Sam 16:12–13). David refers to Saul consistently as "the Lord's anointed one" even after he himself is anointed by Samuel.[24] But once Saul dies and David is anointed publicly (in 2 Sam 2:4), he assumes the title for himself: "Your lord Saul is dead, and now the house of Judah has anointed [*kechriken*] me as king over them" (2 Sam 2:7). While David is referred to as an anointed one in several other places in the LXX,[25] the language of "anointed one" also shifts from David the individual monarch to David as the foundation of a royal lineage. And in these cases, the language of "anointing" becomes nearly synonymous with the very institution of the Davidic monarchy.

In his extensive study of the use and development of messianic language, Matthew Novenson documents this phenomenon in practice. On the "specific" use of the terminology that points toward individual—and not necessarily Davidic—kings, he highlights Psalm 2, which he considers "a coronation hymn . . . for the occasion of the installation of a new monarch." Near the beginning, the psalmist writes that "the kings of the earth set themselves, and the rulers take counsel together, against the Lord and his anointed [*christou*]" (Ps 2:2). Novenson argues that "his anointed" refers to "the sitting king, or rather, the king who is being installed on the occasion of the psalm's performance."[26] We encounter a quite different use of this terminology later in Psalm 132, however. Here the psalmist describes Jerusalem both as the perpetual resting place of God as well as the location of the future Davidic king: "There I

---

24 In 1 Sam 24:7, 11; 26:9; 26:11, 16, 23. Additionally, 2 Sam 1:14, 16; 2:5.
25 See, e.g., 2 Sam 19:22; 22:51; 23:1; 2 Chr 6:42; Pss 17:51; 88:39, 52; 131:10, 17.
26 Novenson, *Grammar of Messianism*, 55.

will make a horn to sprout for David; I have prepared a lamp for my anointed [*christō*]" (Ps 132:17). Novenson observes that in this case, "the [anointed] of the psalm is the king from the house of David, although not, in this case, a particular office-holder but rather the office itself."[27]

In the first-century BCE *Psalms of Solomon*, a collection of non-canonical poetry extant in Greek and Syriac,[28] we again encounter the language of anointing applied to the Davidic monarchy and used to express hope for the monarchy's eventual reestablishment. In the seventeenth psalm, the author asks his god to bring forth a king, whom he calls "the son of David" (*Pss. Sol.* 17:21). The author elaborates: "He will be a righteous king over them, taught by god. During his time there will be no wickedness in their midst, because everything will be holy. Their king will be the Lord's anointed [*christos*]" (*Pss. Sol.* 17:32). Similar language occurs in the psalm that follows: "Let god purify Israel for the day of mercy in bless-ing, for the day chosen for the raising up of his anointed [*christou*]. Happy are the ones born in those days, to behold the good things of the Lord, which he will accomplish in the coming generation under the rod of instruction of the Lord's anointed [*christou*]" (*Pss. Sol.* 18.5–7). Novenson notes that because both passages were writ-ten centuries after the fall of the Davidic monarchy, neither author is writing with a specific king in mind. Rather, "by [*christos*], the psalmist means, roughly, the office of the Judahite king, which he eagerly hopes will soon be occupied once again."[29]

The Magi's question about the "king of the Judeans" and Herod's question about the "anointed one" are meant to complement

---

27 Novenson, 56.

28 English translation of the *Psalms of Solomon* (along with a helpful introduction to the collection) is available in volume 2 (pp. 639–70) of James H. Charlesworth, ed., *The Old Testament Pseudepi-grapha*, 2 vols. (Garden City, NY: Doubleday, 1983–85).

29 Novenson, *Grammar of Messianism*, 57.

each other and to highlight (again) Matthew's emphasis on Jesus's Davidic lineage. But I would also suggest that this pairing is meant to call to mind a hopeful expectation like what we find in the *Psalms of Solomon* and elsewhere. For Matthew, Herod is an illegitimate ruler, not an anointed king. And this sentiment is not unique to Matthew's Gospel; no extant texts from the first century speak of Herod as anointed.[30] In contrast to Herod, whose authority and title depend on the pleasure of Rome, Jesus's authority is his by virtue of his lineage. The politically subversive question "Where is the one born king of the Judeans?" implies that Jesus embodies David's lineage and, with it, the hope that an anointed king—not a puppet of the Roman government—will one day rule again.

What Did They See?

The Magi follow their question about the Judean king with a claim: "We saw his star at its rising and have come to honor him" (Matt 2:2). This is no normal star. The Magi are able to discern some type of significance in its rising, which suggests not only that it is sometimes absent from the sky but also that when it does appear, it does so in a distinctive way. The popular image of the Magi—arguably the most prominent in cinema and Christmas pageants—pictures them seeing the star and trudging westward as it moves on ahead of them, like a carrot on a stick. While this image is rooted in early readings of the Magi story, it does not seem to be what's happening in Matthew's Gospel, at least not during the first leg of the Magi's journey.

---

30 There are some later Christian authors (e.g., Tertullian, Epiphanius, and Jerome) who claimed that some hailed Herod as a sort of messianic figure (discussed in James H. Charlesworth, "Who Claimed Herod Was 'the Christ'?," *Eretz-Israel: Archaeological, Historical and Geographical Studies* 31 [2015]: 29–39), although many of these authors are motivated by anti-Semitic and Judeophobic aims.

Matthew's story suggests that when the Magi see the star at its rising, they understand it to mean that they must travel to find "the one born king of the Judeans." The star *sends* them to Jerusalem, in other words, but it does not *lead* them. But after Herod sends them on their way and they depart Jerusalem for Bethlehem, "the star that they saw at its rising went on ahead of them, until it came and stopped over where the child was" (Matt 2:9). It is at this point that the star *does* become more of a carrot on a stick, leading the Magi to Jesus's precise location (Matt 2:10).[31] Again, this is no normal star.

An impressive amount of energy and ink has been spent determining what type of astronomical phenomenon Matthew may have envisioned. Is he *actually* talking about a star? Or was he thinking of something else that may have resembled a star? Maybe a comet? Or perhaps a supernova? This line of questioning often leads to another: if Matthew was envisioning a specific *type* of astronomical phenomenon—a star, comet, a supernova, or something else—then could it also be the case that he may have had a specific astronomical *event* in mind? Not just a supernova, for example, but a specific supernova significant enough to be known both by Matthew and his audience. Because Matthew uses Herod the Great to situate his broader narrative within a known chronological framework, it is at least possible that he is doing the same thing with the star. But unlike Herod, whose dates can be known with relative certainty, correlating Matthew's star with a singular astronomical event is far more difficult, perhaps even impossible. Of course, this has not stopped people from trying.

---

31 As Daniel Harrington puts it, "Now the movement of the star specifies where precisely the child is. The extent to which the star had served as a guide before this point had not been made clear" (*The Gospel of Matthew*, Sacra Pagina 1 [Collegeville, MN: Liturgical, 2007], 43). See also Brown: "There is no indication that the magi followed the star to Jerusalem. Rather, having seen the rise of the star which they associate with the King of the Jews, they have come to the capital city of the Jews for more information. Only in v. 9 is it clear that the star served as a guide" (*Birth*, 174).

In the early seventeenth century, the German astronomer and mathematician Johannes Kepler witnessed a conjunction of Mars, Jupiter, and Saturn. All these planets are visible to the naked eye on any clear night, but when they align, they appear brighter than normal. What made this conjunction notable for Kepler was that he also saw a "fourth star"—possibly a supernova—appear in the midst of the three planets. This experience lead Kepler to suggest that Matthew's description of the star was based on a similar phenomenon. Because planetary conjunctions are both predictable and recurring, it is possible to calculate not only when they will occur in the future but also when they occurred in the past.[32] Kepler determined that a conjunction like the one he witnessed occurred *three times* in 7 BCE, and he postulated that these conjunctions in some way had also produced a "new star." That new star, he argued, was the star that Matthew describes.[33]

Three hundred years before Kepler, the Florentine artist Giotto di Bondone (ca. 1267–1337) painted his suggestion for the identity of the star onto the walls of the Scrovegni Chapel in Padua, Italy. In a fresco depicting the *Adoration of the Magi*, Giotto situates Mary, Jesus, Joseph, and an angel in a stable in front of a rocky outcropping. The Magi present their gifts and bow before Jesus while the deep blue night sky lingers in the background. The star appears at the top of the scene, in the center. Only it's clearly *not* a star but rather an orange mass streaking through the night sky with a long

---

32 Much of this information is readily available in several media. See, for example, the Wikipedia page that catalogs planetary conjunctions, comets, eclipses, and so on that will occur between now and tens of thousands of years in the future ("List of Future Astronomical Events," https://en.wikipedia.org/wiki/List_of_future_astronomical_events).

33 See Johannes Kepler, *De Stella Nova in Pede Serpentarii* (Prague: Paul Sessius, 1606); also Max Caspar, *Kepler*, trans. C. Doris Hellman (New York: Dover, 1959), 154–57. The "triple conjunction" of 7 BCE has been confirmed by modern astronomers, who estimate dates of May 27, October 6, and December 1 (see Bryant Tuckerman, *Planetary, Lunar, and Solar Positions 601 B.C. to A.D. 1 at Five-Day and Ten-Day Intervals* [Philadelphia: American Philosophical Society, 1962], 330).

tail behind it. Giotto painted a comet. And not just any comet. Giotto painted the famous Halley's Comet, which he would have seen when it passed by Earth in 1301, just four years before he completed the Scrovegni Chapel frescoes. We don't know why Giotto painted the star in this way. One suggestion is that doing so made the scene a bit more "contemporary" for patrons of the chapel. But it is also possible that Giotto believed Halley's Comet to have been Matthew's reference point for the star of the Magi. And because this comet was visible from Earth in 12 BCE, the suggestion isn't unreasonable.[34]

Even if Matthew had a specific astronomical event in mind—and again, it is not clear that he did—there are a couple of difficulties involved in identifying which event it may have been. First and perhaps most importantly, historians are not sure what year Jesus was born in. Tradition specifies that the year is 1 CE, but there are serious issues with this. Herod the Great died in 4 BCE, for example, so if Matthew and Luke are correct that Herod was alive when Jesus was born, then his birth must have happened either during or prior to 4 BCE. Some argue that his birth took place as early as 6 BCE. If Matthew is imagining an astronomical event that occurred close to this window, then the year in which Jesus was born is a significant piece of this puzzle. If Matthew was thinking more broadly in terms of astronomical events that would have happened within a *decade* of Jesus's birth (whenever that was), our situation is not improved. Astronomer Bradley E. Schaefer notes that the decade in which Jesus was born is filled with "starlike"

---

34 See Gary W. Kronk, *Cometography: A Catalog of Comets*, vol. 1, *Ancient–1799* (Cambridge: Cambridge University Press, 1999), 24–25. An argument against proposing Halley's Comet as the reference point for Matthew might be that 12 BCE is a full 6 years before when most scholars peg the birth of Jesus (6 BCE). Yet Brown notes that Matthew is likely not concerned with such things. Matthew, according to Brown, "has reinterpreted by association with Jesus an astral phenomenon which occurred *in the general time period* of his birth" (*Birth*, 172; emphasis added).

phenomena: Halley's Comet in 12 BCE; Uranus passing by Saturn and Venus in 9 and 6 BCE; conjunctions of Jupiter, Saturn, and Mars in 7 and 6 BCE; the stationary points of Jupiter in 5 BCE; a hypernova in the Andromeda Galaxy in 5 BCE; a Chinese nova and comet in 5 BCE; four supernovas in 4 BCE and 2 BCE; and an occultation of Jupiter and Venus in 2 BCE.[35] And this list includes only the events that are known!

It is tempting to conclude from this data that the decade of Jesus's birth was somehow unique, but Schaefer cautions against this conclusion. "All decades," he writes, "are crowded with spectacular astronomical events."[36] Without the ability to date Jesus's birth with precision, attempts to identify the nature of the Magi's star will remain unconvincing. But I would suggest that such exercises tend to skirt a far more interesting and important question: What function does the star serve within the story of the Magi?

The Stars and the Sons of God

Like their question about "the one born king of the Judeans," the Magi's claim about a rising star is polemical and politically subversive. Matthew is participating in a well-known tradition in which stars and other astral phenomena are connected with powerful and important people. There are a few well-known examples of this tradition in the LXX. One is found in the book of Numbers in a speech delivered by Balaam, a prophetic figure whose name is best known to readers today for his talking donkey who, after being struck numerous times, speaks up and reminds Balaam that she is

---

35 All of this data is from Bradley E. Schaefer's chart in "A Critical Look at the History of Interpreting the Star of Bethlehem in Scientific Literature and Biblical Studies," in Barthel and van Kooten, *Star of Bethlehem*, 87.

36 Schaefer, 87. See also Schaefer, "Confluences of Astronomical Spectacles," *Archaeoastronomy* 11 (1989): 91–99.

generally a good donkey who doesn't deserve such treatment (Num 22:22–30).[37] But after this story, Balaam has a confrontation with Balak, the king of Moab. Here he utters a lengthy oracle in which he predicts that a ruler will rise up against the Moabites: "A star [*astron*] will rise out of Jacob, and a man will rise out of Israel; he will crush the borders of Moab, and will plunder all the sons of Seth" (Num 24:17).

The person referenced in this oracle is clearly a military leader of some sort, although it remains unclear who the author had in mind. Because of the reference to the star as coming out of Jacob—who is mentioned in Matthew's genealogy of Jesus—it is not surprising that some have suggested this passage as the primary backdrop for Matthew's star.[38] While Matthew may have been familiar with this, I would argue that it is not his primary reference point. Elsewhere, Matthew goes out of his way to signal to readers when he is alluding to ways in which Jesus's birth "fulfills" certain LXX passages. If he had intended for readers to see the star as a reference to Balaam's oracle, we would expect him to use this fulfillment formula to make that connection explicit for his readers. It is more likely that Matthew has this story in mind as one of many examples of stars being connected with rulers.

Another example of this phenomenon is in Isaiah 14, in which the prophet compares the king of Babylon to a star. As part of a lengthy tirade, Isaiah remarks, "O how the morning star [*heōsphoros*]

---

37 The *she* in this sentence reflects the fact that the Hebrew text of Numbers and its LXX translation both specify that the donkey is a female. The detail doesn't seem to have any clear purpose in the narrative.

38 See Brown, *Birth*, 168, 190–96; and Hagner, *Matthew 1–13*, 25. The alleged connection between the star and Balaam also has ancient roots. Some have suggested that Balaam is the unidentified man on Severa's slab (mentioned at the start of chap. 3). Philo of Alexandria refers to Balaam as a *magos* in *Mos.* 1.50. He uses the same designation earlier to refer to the "magicians" in Pharaoh's court who challenge Moses (*Mos.* 1.16). On the connection between Matthew's Magi and Balaam, Luz notes correctly, "The text makes it relatively easy for its readers to draw on the story of Balaam as an intertext, but whether that was the author's intention must remain an open question" (Ulrich Luz, *Matthew 1–7: A Commentary on Matthew 1–7*, trans. James E. Crouch [Minneapolis: Fortress, 2007], 105).

has fallen from heaven, when it used to rise in the morning! The one who sent light to the nations has been broken into the earth" (Isa 14:12). Christian readers are often trained to interpret this fallen "morning star" as a reference to "the fall of Satan" or "the fall of Lucifer." In fact, the tradition behind the name "Lucifer" comes from such a reading of Isaiah. In Latin translations of Isaiah, the Hebrew word *helel* (Greek: *heōsphoros*), usually translated as "day star" or "morning star," is translated using the Latin word *lucifer*. But in Latin, *lucifer* is a noun, not a name or a title. It means "something that bears light." The interpretation equating Isaiah 14 with the fall of Satan/Lucifer was popularized by John Milton's publication of *Paradise Lost* in 1667, but it is present as early as the book of Revelation, where the author writes, "I saw a star [*astera*] that had fallen from heaven to the earth, and the key to the shaft of the abyss was given to him" (Rev 9:1). In the context of Isaiah, however, there is no question that the "morning star" refers to the king of Babylon. For when Isaiah is told what words to speak just verses earlier, God instructs him, "Take up this lament against the king of Babylon" (Isa 14:2). Notably, in this instance, the star is falling, not rising.

The stars in Numbers and Isaiah indicate different attitudes toward leaders. In Balaam's oracle, the star signifies a leader who is conceived of *positively*. This leader represents divine promises to the people of Israel. In Isaiah 14, by contrast, the star is used to frame another leader in a thoroughly *negative* light. According to Isaiah, the king of Babylon is the one responsible for destroying the Jerusalem temple and for exiling the people in Babylon. Isaiah 14:12, then, is indicative of the author's hope that this king will ultimately be cast down.[39] The language of stars either "rising" or "falling"

---

39 This portion of Isaiah is written long after the fall of the Babylonian Empire, so the author is writing this in hindsight, with full knowledge of what has already happened.

in these two examples likewise contributes to the dichotomy between their referents as either "good" or "bad." But it would be a mistake to say that "a good ruler's star rises and a bad ruler's star falls," because any star that falls must once have risen. It is perhaps more fitting to say that a *current* or *new* ruler's star rises, while the star of a ruler whose rule has come to an end falls. And herein lies the clear polemic in the Magi's words to Herod: "We saw his star at its rising" could be taken to mean "Your star has fallen; your rule is over." It is also possible that Matthew's reference to the rising of Jesus's star is targeting not only Herod but also the empire that gave him power in the first place: Rome.

The emperors of Rome were not a homogenous group. Some were loved, some were hated, and each is remembered for various achievements and atrocities. One thing that they shared is that many were worshipped as gods after their deaths.[40] The first to have received this honor was not technically an emperor but the charismatic military leader and politician Julius Caesar (100–44 BCE). In an event that traditionally marks the beginning of the end of the Roman Republic and the dawning of the Roman Empire, Julius Caesar was assassinated by a group of senators in March of 44 BCE. Only a few months after his death, something extraordinary happened: a comet appeared in the sky. Stories about this comet are attested in Roman sources, and many are quite detailed in terms of when it arrived, when it was visible, and how people reacted to it.[41] Our earliest extant references to this phenomenon are in the poets Virgil (70–19 BCE) and Horace (65–8 BCE); Horace refers

---

40 Emperor worship is sometimes framed by scholars as a sort of distinctive entity, or "imperial cult," but Ittai Gradel (in *Emperor Worship and Roman Religion* [Oxford: Clarendon, 2002], 5) rightly cautions against separating worship of the emperor (or other people for that matter) from other aspects of Roman religious practice.

41 Chinese records likewise describe the appearance of a comet at this point, as noted by John T. Ramsey and A. Lewis Licht in *The Comet of 44 B.C. and Caesar's Funeral Games*, American Philological Association American Classical Studies 39 (Atlanta: Scholars, 1997), 130–31.

to it not as a comet but as the *Iulium sidus*, or "Julian Star" (*Carm.* 1.12.47), and Virgil, similarly, refers to it as the *Caesaris astrum*, or "Star of Caesar" (*Ecl.* 9.47).[42] The Roman historian Suetonius (ca. 69 CE–ca. 122) describes the event in more cometesque language as a "hairy star [*stella crinita*]." He says that it lingered in the sky for close to a week and that it was so bright that it could be seen even in the early evening (*Jul.* 88). Pliny the Elder (ca. 23–79 CE), who wrote several decades before Suetonius, recounts these same details (in *Nat.* 2.94). Both Pliny and Suetonius suggest that the "common people [*vulgus*]" of Rome interpreted the event as a sign that the soul of the great Julius Caesar had ascended into the heavens and had taken a seat among the pantheon of Roman deities. Julius Caesar had been deified.[43]

Pliny notes that there was one Roman in particular who was especially eager to interpret the comet/star event as an indication of Caesar's newly achieved divine status: Caesar's great-nephew, Octavian (63 BCE–14 CE), whom Caesar claimed in his will as his adopted son. Octavian became the first emperor of Rome in 27 BCE, nearly two decades after Julius Caesar's death. He became known by the title Caesar Augustus, which we might translate as "Venerable Caesar." Pliny says that Augustus's public

---

42 The later Roman historian Cassius Dio (155–235 CE) refers to it as a star (*astēr*) while also noting that some called it a comet (*komētēs*) (45.7).

43 The "formal" deification of Caesar took place in 42 BCE with a vote of the senate of Rome. As Nandini Pandey points out, none of this would have seemed strange or improper at the time. Pandey argues,

> The plebs had already been engaged in forms of worship that found their natural culmination in Caesar's apotheosis. Caesar's deification was also a logical extension of honors that the senate granted him in his own lifetime and philosophical and literary ideas popular in Rome at the time, particularly the notion that great men attain divinity through civic virtue. In this sense, while many senators resented Caesar's accumulation of powers and honors during his lifetime, official deification in 42 offered a way to placate and rebuild unity with the populace after the assassination, stabilize disruptive memories, and link Caesar's threatening greatness with his service to the state. (*The Poetics of Power in Augustan Rome: Latin Poetic Responses to Early Imperial Iconography* [Cambridge: Cambridge University Press, 2018], 50)

attitude toward the comet was more subdued than his private one. Publicly, he says, Augustus noted the details of the phenomenon's appearance and how it had been enthusiastically received by the people of Rome as a sign of his late father's deification. Privately, however, Pliny claims that Augustus believed the comet's appearance to be as much about his own fortune as it was about his father's (see Pliny, *Nat.* 2.93–94). Augustus believed that the comet was a sign not only that he was destined to rule Rome but that he would do so as the son of a god. The Roman poet Ovid (43 BCE–ca. 17 CE) echoes this sentiment toward the end of his *Metamorphoses*. Ovid argues that of all the accomplishments credited to Julius Caesar, there is not one greater than his son Augustus. And, Ovid continues, Caesar's deification was meant to ensure that Augustus would be a divine ruler (*Metam.* 15.751–61). While Jupiter may be king of the heavens, Ovid writes, "the earth is under Augustus" (*Metam.* 15.859–60).

The Julian Star was a recognizable symbol that Augustus and others would use to support their claims to power and, in certain cases, their divinity. It was displayed in the Temple of Julius Caesar, which was built by Augustus and dedicated in 29 BCE, just two years before he would assume the role of emperor. The ruins of this temple are still visible in the Roman Forum. The iconography of the comet/star was apparently so prominent in the space that Pliny claims that the comet itself is worshipped there (*Nat.* 2.93). Star/comet symbolism appears outside of Rome as well, perhaps most visibly in Roman Imperial coinage. On silver denarii issued by Augustus, for example, the emperor appears on the obverse with a wreath on his head and surrounded by his title, Caesar Augustus. The coin's reverse is dominated by the comet, whose light radiates outward from a single point, and the words *Divus Iulius*, or "Divine Julius." Such coins circulated throughout the Roman Empire, from

© American Numismatic Society (ANS 1941.131.676)

Image is in the public domain (http://numismatics.org/collection/1941.131.676)

Yugoslavia all the way to Great Britain.[44] The use of star symbolism on Roman Imperial coinage is also not limited to Augustus. In the first century alone, it can be found on various coins of Emperors Tiberius (14–37 CE), Caligula (37–41 CE), Vespasian (69–79 CE), Titus (79–81 CE), Domitian (81–96 CE), and Trajan (98–117 CE).[45]

The Magi's star in Matthew is not necessarily a direct reference to the Julian Star or, for that matter, to any of the other passages noted in this section. Rather, *all* of these references together serve as a potential backdrop for understanding the complex function of the star in Matthew's story. As noted, the Davidic undertones in the genealogy and the Magi's reference to "the one born king of the Judeans" already prime readers to understand Jesus as a king whose legitimate claim to the throne challenges and supersedes that of Herod. The star of the Magi reinforces this claim, especially when coupled with references to stars and their respective

---

44   This and other examples of this style of denarius are catalogued RIC I (2nd ed.) Augustus 37A. Pandey notes (47–48) that Augustus was not the first to employ the Julian Star on coinage. It appears as early as 39 BCE on a denarius of Mark Antony, for example (see Pandey, *Poetics of Power*, 47–48).

45   RIC I (2nd ed.) *Tib.* 23, 24, 70, 71, 72, 73, 91, 92, 93; *Cal.* 1, 2; RIC II, Part 1 (2nd ed.) *Vesp.* 941, 942, 950; Titus 447, 448, 456, 457, 462, 463, 467; Dom. 822, 823, 824; Trajan 770, 772, 804.

rulers like those in Numbers and Isaiah. Adding the Julian Star into this mix—at least as a convention that would be recognizable to Matthew's earliest audiences—introduces a theological dimension alongside the political one. I have noted that the symbolism of the star was used by various Roman emperors to legitimize their claims to power as well as to establish a connection or even oneness with the gods. In this context, the star of the Magi could be seen as functioning in much the same way—namely, as a sign of the legitimacy of Jesus's kingship, but also as somehow signaling his claim to a divine status. And just as Jesus's claim to the throne challenges the false kingship of Herod, so too could this claim of divinity pose a challenge to the emperors of Rome.

As characters in Matthew's story, the Magi are interested in honoring Jesus as the "king of the Judeans." They give no indication that they are interested in worshipping him as a divine being. And yet readers of Matthew have seldom hesitated to interpret the bowing of the Magi as a clear act of worship directed toward a god. Matthew's depiction of Jesus as a divine being elsewhere in his Gospel puts this interpretation of the Magi's actions within the realm of possibility.[46] Viewing this portion of the story through a lens like the Julian Star likewise contributes to this understanding.

But Wait, There's Myrrh

Considering how much of Matthew's story of the Magi is left to the reader's imagination, it is a bit shocking to find relatively precise details during the presentation of their gifts. One might expect unnamed and unnumbered visitors who arrive from an unspecified

---

46 Jesus's healing of the paralytic in Matt 9:1–8 is one example. In this story, Matthew uses the healing of the man's paralysis as "proof" that Jesus is also able to forgive sins.

location to bring, simply, "gifts." But instead, they bring gifts that are oddly specific: "gold, incense, and myrrh" (Matt 2:11). As is the case with so many aspects of the Magi story, the significance of these gifts is not clear, and Matthew shows no interest in connecting those dots for the reader. But there are at least three possible ways to understand how the gifts function within the story of the Magi and in Matthew's Gospel more broadly.

Gold (*chrusos*) is the most recognizable gift that the Magi bring, and readers today will understand it much like a first-century audience would have. Gold is heavy and malleable. It doesn't tarnish or rust. But it is also rare and, consequently, it is expensive. *Incense* is likewise a word that modern readers will recognize. Today, one can find incense—or, at least, substances sold as incense—at grocery stores and gas stations, and for not a lot of money. But in the ancient world, it was neither affordable nor widely available. When Matthew speaks of incense (*libanos*), he is referring to the dried resin (*libanōtos*) of the frankincense tree that grows in the Arabian Peninsula. In the LXX, it is often linked to sacrificial offerings or other cultic rituals.[47] Much like gold, incense was considered a precious, valuable substance, and not something that you could pick up for spare change at your local corner store.[48]

Of all the gifts presented by the Magi, myrrh (*smurna*) is probably the least familiar to modern readers. Like incense, myrrh is a strong-smelling substance that is made from the resin of a tree—in this case, the myrrh tree—that also grows in the Arabian Peninsula. Myrrh appears to have had a few different applications in the ancient world. The Greek physician Hippocrates (ca. 460–370 BCE)

---

47 See, for example, Lev 2:1–2, 15–16; Num 5:15; Neh 13:5; and Isa 43:23.

48 Pliny, for example, describes the production, refinement, and sale of incense and notes that it was often in high demand because of the limited locations in which the frankincense trees can grow and the times at which the resin can be harvested (*Nat.* 12.30–32).

prescribed myrrh as a treatment for stomach ulcers (*Ulc.* 5). Toward the end of the Gospel of Mark, Roman soldiers offer Jesus wine that has been "myrrhed [*esmurnismenon*]" before they crucify him (Mark 15:23). Here myrrh functions as a spice, or perhaps a sedative or anesthetic. Herodotus says that it is one of the substances that Egyptians used to embalm the dead (*Hist.* 2.86). Such usage is also reflected in the Gospel of John when Nicodemus brings a large amalgamation of myrrh (*smurna*) and aloe (*aloē*) to prepare Jesus's postcrucifixion body for burial (in John 19:39). Passages like the one in John have led to the popular misconception that myrrh is a type of lotion or balm.[49] It is far more accurate to think of myrrh as an expensive ingredient that was used to scent or flavor various substances and that also had medicinal value in some contexts.

The significance of the gifts in Matthew's story is a topic of ongoing debate among scholars. Why these three? One suggestion is that the gifts and the Magi's journey more broadly are meant to allude to specific LXX texts about people coming to pay tribute to kings. Two such passages are generally noted: LXX Psalm 71 (Ps 72 in the Hebrew Bible) and LXX Isaiah 60. In LXX Psalm 71, the author writes about "foreign" kings who come to honor a new king of Israel, David's son Solomon: "Kings of Tarsus and the islands will bring gifts, and kings of Arabs and Sheba will bring gifts. All the kings will honor him, and all the nations will be slaves [*douleusousin*] for him" (Ps 71:10–11 LXX). Something similar takes place in LXX Isa 60:6: "All those from Sheba will come bearing gold [*chrusion*]. They will bring incense [*libanon*] and will announce the good news of the salvation of the lord." If Matthew were alluding to

---

49 See, for example, the opening scene from *Monty Python's Life of Brian*, in which Brian's mother asks what myrrh is, and one of the Magi responds, "It is a valuable balm." Believing him to have said "bomb," she becomes worried, and he clarifies, "It is an ointment."

these passages, then the view that the Magi are foreign kings from Arabia would be plausible.[50]

Stories like these in which various nations and their leaders travel to pay tribute to a king are not uncommon in antiquity, and it is almost certain that Matthew and his earliest audience were influenced by them.[51] However, it is unlikely that Matthew intends to allude to any of the aforementioned passages, and for a couple of reasons. First, as I have noted, when Matthew consciously alludes to something from the LXX, he tends to let his readers know by means of a fulfillment formula. Second, and more significantly, the Magi in Matthew are not kings; they are Magi. As such, a connection between their journey and a text like LXX Psalm 71 seems tenuous. It is undeniable that there are similarities between these passages and Matthew's story, and these "family resemblances" may well explain why the Magi *do* develop into kingly figures in later retellings of the story. In these later retellings, the Magi will also be linked with specific geographical regions, including Arabia, and possibly because of alleged connections like those proposed here. But such connections are far from certain.

Another suggestion for understanding the significance of the Magi's gifts is that they are allegorical, pointing toward various aspects of Jesus's identity in Matthew. The gifts are not an indication of who or what Jesus might *become* but an expression of who and what Jesus actually and already *is*. The gold signifies royalty,

---

50 See Brown, *Birth*, 187; Hagner, *Matthew 1–13*, 31; Harrington, *Gospel of Matthew*, 42.

51 Josephus tells of how people flocked to celebrate Herod the Great's completion of Caesarea Maritima (in ca. 10/9 BCE), for example, and he claims that the wife of Caesar sent expensive things (*polytelestatōn*) as tribute to Herod (*Ant.* 16.136–41). There is also the story of Tiridates, the king of Armenia, who travels to Rome in 66 CE to honor Caesar Nero. In Pliny's retelling of this story, he even refers to Tiridates as a *magus* and the envoys that travel with him as *magi* (*Nat.* 30.16–18)! In the broader context of *Nat.* 30, it is clear that the designation *magus* is not meant to be a flattering one. The story of Tiridates appears also in Tacitus (*Ann.* 15.24), Suetonius (*Nero*, 13), and Cassius Dio (63.1–7).

while incense is meant to signify divinity. And because of its connection with embalming practices, myrrh is meant to signify death and mortality. On this interpretation, the gifts of the Magi highlight the three important facets of Jesus's identity: he is a king, he is a deity, and he is going to die. Of course, this final detail does not in itself make Jesus unique, as death comes for all who live. The force of the claim is not simply that Jesus will die but that his death is somehow an integral component of who he is as a person. An allegorical reading like this is alluring, and in chapter 6, I will note that it was immensely popular with several early Christian authors. Our question at this point, however, is whether or not it helps us make sense of the story in the context of Matthew's Gospel. Is this what Matthew had in mind?

Connecting gold with Jesus's kingly status is appealing in light of the strong Davidic undercurrents highlighted earlier. There is no doubt that Matthew intends to cast Jesus as king. Yet it is not clear whether Matthew intends for the gift of gold to contribute to that portrait. The connection of incense with divinity is likewise unpersuasive. While incense is connected with various types of cultic practice—the serving of the gods—this is not its only use. Ulrich Luz notes that like myrrh, incense was also used "for magical practices, at wedding ceremonies, for cosmetic purposes, and as seasoning or medication."[52]

The presence of myrrh among these gifts may be the most important part of the argument *against* interpreting them allegorically in the context of Matthew's Gospel. Let's assume that the only use for myrrh in the ancient world is the preparation of bodies for burial (as noted by Herodotus in *Hist.* 2.86 and in John 19:39). This isn't true, but let's pretend that it is. If Matthew had intended

---

52 Luz, *Matthew 1–7*, 114.

for myrrh to point toward the death and burial of Jesus, he had a clear opportunity to make this connection. But he didn't take that opportunity. In fact, he made a conscious decision to destroy it. Earlier I noted Mark's reference to the "myrrhed [*esmurnismenon*] wine" that Jesus is offered at the crucifixion (Mark 15:23). Matthew draws from Mark's story of Jesus's death when writing his own version, and he includes Mark's detail of Jesus being offered wine at the crucifixion. But Matthew does not copy this detail verbatim. Rather, he alters it in a fairly dramatic way. In Matthew's account, the wine that Jesus is offered is not "myrrhed" but rather "mixed with gall [*cholēs*]" (Matt 27:34).[53] Whatever the reason for Matthew's decision to alter Mark's account, the fact that he did indicates that an allegorical connection between myrrh and the death of Jesus simply was not on his mind.

We come now to a final option which is both the simplest of the three and, in my view, the most fitting: the gifts of the Magi have no real significance outside of their cost. The common thread that binds gold, incense, and myrrh together is not where they originate, what they are used for, or what they symbolize. What they share is that none of them is easy to obtain and, as a result, all of them are exceedingly valuable. There is little evidence in Matthew's Gospel to suggest that any of these gifts are meant to be read allegorically or as literary allusions. Moreover, the story of the Magi—and Matthew's Gospel more broadly, for that matter—does not require these types of interpretations to make sense. One way to interpret the expensive nature of the gifts is that Matthew imagines the Magi as being wealthy. After all, costly gifts are generally given by

---

53 Noted in Davies and Allison, *Matthew 1–7*, 249. Matthew likely changes this detail in order to form a connection between LXX Ps. 68:22 (Ps. 69:21 in the Hebrew Bible): "They gave me gall [*cholēn*] for food, and for my thirst, vinegar [*oxos*] to drink." Luke and John likewise have Jesus being offered wine at the crucifixion, but they (also following LXX Ps. 68:22) specify "vinegar [*oxos*]" (Luke 23:36; John 19:29).

those who have the means to purchase them in the first place. Or perhaps the Magi are not wealthy but instead more like the person in the Matthean pearl of great price parable who sells all that he has to acquire something of great value (Matt 13:45–46). Whether the Magi are themselves wealthy is an unanswerable question, but it also distracts from the main point of Matthew's story: the Magi embark on their journey with the goal of honoring a king, and the gifts that they bring with them are recognizably appropriate for that occasion.

The Coronation

As Jesus's mission in Matthew plays out, readers discover that his kingship leads to an unexpected and violent place. For after it appears on the lips of the Magi, the title "king of the Judeans" does not occur again until the Passion Narrative, in which Jesus is arrested, tortured, and executed by the Romans. The bookending of these titles encourages readers to understand the episodes with reference to each other. I close with a few thoughts to this effect.

Pontius Pilate—the Roman governor of Judea—is the first to use this title in Matthew's Passion Narrative. He questions Jesus, "Are you the king of the Judeans?" Jesus responds, "So you say" (Matt 27:11). When Pilate hands Jesus over to the Roman soldiers to be crucified, they put a crown of thorns on his head and bow before him, saying, "Hail, O king of the Judeans!" (Matt 27:29). His abuse in this setting becomes a sort of mock coronation, and his title, a bitter and painful irony. This is not the coronation that one would expect or hope for, but I would argue that for Matthew, there is a sense that even in this moment—maybe even especially in this moment—Jesus is the king of the Judeans. The title appears one last time, on a placard that hangs over his head when he is crucified: "This is Jesus, the king of the Judeans" (Matt 27:37).

From the opening lines of his Gospel, Matthew primes his readers to understand Jesus as the rightful king of the Judeans. I have argued in this chapter that every aspect of the Magi's story—from their question to Herod, to the star, to the gifts that they bring—is meant to clarify and strengthen that identity. What changes over the course of Matthew's Gospel is not the legitimacy of this title but how readers are meant to understand its implications. Jesus's kingship poses a challenge to the legitimacy of Herod's rule, which is why Herod attempts to kill him. So too does this same kingship challenge the authority of the Roman Empire. While Rome succeeds where Herod did not, their destruction of Jesus's body on the cross is ultimately not a tragedy but a profound irony. The placard on Jesus's cross is posted as a warning, but for Matthew, perhaps it is better read as an affirmation: "This is Jesus, the king of the Judeans."

5

Mushrooms, Armies, and Secrets as Old as the World

THE YEAR IS 1164, AND a convoy of Frederick Barbarossa (1122–1190 CE), Holy Roman emperor and king of Germany, is on its way from Milan to Cologne. Their month-long journey of more than five hundred miles will take them through rugged terrain, across the Alps, and then north along the Rhine River. Their cargo? Human remains pillaged from Milan after it was besieged and then destroyed, a gift from Frederick to the archbishop of Cologne, Rainald of Dassel (ca. 1120–1167). These were not just *any* human remains. These were believed to be the bones of the Magi.

For hundreds of years, pilgrims have flocked to Cologne in order to gaze at the Dreikönigenschrein, or "Shrine of the Three Kings," a gilded sarcophagus that has held the alleged relics of the Magi since its completion in the early thirteenth century. Since the sixteenth century, Cologne's coat of arms has featured three crowns, an homage to the city's most famous and hallowed residents. In 1948, the shrine was paraded through the city's war-damaged streets and rubbled buildings before being placed in its current location, behind the high altar of the Cologne Cathedral Church of Saint Peter. One last journey—at least for now—come to an end.

According to the fourteenth-century Carmelite friar John of Hildesheim (d. 1375), the story of how these relics first came to be in Milan begins during the reign of the Roman emperor Constantine (ca. 272–337 CE). Toward the end of his *History of the Three Kings*, Hildesheim writes that one year, just before Christmas, the star that had prompted the Magi's journey appeared again in their native land, and they knew that this was a sign that their time on earth had run out. They died within days of one another. Melchior on the Feast of the Circumcision, and Balthasar on Epiphany. Both, Hildesheim says, were more than one hundred years old. Gaspar died six days later. They were then buried in the same tomb, which they had selected together. Not long after this, Constantine's mother, Helena, traveled eastward with the goal of locating and acquiring the bodies of the Magi. She had them exhumed, brought to Constantinople, and deposited in the Church of Holy Wisdom, which was ostensibly located where the famed Hagia Sophia stands today. Surely a fitting resting place for the so-called wise men.

Hildesheim says that the relics of the Magi were brought from Constantinople to Milan in the mid-fourth century CE, after the deaths of Helena and Constantine, when Christians in Constantinople were being persecuted. The Roman emperor entrusted them to a man named Eustorgius, then Bishop of Milan, who enshrined them in a Milanese church that still stands today: the Basilica of Sant'Eustorgio. Visitors to the Basilica will find in the right transept a large, stone sarcophagus with a comet carved into the lid, accompanied by the Latin inscription *Sepulcrum trium Magorum*, or "Tomb of the Three Magi." Today the sarcophagus is empty because the relics of the Magi are now in Cologne. Or so they say.

The postmortem adventures of the Magi make for great stories. And like most great stories, they are a mixture of truth and fiction. Some facts, but coupled with generous, creative embellishment. Human remains were in fact brought to Cologne in or around 1164 CE, and presumably, these same remains are enshrined in the gilded sarcophagus that is currently on display in Cologne Cathedral.[1] Helena and her son Constantine were real people. So were Frederick Barbarossa and Rainald of Dassel. There are three crowns on the Cologne coat of arms, and we have photographs of the shrine's 1948 procession through the war-torn streets of the city. The Basilica of Sant'Eustorgio exists, and so does the stone sarcophagus in its right transept. But this is where much of our certainty ends. We don't know *who* the remains in Cologne belonged to, and we don't know if they are the same ones that were allegedly housed in Milan. Moreover, if there *were* remains housed in Milan at some point—which is far from sure—we don't know how those remains got there, who brought them, when they got there, or where they came from.

Stories like these develop over time, and they are not necessarily created to deceive. Often, they are born from a desire to understand or to address lingering, unanswered questions. Matthew's story of the Magi, as we have seen, leaves us with plenty of unanswered questions. We still do not know where the Magi in Matthew are from, aside from "the East." We know they came to honor the king of the Judeans, but we don't quite know why. We know that Herod

---

1 The sarcophagus was unsealed in 1864, its contents removed, and an eyewitness reports that experts were able to assemble these bones into three "almost complete bodies" (Heinrich Joseph Floss, *Dreikönigenbuch: Die Übertragung der hh. Dreikönige von Mailand nach Köln* [Cologne, Germany: DuMont-Schauberg, 1864], 108).

and the people of Jerusalem panicked when they arrived, but we don't know what caused this reaction. We also don't know what happened to them after they left Bethlehem and returned home "by another route." One of the ways to answer questions like these is to retell the story in a way that addresses them.

Our primary concern up to this point has been Matthew's Gospel and how to understand the story of the Magi as we find it in that context. What could Matthew as an author have intended to convey through this story, and what possible meanings could a first-century reader have deciphered? We now shift attention to how this story was told and retold in the second century and beyond. In a body of texts known to scholars as "Christian apocrypha," we find many versions of the Magi story. Some adhere closely to what we find in Matthew, while others wildly diverge. All of them serve to make sense of the Magi story by adapting it to their own theological contexts and by "filling in the gaps" of Matthew's narrative.

What Is Christian Apocrypha?

Broadly speaking, Christian apocrypha refers to early Christian texts that share much in common with New Testament literature in terms of both genre and characters.[2] There are apocryphal gospels, apocryphal acts, apocryphal letters, and apocryphal apocalypses. Some of these texts were written as early as the first century, maybe even around the same time as some New Testament texts, but most were written later, and sometimes hundreds of years later.

---

2   As a category, Christian apocrypha is distinct from the additional texts found in Orthodox and Roman Catholic Bibles. These texts—often labeled "Apocrypha"—are typically not part of Protestant canons. They include Tobit, Judith, Sirach, and 1 and 2 Maccabees, among others. Readers interested in a more thorough overview and introduction to Christian apocrypha should consult Tony Burke, *Secret Scriptures Revealed: A New Introduction to the Christian Apocrypha* (Grand Rapids, MI: Eerdmans, 2013); or Brandon Hawk, *Apocrypha for Beginners: A Guide to Understanding and Exploring Scriptures beyond the Bible* (Emeryville, CA: Rockridge, 2021).

Characters in apocrypha are often similar to those we find in the New Testament. Jesus frequently appears, but his disciples also show up quite often. Many apocryphal texts feature Mary, and as we will see, quite a few include the Magi.

The word *apocrypha* means "secret" or "hidden," but it is also sometimes used to mean "fake." When sharing a story, a person may start with the caveat, "This story may be apocryphal." What they generally mean by this is "I'm not sure that this ever actually happened." When scholars of early Christian literature speak of "apocrypha," it is not a judgment on whether a text is historically accurate. Rather, it is a way of acknowledging that a text is outside the boundaries of what most consider to be the New Testament canon.[3]

The process of canonization, of determining what texts would be included in the New Testament and which would be excluded, was complicated and lengthy. Some popular books describe it as a shady exercise in which a small group of white-haired, generously bearded men gather in a candlelit room to select a handful of texts that conform to their own political and theological biases. Whatever texts are left over are burned in a smoldering rubbish bin while a raspy cackle echoes in the distance. There is much about the canonization of biblical texts that remains mysterious and inaccessible to historians, but we are relatively confident that it was not as sinister as what is described here. The process happened over many hundreds of years and was more organic than many accounts would suggest.

---

3 Today, the New Testament canon generally consists of twenty-seven texts: four Gospels, Acts, twenty-one letters, and one Apocalypse. Two influential "Bibles" from the fourth century—Codex Sinaiticus and Codex Vaticanus—illustrate the flexibility of the canon in the earliest centuries CE. Sinaiticus includes two apocryphal texts: the Shepherd of Hermas and the Epistle of Barnabas. Vaticanus includes neither of these, and it omits four texts included in Sinaiticus: 1 and 2 Timothy, Titus, and Philemon.

Texts were included in the earliest biblical canons not only on the basis of the ideologies they promoted but because of how popular and influential they were. Because people are bound to gravitate toward things that confirm and reinforce their beliefs rather than challenge them, the question of popularity is also linked to the question of ideology. This creates a snowball effect; the more popular a work becomes, the more that work's ideology will become mainstream. If you set out with the goal of assembling an anthology of twentieth-century US literature, you would ask when and where a text was written, who wrote it, and in what language it was written. But the most important question, and the one that you would pose before any other is this: Were people in the United States actually reading this text in the twentieth century? A short story by Kurt Vonnegut would make the cut rather easily, while the Bokonon fan fiction that I wrote when I was seventeen almost certainly would not. Millions have read (and adored) *Cat's Cradle*, while my fan fiction was skimmed (begrudgingly) by my high school English teacher and two close friends.

Some apocryphal texts contain ideas or concepts that were seen as theologically problematic by some early Christians. One example is the *Infancy Gospel of Thomas*, a collection of stories featuring Jesus as a young child. This text presents the young Jesus as irascible and violent. He is easily irritated by his playmates and teachers, and he injures and even kills those who would dare challenge him or disturb his play. Portions of this text have enjoyed popularity through the years. One of its calmer episodes—in which Jesus brings clay birds to life with a clap of his hands—appears in the *Qur'an* (5:110) as well as on a ceiling tile in St. Martin's Church in Zillis, Switzerland (*Inf. Gos. Thom.* 2.1–4). But the text's portrait of Jesus as a potentially murderous child makes it an obvious ideological outlier among other apocrypha as well as literature that would eventually become canonical.

Other apocryphal texts are tame by comparison and by many standards are as "orthodox" as their canonical counterparts. The *Didache*, for example, is a late first-century document that purports to be a collection of teachings handed on from the disciples of Jesus. Similarly, a text like *1 Clement*, while not included in the New Testament canon, can easily be read alongside various letters of Paul. When we speak of Christian apocrypha, we are speaking about a body of literature with a variety of ideas, goals, and audiences.

Some apocryphal texts were condemned by various authorities in the past because they espoused ideas that deviated from prevailing theological norms.[4] But many of them continued to exert an enormous influence on the development of Christian theologies even after their condemnation. Some of their stories survived and thrived in religious iconography. In their study of Christian apocrypha and art, David R. Cartlidge and J. Keith Elliott note that "the pictorial art of the church has had such an influence on its theology and piety that it would not be inappropriate to insist that this art formed a Bible of its own, a sacred scripture which was handed down in parallel to the written Bible."[5] The mere existence of many of these texts today is itself a testimony to the fact that they continued to circulate and be read. If this were not the case, then they would have faded into obscurity along with the material on which they were originally penned. But as it stands, scribes saw fit to copy aging manuscripts to ensure that they were preserved for future generations.

---

4 See, for example, the lengthy catalog of apocryphal texts that are rejected as heretical by the so-called Gelasian Decree (*Decretum Gelasianum*), a document that purports to have been written in the fifth century by Pope Gelasius I but is itself a forgery by someone writing decades after Gelasius's death.

5 David R. Cartlidge and J. Keith Elliott, *Art and the Christian Apocrypha* (London: Routledge, 2001), xv.

Because we are concerned with understanding the Magi as *literary* characters and not *historical* ones, we are not interested in Christian apocrypha as reliable sources of data on who the Magi *actually* were, where they *actually* came from, and what *actually* prompted their journey. Some apocryphal authors may have believed that they were providing such information, but this is not why we are interested in what they wrote. Scholars of early Christianity value these texts for many reasons. Foremost among them is that they provide glimpses into the diverse beliefs and practices of early Christians. It is tempting to view early Christianity as a unified community with unified beliefs that fractured over time over various disputes. As H. L. Mencken would say, this story is clear, simple, and wrong. Evidence suggests that diversity is a hallmark of the earliest strata of the Christian movement. One can see it on display in the pages of the New Testament: There are four canonical Gospels instead of just one, while Paul's letters are filled with attempts to justify his theological positions against those of various "false teachers." Through their creative retellings of biblical narratives, authors of apocrypha contribute to this diversity. And by studying their writings, we learn how they thought about texts like Matthew and his story of the Magi.

When stories are retold and rewritten, details are bound to change. This is as true for Christian apocrypha as it is for storytelling in general. Sometimes changes are major, obvious, and intentional. An author might add a character or characters, provide backstories or commentary, or even create entirely new episodes. Other times, changes may be small and incidental and have no effect on the story's overall sense. But even minor changes can sometimes be of great consequence. One of our goals in examining apocryphal retellings of the Magi story is to highlight the types of changes that authors make to Matthew's account. What do they clarify? What do they change? What do they add? What do they omit? In addition to revealing how these authors have understood the story of the Magi, questions like these may also betray a certain dissatisfaction with how Matthew tells the story or with the details that he fails to include. Apocryphal literature therefore shows us how Matthew's story was read and understood, and it also has the capacity to highlight parts of the story that may otherwise have gone unnoticed.

This chapter focuses on four apocryphal texts that feature the Magi: the *Protevangelium of James*, the *Gospel of Pseudo-Matthew*, the *Armenian Gospel of the Infancy*, and the *Revelation of the Magi*. These are not the only apocrypha that mention the Magi.[6] They are included in this chapter because each of them approaches the story of the Magi in unique ways. Their ordering in the following pages is based loosely on their date, but more so on the degree to which they adapt and add to Matthew's story.

The *Protevangelium of James*

The *Protevangelium of James* is an "infancy gospel" written in the latter half of the second century CE.[7] It claims to be the work of James, known in various Christian traditions as the younger brother of Jesus. In this text, James is *older* than Jesus and is quite explicitly understood as a stepbrother, the son of Joseph from his

---

6 Some of these other texts are outlined in Witold Witakowski, "The Magi in Ethiopic Tradition," *Aethiopica* 2 (1999): 69–89; and Witakowski, "The Magi in Syrian Tradition," in *Malphono w-Rabo d-Malphone: Studies in Honor of Sebastian P. Brock*, ed. George A. Kiraz (Piscataway, NJ: Gorgias, 2008), 809–43. See also the fascinating Irish infancy traditions, most notably the *Leabhar Breac*. The *Liber Flavus Fergusiorum* is another fascinating Irish text, although the Magi are not mentioned in it.

7 Translations of the *Protevangelium* in this section are my own. Readers interested in a full English translation with commentary should consult Lily Vuong, *The Protevangelium of James*, Early Christian Apocrypha 7 (Eugene, OR: Cascade, 2019).

first marriage. The title *Protevangelium*, or "Proto-Gospel," implies that this text is a precursor to stories about the life and ministry of Jesus.[8] The *Protevangelium* is first and foremost a collection of tales about Jesus's mother, Mary.[9] The narrative begins before her birth, with her parents Anna and Joachim, and then catalogs her childhood, her marriage to Joseph, and the birth of Jesus as well as the events that follow. It is the earliest apocryphal retelling of the Magi story, and the changes that the author makes to this story enhance the political rhetoric that we saw in our analysis of Matthew.

The story of Jesus's birth spans several chapters near the end of the text (*Prot. Jas.* 17–21). The author is familiar with both Matthew and Luke and attempts to harmonize these two accounts. Mary and Joseph live in Bethlehem (as they do in Matthew), but they still travel for the census (as they do in Luke). When Mary goes into labor, she and Joseph stop and take shelter in a cave. The account of Jesus's birth is more detailed than anything we find in Matthew or Luke; there are new characters (Joseph's sons, a midwife, and a woman named Salome) as well as additional stories.[10] The Magi arrive not long after.

---

8   *Protevangelium* is a modern label that dates to the sixteenth century CE. The text circulates in the ancient world under dozens of titles. A discussion of its date of composition is available in Eric Vanden Eykel, *"But Their Faces Were All Looking Up": Author and Reader in the "Protevangelium of James,"* Reception of Jesus in the First Three Centuries 1 (London: T&T Clark, 2016), 23–24; and Lily Vuong, *Gender and Purity in the Protevangelium of James,* Wissenschaftliche Untersuchungen Zum Neuen Testament 2 (Tübingen, Germany: Mohr Siebeck, 2013), 32–39.

9   Mary in this text is a remarkable character. She takes her first steps when she is only six months old, and she spends the majority of her childhood living in the Jerusalem temple. The author's chief aim is to establish her in the reader's mind as an utterly pure creature and as one whose virginity is a permanent and unchanging reality. One of the ways that he accomplishes this is by portraying Joseph as an elderly widower with little to no interest in being wed to Mary. His children from a previous marriage are mentioned at a few points, and when he does agree to take Mary as his wife, it is with the acknowledgement that the whole thing is quite an embarrassing spectacle because of how young she is.

10   One of the most vivid and memorable episodes is when Joseph departs the cave in search of a midwife. When he looks around, he sees that everything in creation that moves has ceased: birds paused mid-flight, a river stopped as if frozen, and a group of shepherds lounging in the field and staring up at the heavens.

Their visit causes chaos in Bethlehem: "Joseph was preparing to depart for Judea, but there was a great confusion in Bethlehem of Judea. For behold, Magi came, saying, 'Where is the king of the Judeans? For we saw his star at its rising and have come to honor him'" (*Prot. Jas.* 21.1–2). When Herod hears of this, he sends for the Magi and questions his advisers about where the anointed one (*christos*) is to be born (*Prot. Jas.* 21.4). They answer as they do in Matthew: "Bethlehem" (*Prot. Jas.* 21.5). Herod interrogates the Magi when they arrive, but unlike in Matthew, where he asks when the star (*astēr*) had appeared (Matt 2:7), he doesn't mention the star in the *Protevangelium*. Instead, he asks what sign (*sēmeion*) the Magi had seen that had indicated the birth of a king (*Prot. Jas.* 21.7). They respond, "We saw an enormous star [*astera*] shining among the other stars and dimming them, so that they didn't even appear. Therefore, we knew that a king had been born for Israel, and we came to honor him" (*Prot. Jas.* 21.8). Herod sends them on their way and orders them to return once they have found the king (*Prot. Jas.* 21.9). The star then reappears, leads them to a cave, and stops over Jesus's head (*Prot. Jas.* 21.10). They present their gifts and then depart, going home by another route (*Prot. Jas.* 21.11–12).

The *Protevangelium*'s story of the Magi is like Matthew's, but with a few notable differences. One of the most glaring is that in the *Protevangelium*, the Magi travel first to Bethlehem, not Jerusalem. Scholars of this text have long concluded that its author was unfamiliar with the geography of the region, which is a fair assessment. For example, the author notes that Joseph "was preparing to depart for Judea" but that his plans were delayed because of "a great confusion in Bethlehem of Judea." The issue with this is that Bethlehem is *in* Judea, and Joseph is already in Bethlehem. Just as it would make little sense to say that someone in Virginia was preparing to go to the United States, it is similarly nonsensical to say that someone in

Bethlehem was preparing to go to Judea. It is tempting to dismiss the Magi's stop in Bethlehem instead of Jerusalem as further evidence of the author's ignorance of geography. But it would be out of character for this author to err on two details that Matthew spells out so clearly: first, that Bethlehem and Jerusalem are distinct cities and, second, that in Matthew, the Magi go to Jerusalem first. This change does not seem accidental.

By moving the destination of the Magi from Jerusalem to Bethlehem, the author of the *Protevangelium* highlights one of the central themes of Matthew's story: the illegitimacy of Herod's kingship. This comes into focus when the Magi pose their question: "Where is the king of the Judeans?" (*Prot. Jas.* 21.1). This is like their inquiry in Matthew, but it is missing an important qualifier.[11] In Matthew, they aren't looking for "the king of the Judeans"; they are looking for "*the one born* king of the Judeans" (Matt 2:2; emphasis added). This question contributes to Matthew's portrait of Herod as a king who serves not by right but at the pleasure of Rome; Jesus, on the other hand, is king by virtue of birth. With two amendments to Matthew's story, the *Protevangelium* amplifies this polemic. Whereas in Matthew, the Magi travel to Jerusalem because this is where one could expect to find the king of the Judeans, in the *Protevangelium*, the Magi travel to Bethlehem directly because there are no kings to be found in Jerusalem. And by omitting Matthew's reference to "*the one born* king of the Judeans," the author of the *Protevangelium*

---

11 The precise wording of the Magi's question in the *Protevangelium* fluctuates in the Greek manuscripts. Are they looking for "the king of the Judeans" or for "*the one born* king of the Judeans"? Constantin von Tischendorf's Greek text (in *Evangelia Apocrypha, adhibitis plurimus codicibus Graecis et Latinis maximam partem nunc primum consultis atque ineditorum copia insignibus*, 2nd ed. [Leipzig, Germany: Mendelssohn, 1876]) has the latter reading, which is followed by Ronald Hock (in *The Infancy Gospels of James and Thomas*, Scholars Bible 2 [Santa Rosa, CA: Polebridge, 1995], 70). The oldest extant copy of the *Protevangelium* (Papyrus Bodmer V), by contrast, has "the king of the Judeans." This shorter reading, which I adopt here, is also preferred by Émile De Strycker (*La Forme la plus ancienne du Protévangile de Jacques*, Subsidia Hagiographica 33 [Brussels: Société des Bollandistes, 1961], 166) and Vuong (*Prot. Jas.*, 21).

obliterates the distinction between "the one who is king by procla-
mation of Rome" and "the one who is king by right of birth." The
message of the Magi in the *Protevangelium* is clear: there is only one
king of the Judeans, and he is not in Jerusalem.

Another difference between the *Protevangelium* and Matthew,
and one that further amplifies this rhetoric, is the level of detail that
the author provides when discussing the star. Because it prompts
their journey from the East, the star is an indispensable part of
Matthew's story. But aside from noting its existence in their original inquiry—"We saw his star at its rising" (Matt 2:2)—and then
again when it guides them to Bethlehem (Matt 2:9–10), Matthew
doesn't say anything about it. The author of the *Protevangelium*, by
contrast, emphasizes the star's brightness and how that brightness
obscures the light of the other stars (*Prot. Jas.* 21.8).[12] The notion
that important and powerful rulers are linked with stars would have
been familiar to the author of the *Protevangelium*. The Magi's interpretation of the star for Herod—"Therefore we knew that a king
had been born for Israel"—leaves no doubt that this is how they
understand it.

By emphasizing the star's brightness and by mentioning the
other stars, the author develops its political implications beyond
what we see in Matthew. In Matthew's story, the star is not a "normal" star, but there is also nothing particularly noteworthy about
it, at least not to the untrained eye. Herod and the residents of
Jerusalem are panicked, but the source of their panic is not in the
night sky. They panic because of the Magi's interpretation of the night
sky. Matthew's Magi draw significance from the star not because it
stands out in some obvious way but because they are diviners who

---

12 The *Protevangelium* is one of the earliest texts to be concerned with the brightness of the Magi's
    star, but it is probably not the first. In the following chapter, we examine the "Star Hymn" in
    Ignatius of Antioch's *Letter to the Ephesians*, which also emphasizes the star's brightness.

can see the hidden significance of ordinary things. In the *Protevangelium*, by contrast, the star that they see is noticeably brighter than all the others. It is so bright, in fact, that when it appears, none of the other stars are even visible.

The Magi in Matthew are interested in the rising of a single star that indicates the dawn of a new, legitimate Judean king. The same is true in the *Protevangelium*, only in this text, this new king is not alone. Just as the star is surrounded by a multitude of others, so too does this king exist alongside other rulers. Yet the brightness of this star is such that once it appears, the others fade away and become invisible. Jesus's kingship in the *Protevangelium* continues to stand as a challenge to other earthly rulers. The star's brightness may also indicate that this author understands Matthew's story against one of the potential backdrops proposed in the previous chapter: the Julian Star. In addition to noting that its arrival was understood as a sign of Julius Caesar's deification, both Pliny (in *Nat.* 2.94) and Suetonius (in *Jul.* 88) suggested that one of the things that made this phenomenon notable in the first place was that it was so bright that it was visible in the early afternoon. The star in the *Protevangelium* is already understood as a challenge to kings in general, but if it is the case that this author is also alluding to the Julian Star, then the rhetoric becomes even more focused on Rome and the veneration of its emperors.

In the *Protevangelium*, the star leads the Magi not to a house but to a cave. On the one hand, the cave could be read as a means of harmonizing the stories of Jesus's birth in Matthew and Luke. In order to have Joseph and Mary live in Bethlehem (as they do in Matthew) and be traveling for a census when Jesus is born (as they are in Luke) and still have Jesus be born in Bethlehem, the author creates a location just outside the city as the setting for the nativity. The harmonizing impulse is undeniably present, but the question remains: Why a cave? Why not someone else's house? Or maybe a stable? Elsewhere in the *Protevangelium*, the cave seems to take on theological significance as a possible foreshadowing of Jesus's postcrucifixion burial in a rock-cut tomb.[13] Perhaps the Magi's visit to the cave is meant to contribute to this grizzly subplot. A reading like this makes sense in the *Protevangelium*, but it also fits well with our analysis of Matthew. The Magi seek "the one who has been born king of the Judeans" (Matt 2:2), and the only other time in Matthew's Gospel where Jesus is called this is when he is executed (Matt 27:11, 29, 37). There is no crucifixion story in the *Protevangelium*. The story ends when Jesus is still a child. But if this author were interested in pointing readers to where Jesus's kingship will lead, then having the Magi visit him in the cave is a subtle way of doing so.

The *Gospel of Pseudo-Matthew*

The *Gospel of Pseudo-Matthew* was written in Latin in the sixth or seventh century CE, and like the *Protevangelium of James*, it is primarily concerned with stories that involve Jesus's mother. In fact, while this author is familiar with Matthew (as well as Luke), many of its episodes are patterned off those in the *Protevangelium*. Yet it would be a mistake to think of *Pseudo-Matthew* as merely a Latin translation of this earlier Greek text. The *Protevangelium* is one of the primary sources that the author uses to build their narrative, but the world that they create is their own.

The birth of Jesus in *Pseudo-Matthew* happens in a cave, as it does in the *Protevangelium*. Jesus can stand on his own immediately

---

13 The story of Jesus's burial is found in Matt 27:59–65; Mark 15:43–46; Luke 23:50–53; and John 19:40. For an account of the parallels between Jesus's birth in the *Protevangelium* and his death in the canonical Gospels, see Vanden Eykel, *"Their Faces,"* 158–66.

after being born, at which point angels fill the cave and begin to worship him (*Ps.-Mt.* 13.11).[14] The Magi appear in Jerusalem several chapters later, after the presentation of Jesus in the temple (from Luke 2:22–40),[15] but their story begins not long after Jesus is born. The author mentions the shepherds (from Luke 2:8–20) and comments, "Also, an enormous star shone from evening until morning" (*Ps.-Mt.* 13.30). The Magi arrive in Jerusalem a full two years after this star, asking, "Where is the king who is born to us [*nobis*]? For we saw his star in the East and have come to worship him" (*Ps.-Mt.* 16.1).

Already there are a few points worth pausing to highlight. The first is the specific, drawn-out timeline the author gives for the Magi's arrival. Matthew does not indicate how much time passes between the birth of Jesus and the Magi's arrival; he simply states that it happened "after Jesus was born in Bethlehem of Judea" (Matt 2:1). "After" here could imply hours, days, or years. The author of the *Protevangelium* is similarly vague in terms of timing. The addition of this detail in *Pseudo-Matthew* may be the author's attempt not only to be more specific but also to make sense of a detail in Matthew's account that they found odd or unclear. In Matthew, after the Magi depart Bethlehem and avoid going back through Jerusalem, Herod orders the murder of male children in and around Bethlehem. But the order applies only to those children who are two years old or younger. This story—traditionally called the Massacre of the Innocents—is meant to evoke a comparison between Herod the Great and the Egyptian pharaoh at the start of

---

14 English translations of *Pseudo-Matthew* in this section are taken from Brandon Hawk, *The Gospel of Pseudo-Matthew and the Nativity of Mary*, Early Christian Apocrypha 8 (Eugene, OR: Cascade, 2019).

15 The episode of Jesus's presentation in the temple is one example of how *Pseudo-Matthew* differs from the *Protevangelium*. Presumably, Joseph is preparing to take Mary and Jesus to the temple at the start of *Prot. Jas.* 21, but then the Magi show up.

Exodus. Fearing that his Hebrew slaves are becoming too numerous, Pharaoh slaughters their male children as a means of population control (Exod 1:22). Matthew's reference to a specific age after which children should be spared is absent from the Exodus story. He justifies including this detail by explaining that Herod made his decision "according to the time that he had received from the Magi" (Matt 2:16).

The conversation between Herod and the Magi in Matthew happens "off-screen" (see Matt 2:7), so the information that Herod receives from that conversation is uncertain. Matthew imagines either that the star appeared and gave the Magi a two-year head start so that they would arrive in Bethlehem shortly after Jesus was born or that the star appeared when Jesus was born and it took the Magi two years to make it to Bethlehem. *Pseudo-Matthew* chooses the latter of these options. The star appears in the sky immediately after the birth of Jesus (in *Ps.-Mt.* 13.30), and the Magi arrive two years later, having seen it all the way in the East. This, of course, raises another question: How far did these visitors travel that it took them two full years to complete their journey? This is not a question that the author of *Pseudo-Matthew* is interested in addressing, but it will be taken up and explored by other apocryphal authors.

Another detail in *Pseudo-Matthew* that stands out is the question that the Magi pose when they arrive in Jerusalem. They are not looking for "the one who has been born king of the Judeans" (Matt 2:2) or even "the king of the Judeans" (*Prot. Jas.* 21.1). The Magi in *Pseudo-Matthew* are looking for "the king who has been born to us [*nobis*]" (*Ps.-Mt.* 16.1). One possibility for how to understand the "us" in their question is that this author understands the Magi as Diaspora Jews from the East—perhaps even descendants of Daniel and the others from Babylon—returning to Judea as an acknowledgment that the new, rightful king has been born. A more likely explanation, however, is that the "us" is the author's attempt to broaden the kingship of Jesus to include non-Judeans as well as Judeans. In Matthew and the *Protevangelium*, the Magi indicate that they are looking for someone else's king (the king of the Judeans), but here in *Pseudo-Matthew*, Jesus's kingship is universalized. This dynamic is articulated earlier as well, when the author first mentions the star and then comments on its significance: "This star made known the birth of Christ, who would restore not only Israel but also all peoples as he had promised" (*Ps.-Mt.* 13.30). This author does not include the *Protevangelium*'s emphasis on the brightness of the star eclipsing all the others, but the broadening of his kingship has the same rhetorical effect: other kings continue to exist, but they pale in comparison to Jesus.

When the Magi depart Jerusalem for Bethlehem, the star that they had seen two years earlier has reappeared and gone on ahead of them. Because two years have passed, Jesus is no longer in the cave where he was born, so the star leads them instead to "where the child was" (*Ps.-Mt.* 16.7). The Magi find Jesus perched on his mother's lap, and they proceed to offer their gifts. In this scene, we encounter two more alterations to Matthew's story. The three traditional gifts of gold, incense, and myrrh are all present, but in this text, they are understood not as gifts for Jesus but as gifts for Joseph and Mary. In addition to these gifts, however, the Magi also bring something special for Jesus; each gives him "a single gold coin [*singuli singulos aureos*]" (*Ps.-Mt.* 16.9). In his English translation of *Pseudo-Matthew*, Brandon Hawk notes the grammatical obscurity of this Latin phrase as well as the fact that this strange detail of the gold coins occurs neither in Matthew nor in the *Protevangelium*.[16] An alternate translation of *singuli singulos aureos* might be "a

---

16 Hawk, *Pseudo-Matthew*, 73.

single piece of gold," but even here the meaning is elusive. What is the purpose of these additional gifts?

One way of exploring this detail is to ask whether the text of *Pseudo-Matthew* is somehow corrupt. Did a scribe who was copying the text make a mistake or change a detail that resulted in the obscurity that we see here? Textual corruption of this sort is common in both canonical and apocryphal texts.[17] Perhaps in the "original" version of *Pseudo-Matthew*, the Magi are understood as presenting their three traditional gifts, and the author meant to describe not an additional gift but the types of containers in which these gifts were housed. Matthew describes these containers as "chests [*thesaurous*]" (Matt 2:11), and the *Protevangelium* describes them as "pouches [*pēras*]" (*Prot. Jas.* 21:11). *Pseudo-Matthew* follows Matthew's reading: "Then they revealed their treasures [*thesauros*] and presented Mary and Joseph with remarkable gifts [*muneribus munerauerunt*]" (*Ps.-Mt.* 16.9). It is possible that the author originally described these containers as themselves being made of gold. In his critical edition and commentary on *Pseudo-Matthew*, Jan Gijsel notes that several scribes tampered with this section of the text, but he concludes that their tampering seems to have been prompted more by the fact that they also didn't quite understand what *singuli singulos aureos* was supposed to mean.[18] The textual corruption hypothesis remains alluring, but in the absence of additional manuscript evidence, it also remains unverifiable.

Assuming this detail of the gold coins is an original and intentional piece of *Pseudo-Matthew*'s story, it is possible to read it as another attempt by the author to further intensify the politicizing

---

17 An overview related to the transmission and corruption of texts can be found in Bruce M. Metzger and Bart D. Ehrman, *The Text of the New Testament: Its Transmission, Corruption, and Restoration*, 4th ed. (Oxford: Oxford University Press, 2005).

18 Jan Gijsel, *Libri de nativitate Mariae: Pseudo-Matthaei Evangelium, textus et commentarius*, Corpus Christianorum Series Apocryphorum 9 (Turnhout, Belgium: Brepols, 1997), 442.

rhetoric present in Matthew and the *Protevangelium*. The Magi's question—"Where is the king who is born to us?"—suggests that this author understands the kingship of Jesus as universal rather than more localized; Jesus is a king not just for the Judeans but for all. If the Magi are understood as representatives of "all peoples" (*Ps.-Mt.* 13.30) coming to honor this new king, then perhaps the "single gold coin" that each of them gives to Jesus is meant to be understood as their paying some sort of tribute or tax and an indication that they are now his subjects. We see this interpretation play out in a more dramatic way in the two apocrypha outlined in the following sections. In these texts, the Magi themselves become royal figures who travel to subject themselves to the new king.

The *Armenian Gospel of the Infancy*

The *Armenian Gospel of the Infancy* (here *[Arm.] Gos. Inf.*) is the lengthiest text surveyed in this chapter. As its name implies, the text survives in Armenian translation, and while it is difficult to date with any precision, it has been suggested that this translation was made in the late sixth century CE from an older and no longer extant Syriac text.[19] One thing that distinguishes this text from those surveyed above is the author's concern with precision. Whereas Matthew implies and *Pseudo-Matthew* specifies that the Magi arrive roughly two years after the birth of Jesus, for example, neither of them indicate when Jesus's birth takes place, so the timeline remains imprecise. The *Armenian Gospel of the Infancy*, however, names an exact date for the Magi's arrival in Jerusalem: January 8 (*[Arm.] Gos. Inf.* 11.1). This text also indicates that there

---

19 Abraham Terian, *The Armenian Gospel of the Infancy* (Oxford: Oxford University Press, 2008), xviii–xxvi. English translations of the *(Arm.) Gos. Inf.* in this section are taken from Terian.

are three Magi and that they are brothers. The author also refers to them as "kings," and they are given names and territories: "The first, Melkon, was king of the Persians; the second, Gaspar, was king of the Indians; the third, Baltasar,[20] was king of the Arabians" (*[Arm.] Gos. Inf.* 11.1).

The story of the Magi in the *Armenian Gospel of the Infancy* appears mostly in chapter 11, although they are first mentioned earlier, in chapter 5. The bulk of chapter 5 is a retelling of the angelic announcement of Jesus's birth to Mary, which is based loosely on the annunciation narrative in Luke 1:26–38. The author of the *Armenian Gospel of the Infancy* adds to Luke's brief story a lengthy dialogue between Mary and the angel as well as a description of the conception of Jesus: "At that very moment when this word was spoken, as the holy Virgin consented, God the Word penetrated through her ear . . . at that same time began the pregnancy of Mary" (*[Arm.] Gos. Inf.* 5.9). The author introduces the Magi when the same angel who spoke to Mary travels east to Persia. This angel reports the news of Mary's conception and instructs the Magi to go and worship the baby that will soon be born. The author then fills out the story of the Magi with dramatic details: They are not astrologers, magicians, or sages. Rather, they are powerful military leaders whose strength and prowess surpass other kings in the East. And in this text, they do not travel alone, but with armies (*[Arm.] Gos. Inf.* 5.10).

The nine-month journey of the Magi is not described in the *Armenian Gospel of the Infancy*, but they arrive in Jerusalem just days after the birth of Jesus. Here, for the first time, the armies of the Magi are numbered at twelve thousand troops. The light

---

20 The names Melkon and Baltasar in Terian's English translation are different from the more traditional Melchior and Balthasar. For the sake of continuity, I have chosen to retain these alternate spellings in this section.

of their guiding star fades, and they set up camp outside the city walls (*[Arm.] Gos. Inf.* 11.1–3). One of the more curious elements of the Magi story in Matthew is the panic that overtakes Herod and the entire city of Jerusalem when the Magi show up (Matt 2:3). In Matthew, it is understood as concern that Herod's position as king of the Judeans is threatened by the birth of a new king who will rule by birthright rather than at the pleasure of Rome. The author of *Armenian Gospel of the Infancy* has another explanation for why Herod and the residents of Jerusalem are panicked at the Magi's arrival: they believe that they are under siege by a potentially hostile force (*[Arm.] Gos. Inf.* 11.4).

The *Armenian Gospel of the Infancy* develops the Magi as literary characters beyond anything that we have seen up to this point. Herod sends a convoy of princes, for example, to meet with the Magi, determine their motives, and negotiate with them. A lengthy conversation ensues. The Magi tell the princes where they are from, and they indicate that they wish to be on their way the next day, while the princes insist that it was improper for them to set up camp and not request an audience with Herod. "He wished to meet you," they say, "and to hear a word spoken or told by you. But you were indifferent, unwilling to come to him. So he sent us as ambassadors to invite you with great honor to the palace, to examine and to learn your intentions, as to what you seek" (*[Arm.] Gos. Inf.* 11.5). The Magi respond that they didn't seek out Herod because they have nothing to say to him. The princes persist and ask them about their motives: "Did you come here with love or with hostility?" (*[Arm.] Gos. Inf.* 11.6). The Magi respond with offense: "From our land to this place we have come with joy, and no one has interrogated us as much as this, and you have come here to test us" (*[Arm.] Gos. Inf.* 11.6).

Sensing that they have annoyed their guests, the princes attempt to change the subject, from the Magi's motives to possibilities for commerce. They note that the Magi "are filled with every desirable fragrance of flowers," and they ask whether they are merchants and if they would be interested in having a forum in which to sell their "treasures" (*[Arm.] Gos. Inf.* 11.6). This reference to "fragrance" is meant to remind readers of the Magi's incense and myrrh, both of which are substances with a strong and pleasing aroma.[21] In other texts, these gifts are only mentioned once the Magi arrive in Bethlehem and find Jesus and his family, but in the *Armenian Gospel of the Infancy*, they appear while the Magi are still in Jerusalem. On the one hand, this could be meant to highlight the generosity of the Magi, expressed by the quantity of the substances that they bring with them. They have enough incense and myrrh that people can detect the aroma from a distance. This may also be the author's way of drawing a contrast between the Magi and the princes of Herod. Readers know that the Magi are traveling to present their gifts to Jesus, but of course, Herod's princes are not aware of this, at least not yet. In the moment, they are interested only in the monetary value that their treasures might have.

The conversation takes a theological turn when the Magi indicate that they are not interested in trade. "All we seek is our way," they remark, and this is met with a simple question from the princes: "Which way?" Until now, readers have been given no indication that the Magi are anything but leaders from the East. But their answer complicates this presumed identity. "That in which the Lord leads us in righteousness," they say. "Into the land of uprightness. For we have come here by God's command" (*[Arm.] Gos. Inf.* 11.8). The conversation continues along this trajectory when Herod visits the Magi to clarify what they are seeking. "We heard while in

---

21 The author refers to this aroma again when the Magi present their gifts to Jesus (in *[Arm.] Gos. Inf.* 11:17).

our land," they say, "that a king's son is born in the land of Judea, and we have come to worship him" (*[Arm.] Gos. Inf.* 11.9).

Readers know that the Magi received this news from an angel (in *[Arm.] Gos. Inf.* 5), but here they indicate that they are also in possession of a secret document that has been passed down to them from generation to generation (*[Arm.] Gos. Inf.* 11.9). Herod is intrigued, and they begin to retell the document's dramatic story. They claim that it was sent directly from God and that they were the ones entrusted with its protection. The story begins with Adam's expulsion from the garden of Eden (Gen 3:24), at which point the document was sealed and then given to Adam's son Seth, who protected it and then passed it down to his descendants. During the flood (Gen 6–9), it accompanied Noah on the ark, and when the waters receded, Noah give it to his son Shem. Eventually, the text comes to Abraham, who gives it to Melchizedek, the priest-king of Jerusalem (Gen 14:18–20).

The Magi say that the document made its way to their land via the Persian king Cyrus. Since its arrival there, they say, it has been stored and protected in a special chamber (*[Arm.] Gos. Inf.* 11.11). During this initial description of this document and its centuries-long journey, the Magi give no indication of what the document is or what sort of information it is supposed to contain. In fact, it is unclear whether they themselves know either of these things, for when they first mention it, they indicate that it is "sealed" (*[Arm.] Gos. Inf.* 11.10). What they do indicate is that the goal of their quest is to present this document to the newborn king that they are seeking (*[Arm.] Gos. Inf.* 11.11). When he hears all of this, Herod attempts to have the Magi arrested so that he can investigate the matter further. The building that they are in begins to shake, and it crumbles to the ground, killing seventy-two people.

Herod and the Magi escape unharmed, or so it would seem, and the crowds plead with Herod to let the Magi go (*[Arm.] Gos.*

Inf. 11.12). He summons the Magi one last time, and in the *Armenian Gospel of the Infancy*, it is the Magi who ask Herod, "Where will Christ, the king of the Jews, be born?" The priests and scribes answer, "In Bethlehem of Judea, in the city of King David." Herod then instructs the Magi, as he does in Matthew, to find the child and then report back to him. The star reappears as the Magi set out for Bethlehem, and it leads them to the cave where Jesus, Joseph, and Mary are resting.[22] When they see the star stop, they dismount their horses and begin to celebrate. They and their armies dance in celebration. Mary and Joseph behold this spectacle, and they flee the cave in fear and leave Jesus behind. The Magi ask Joseph about the whereabouts of the newly born king, and Joseph gestures toward the cave. They enter joyfully and begin to worship (*[Arm.] Gos. Inf.* 11.15–16).

Like their interactions with Herod and others in Jerusalem, the Magi's visit to Bethlehem in the *Armenian Gospel of the Infancy* is more detailed than what we have seen in other texts. When the Magi present their gifts, the author of the *Armenian Gospel of the Infancy* adds to the traditional three gifts and specifies what gifts come from which person. Gaspar presents an assortment of incense and spices, and a powerful, pleasing aroma fills the cave. Baltasar gives gold, silver, and precious stones. Melkon's gifts are myrrh and other balms, along with fabrics. The Magi do not linger in the cave for long, and when they depart, they begin to reflect on the nature of their journey. Noting that Jesus's family is poor and, at least at this point, homeless, they begin to wonder if perhaps the entire trip had been in error. "Why did we come from far away to see them?" they ask. "What wondrous sign did we see there? Let us tell one another what was revealed to us" (*[Arm.] Gos. Inf.* 11.18).

---

22 The cave is mentioned at the birthplace of Jesus earlier, in *(Arm.) Gos. Inf.* 8.

As they begin to share their experiences, it becomes clear that what had just transpired in the cave was far from ordinary, for each of them saw a different vision of Jesus as they presented their gifts to him. Gaspar shares his vision first and reports, "I saw him as Son of God embodied, seated on the throne of glory and armies of bodiless beings were serving him." Baltasar goes next: "Physically, I saw him as Son of Man, son of a king, seated on the highest of the thrones and countless armies before him." Melkon speaks last: "I saw him bodily tortured and dead, and risen from the dead." All of them are amazed (*[Arm.] Gos. Inf.* 11.19). These visions of the Magi correspond with their various gifts and are meant to emphasize certain aspects of who this author believes Jesus to have been, as the Magi themselves reveal just a few verses later: "[Jesus] appeared to us in like semblance to the symbolism of the gifts which we presented him" (*[Arm.] Gos. Inf.* 11.21). In Matthew, the gifts of the Magi do not seem to have any significance outside of their cost, but this author explains the significance of these gifts in terms of what they see as the most important facets of Jesus's identity. Gaspar's incense, associated with temple worship, is offered to a divine Jesus who is enthroned in heavenly glory. Baltasar's gold and silver, associated with wealth and power, are given to Jesus the earthly king who is surrounded by armies. And Melkon's myrrh, associated with burial, is presented to one who has died and then been raised.

The Magi return to the cave the next day with the secret document that they described to Herod. Melkon presents it to Jesus, and the contents of the document are then outlined for the reader. It begins immediately after Adam's expulsion from the garden of Eden, as he laments the murder of his son Abel. The document goes on to mention Adam's son Seth, who is here interpreted as consolation for Adam's loss of Abel. The document is a theological attempt to frame Jesus's birth as a consequence of and response to the transgression of Adam: "Since Adam first desired to become divine, God condescended to become human because of his abundant compassion and love for humankind" (*[Arm.] Gos. Inf.* 11.23). We find a divine promise of Jesus's birth: "I shall send my Only-begotten Son, God the Word, who shall come to take body from your progeny; and my Son shall become Son of Man" (*[Arm.] Gos. Inf.* 11.23). It ends with a foreshadowing of Adam's eventual glorification: "Then shall you, Adam, become bodily immortal, united with God as one of us, knowing good and evil" (*[Arm.] Gos. Inf.* 11.23).

Directly before the contents of this document are outlined, a narrative gloss explains why the Magi have never bothered to open it and read it for themselves. They "considered themselves unworthy, since they were not children of the kingdom and were to denounce the savior" (*[Arm.] Gos. Inf.* 11.22). This comment is unsubtly Judeophobic, and it generates some tension with the author's portrait of the Magi elsewhere in the story. Throughout the *Armenian Gospel of the Infancy*, the Magi are described in terms that suggest their faithfulness to the god of Israel. Their connection with this god is admittedly unconventional, but it is also undeniably present. Yet the author says that "they were not children of the kingdom and were to denounce the savior" (*[Arm.] Gos. Inf.* 11.22). Immediately before this scene, they have joyful visions of the fullness of Jesus's identity as "Son of God," which includes his death. Earlier, they spoke to Herod's princes about their pursuit of righteousness, and they believe that their journey to find the newborn king of the Jews is commanded by God (*[Arm.] Gos. Inf.* 11.8). Yet this comment suggests that this is not how their story will end. Readers are left to presume—in the absence of further details—that their eventual denouncing of Jesus will be a consequence not of some choice that they make but of who they are as people.

It is possible that the *Armenian Gospel of the Infancy* presumes knowledge of another facet of the Magi tradition in which they return home and disavow all they experienced and saw on their journey. It is also possible that this commentary was added to the text by a later scribe. Regardless of its origin, this Judeophobic rhetoric likely reflects what some scholars refer to as "the parting of the ways." Historians generally agree that Christianity began as a grassroots movement within first-century Judaism. Jesus was Jewish, after all, and the same is true for his earliest followers. Yet we also know that by the second century, Christianity had become predominantly a gentile movement. A split must have happened at some point, although the precise details are unclear and are the subject of ongoing debate. Certainly, it is something that transpired over a period of time rather than overnight. Comments like this one in the *Armenian Gospel of the Infancy* illustrate some of the harmful rhetoric that develops as a result.

The Magi end up spending three days at the cave with Jesus and his family. They enter the cave one last time before they depart to make a final confession: "You are true God, and Son of God" (*[Arm.] Gos. Inf.* 11:24). They leave joyfully, at which point they learn from an angel about Herod's plot, and they choose to return to their land by another route. In addition to amplifying the political rhetoric of the Magi story, the *Armenian Gospel of the Infancy* illustrates the extent to which gaps in the narrative give rise to wild and sometimes odd speculation. It is unlikely that the additional details in the *Armenian Gospel of the Infancy* were all fabricated by the author; many of them were likely already part of the story that the author was familiar with.

The *Revelation of the Magi*

The *Revelation of the Magi* is a lengthy account of the Magi's journey that survives in Syriac, in a single manuscript housed in the Vatican Library in Rome (Vaticanus Syriacus 162).[23] This manuscript dates to the eighth century CE, but scholars have argued that the story of the Magi that it contains may have originated several hundred years earlier.[24] It is unique among the others surveyed here. Its author considers what the story of the Magi would look like if they themselves were the ones telling it. So here we find their adventures narrated almost entirely in the first person. At the start of this text, the author introduces the Magi with a few biographical details. There are twelve Magi, and they are described as "kings" and "sons of kings" (*Rev. Magi* 2.3, 5). All of them are named along with their fathers: "Zaharwandad son of Artisan; Hôrmizd son of Sanatruq; Auštazp son of Gudaphar," and so on (*Rev. Magi* 2.3).[25] They are called *Magi* because they worship their god in silence (*Rev. Magi* 2.1), and they come from a mythical land called "Shir," which the author describes as "the outer part of the entire East of the world inhabited by human beings, at the Ocean, the great sea beyond the world, east of the land of Nod, that place in which dwelt Adam head and chief of all the families of the world" (*Rev. Magi* 2.4). Their ritual practices in Shir are also described. Every month, for example, they bathe in a specific spring as a means of purification (*Rev. Magi* 5.2–3).

---

23 The *Revelation of the Magi* is a small part of a much longer tale called the *Chronicle of Zuqnin*, which is a retelling of the history of the world from creation up until the eighth century, when the document cuts off.

24 A fifth-century CE Latin text knowns at the *Opus Imperfectum in Matthaeum* (addressed in the next chapter) seems to refer to the *Revelation* at one point, which suggests that the story may be centuries older than the copy that survives today.

25 English translations of the *Revelation of the Magi* in this section are taken from Brent Landau, *The Revelation of the Magi: The Lost Tale of the Wise Men's Journey to Bethlehem* (New York: HarperOne, 2010).

Like the *Armenian Gospel of the Infancy*, this author attempts to link the Magi with Adam. Geography is the first means of achieving this goal. The Magi in this text live in a land that is on the outskirts of the inhabited world, far from civilization, and close to the theological cradle of humankind. The author also depicts them as keepers and protectors of an ancient mystery passed on from the foundation of the world. The *Armenian Gospel of the Infancy* introduces this detail only late in the story, almost as a surprise for the reader, but the *Revelation of the Magi* leads with it. Seth receives a testimony from his father, Adam, and he is given the task of recording this testimony in writing and then ensuring that it is passed down faithfully from generation to generation until it comes to reside in the land of the Magi (*Rev. Magi* 3.1–8).

A significant location in the *Revelation of the Magi* is the "Cave of Treasures of Hidden Mysteries."[26] The cave in this text is located in the land of Shir, in the "Mountain of Victories." It is a place for storing valuable things—including the written testimony that Seth receives from Adam—but also a location where the Magi worship and encounter the divine (*Rev. Magi* 5.6–8). As the story progresses, it becomes clear that there are actually *two* Caves of Treasures, at least in a sense. When the Magi arrive in Bethlehem, the star leads them to a cave, as it does in other apocryphal stories. But in this text, the Magi recognize it as being similar in "form and appearance" to the Cave of Treasures in their native land of Shir (*Rev. Magi* 18.2). In the *Protevangelium of James*, the cave of Jesus's birth was first and foremost a convenient location to seek shelter, but in the *Revelation of the Magi*, the cave is a mirror of the one in the Magi's homeland. Their journey begins at their own Cave of

---

26 A similar location features prominently in another Syriac text known to scholars as *The Cave of Treasures*. In this text, which likely dates from the early-seventh century CE, the Cave of Treasures is the burial place of Adam. The story of the Magi appears toward the end of this text as well.

Treasures, and they know that they have reached the object of their quest when the star arrives at an identical cave.

The star in the *Revelation of the Magi* is one of the hallmarks of the story, and it is introduced as a sort of folktale prophecy: "Our fathers commanded us as they also received from their fathers, and they said to us: 'Wait for the light that shines forth to you from the exalted East of the majesty of the Father, the light that shines forth from on high in the form of a star over the Mountain of Victories and comes to rest upon a pillar of light within the Cave of Treasures [of] Hidden Mysteries'" (*Rev. Magi* 4.2). The author of the *Revelation* says that the story of the star goes all the way back to the beginning: "Adam instructed Seth his son about . . . the light of the star and about its glory, because he [saw] it in the Garden of Eden when it descended and came to rest over the Tree of Life" (*Rev. Magi* 6.2). Because of the role that the star plays in the story of the Magi more broadly, it is possible to think about it as a sort of character alongside the Magi, Herod, and others. In this text, however, the star actually *does* become a character. And not a minor character. In the *Revelation of the Magi*, the star is Jesus himself.

The star appears to the Magi while they are engaged in their monthly bathing ritual (*Rev. Magi* 11.1–4). Like the author of the *Protevangelium of James*, the author of the *Revelation of the Magi* notes the star's brightness. But whereas in the *Protevangelium*, the star is so bright that it eclipses the other stars (*Prot. Jas.* 21.8), in the *Revelation*, the star is so bright that it outshines even the sun (*Rev. Magi* 11.5, 7). When the Magi are on their way to Jerusalem, they comment, "We had no need of the light of the sun or of the moon, because their light became diminished in [the star's] sight, and by night and by day we walked in its light" (*Rev. Magi* 16.4). And yet despite the star's apparent brilliance, they also claim that it was visible only to them. They alone are considered "worthy" to see it (*Rev. Magi* 11.7).

When the star descends, the Magi watch in awe as it enters the Cave of Treasures and illuminates the space. A voice comes from inside: "Enter inside without doubt, in love, and see a great and amazing vision" (*Rev. Magi* 12.5). When they enter, they see that the star has taken the form of a tiny human. It tells them that what they are looking at is the "ineffable light of the voice of the hidden Father of heavenly majesty" (*Rev. Magi* 13.1). It appears to them in its present form, it says, because this is an image that people can see and comprehend. The star then identifies itself with the soon-to-be-born Jesus but then claims a sort of omnipresence: "Even now, as I am speaking with you I am also there" (*Rev. Magi* 13.8). The theme of Jesus's omnipresence appears later as well, after the Magi arrive in Bethlehem and the star speaks to them again: "Yet even now, while I am speaking with you, I am with him and have not become separated from the majesty of the Father" (*Rev. Magi* 19.7).

In much the same way that the Magi in the *Armenian Gospel of the Infancy* had different visions of Jesus when they visited him in Bethlehem, the Magi in this text likewise see different things when they look at the star. "Each of us was speaking about the revelations and visions that had appeared to him," the author writes, "but our visions did not resemble each other" (*Rev. Magi* 14.3). Six of these visions are described by the author. One of the Magi saw "an infant who had unspeakable forms" (*Rev. Magi* 14.4), while another saw "a youth who did not have a form in this world" (*Rev. Magi* 14.5). One saw "a human being who was humble, unsightly in appearance, and poor" (*Rev. Magi* 14.5), and another still saw "a cross and a person of light who hung upon it, taking away the sins of the entire world" (*Rev. Magi* 14.6). Finally, one saw "that he went down to Sheol with force and all the dead rose and worshiped him" (*Rev. Magi* 14.6), and the last one saw "that he ascended in glory, and he opened the graves, and he raised up our dead" (*Rev. Magi* 14.7).

The star's polymorphism and omnipresence in the *Revelation of the Magi* lead to several interesting interpretations. Because the star is a kind of deity, it can do things that are otherwise impossible within space and time. But the fact that the Magi in this text are chosen to interact with it in such a direct way is perhaps the more significant point. The star is first introduced as a beacon that once hovered over the Tree of Life in the garden of Eden but is taken away because of the humans' transgression (*Rev. Magi* 6.3). As was the case in the *Armenian Gospel of the Infancy*, the Magi in this text exist to protect this promise and keep it secret. When the day comes, they are charged with helping welcome the light back into the world and to facilitate its arrival. After an extended theophany and theological reflection on the nature of Jesus, the Magi remove gifts from the Cave of Treasures and then embark on their journey, guided by the star that goes before them (*Rev. Magi* 16.3).

The star in this text does more than just announce the birth of Jesus to the Magi and then indicate the direction they are supposed to travel. It prepares campsites for them to use at night, levels mountains that could stand in their way, enables them to cross rivers without worry, and gives them the ability to trample over snakes and beasts without fear. Its light also multiplies their food rations (*Rev. Magi* 16.5–6). These specific actions of the star are reminiscent of various biblical scenes. The star behaves much like the pillar of fire that guides Moses and the Hebrews (in Exod 17:21–22), and its ability to level mountains echoes prophetic language found in Isaiah (40:4–5). Luke uses this same language to introduce the ministry of John the Baptist: "Every valley will be filled up, and every mountain and hill will be humbled" (Luke 3:5). Because the star is Jesus, its ability to multiply the provisions of the Magi could be understood as referring to stories about Jesus feeding thousands of people with only a small amount of food. In all four of the canonical Gospels, for example, he uses five loaves and two fish to feed thousands (Matt 14:13–21; Mark 6:31–44; Luke 9:12–17; John 6:1–14).

Brent Landau proposes another layer of understanding for this multiplied "food" that is worth considering. His argument is that this part of the story may refer to an early Christian ritual involving psychotropic edibles, possibly mushrooms.[27] Landau notes that when the Magi return home from Bethlehem, the people of Shir are eager to hear about all that the Magi had experienced on their journey. The Magi share their stories, including how their provisions were multiplied by the star. They even show their filled containers to the people: "Behold, they are sitting filled before your eyes, our vessels overflowing from them, because of the power of his blessings, which settled upon us" (*Rev. Magi* 27.9). The Magi then invite the people to eat some for themselves (*Rev. Magi* 27.11). When they do, it causes them to see visions of Jesus in various forms, not unlike those seen by the Magi in Bethlehem and at the Cave of Treasures of Hidden Mysteries (*Rev. Magi* 28.1–4). Because this "star food" has the ability to alter the peoples' consciousnesses and make them see things, Landau proposes that it may refer to a hallucinogen. And because this substance seems to multiply at night, "when the light of the star shines upon it," he suggests a mushroom as the most likely candidate.[28] More importantly, though, Landau suggests that the *Revelation of the Magi* depicts induced, ritualized hallucination among the Magi and the people of Shir because this may have been part of the author's own religious experience.[29]

---

27 Brent Landau, "Under the Influence (of the Magi): Did Hallucinogens Play a Role in the Inspired Composition of the Pseudepigraphic *Revelation of the Magi*?," in *Fakes, Forgeries, and Fictions: Writing Ancient and Modern Apocrypha: Proceedings from the 2015 York University Christian Apocrypha Symposium*, ed. Tony Burke (Eugene, OR: Cascade, 2017), 79–94.

28 Landau, 94.

29 Landau, 80.

As a way of highlighting the strangeness and distinctiveness of the Magi, the author notes that they were objects of curiosity the moment they arrive in Jerusalem, and they say that they are immediately labeled as "Magi" because the people "did not understand [their] mysteries" (*Rev. Magi* 17.2). When they explain why they have come, the Magi describe their quest in purely theological terms. They are not in search of a king alone, but "a messiah, and a life giver, and a savior who gives himself to death for the sake of the entire world" (*Rev. Magi* 17.3). Herod—here "governor of the region"—calls for the elders of Jerusalem and asks about the birthplace of such a person (*Rev. Magi* 17.6). The answer in this text is the same as it is in all others: Bethlehem. The Magi rejoice, and Herod tells them to return and tell him where he can find the child. The Magi comment immediately in an aside, "Because he was not worthy for the worship of the light that was born, because he was a dwelling of error, it was said to us by our guide and our light that we should not return to him" (*Rev. Magi* 17.9).

When the Magi arrive at the cave in Bethlehem, the star descends in a pillar of light, flanked by angels on each side (*Rev. Magi* 18.3). The Magi enter the cave, kneel before Jesus, and in acknowledgment of Jesus's "everlasting kingdom," they remove their crowns and place them under his feet. Building off the parallelism between this cave and the Cave of Treasures in the land of Shir, the *Revelation of the Magi* frames the giving of gifts as more of an exchange: "We brought forth our treasures before him, who is the treasure of salvation, that we might receive them from him in the kingdom by many-fold before his own judgment seat of salvation" (*Rev. Magi* 18.8).[30] Jesus speaks to the Magi about their journey and their

---

30 Reciprocity of gifts is a theme in other apocrypha as well. In the *Arabic Gospel of the Infancy*, Mary gives the Magi a piece of swaddling cloth. After they attempt to burn it as a fire sacrifice and discover that it is apparently indestructible, they include it among their own treasures (*[Arab.]*

worthiness to have embarked on it in the first place (*Rev. Magi* 19:2–4). He then gives the Magi another sign to watch for that will foreshadow his crucifixion: "In the hour that you see the sun darkened in the daytime light the night, and there is a great earthquake upon the earth, and the voice of the dead is heard from their graves giving praise, then at that time know that all the times and seasons have come to an end in my coming to you" (*Rev. Magi* 19:8). Jesus sends the Magi back to their own land with instructions to be "witnesses" to their people in the East (*Rev. Magi* 21.1–5). The star reappears as they leave Bethlehem and leads them back to the land of Shir (*Rev. Magi* 26).[31]

Conclusions

Apocryphal retellings of the Magi story make clear that Matthew's version leaves much to the imagination. But in addition to showing us how authors supplied missing details and bridged narrative gaps, these texts also demonstrate how the story of the Magi has been made to conform to various settings and ideologies. The political dimension of Matthew's story—Jesus's kingship—is present in all these texts, at least to some degree. But each of these authors also understands this kingship and its implications in their own way. The role that the star plays for these authors is also notable. The *Protevangelium* uses the star's brightness as a commentary on the superiority of Jesus's kingship, and in the *Revelation of the*

Gos. Inf. 7–8). In the Old Turkic *Adoration of the Magi* (see Adam Carter Bremer-McCollum, "The Adoration of the Magi: A New Translation and Introduction," in *New Testament Apocrypha: More Noncanonical Scriptures*, vol. 2, ed. Tony Burke [Grand Rapids, MI: Eerdmans, 2020], 3–12), Jesus breaks off a corner of his stone crib and gives it to the Magi. It ends up being too heavy for them to carry, but when a well materializes nearby, they throw it in, which causes some type of explosion (*Ador. Magi* 5–6).

31 The notion that the star leads the Magi back to their homeland is present as well in the *(Arab.) Gos. Inf.* (7).

Magi, the star is Jesus himself. While present and important in both *Pseudo-Matthew* and the *Armenian Gospel of the Infancy*, the star is not noteworthy in either of the texts.

These texts also illustrate the ways in which the Magi story comes to be understood in more theological terms. In the *Revelation of the Magi* and the *Armenian Gospel of the Infancy*, the Magi come to worship a god, not simply to honor and validate a king. This reading is not incompatible with Matthew's story, but neither is it the primary focus. Over time, this theological turn gives way to Judeophobic readings of the story. In the *Armenian Gospel of the Infancy*, this was directed toward the Magi themselves. In other readings, however, the Magi become gentiles who are eager to worship Jesus, while Herod and the others are disinterested at best and murderous at worst. Interpretations like this did not originate in Christian apocrypha, nor are they unique to this body of literature. As the material surveyed in the following two chapters will make clear, such readings are pervasive, from the earliest centuries of Christianity all the way until the present.

6

Horoscopes, Hymns, and Shifting Ground

As trumpets blast and angelic voices sound, stars begin to twinkle against a dark sky. A new star flashes and begins to move, coming to rest over a sleepy city just as three men arrive on camels. They make their way down a dark and cramped alley, eventually arriving at a stable. As they enter, a woman sits asleep in her chair. When she wakes up, she is startled by the sight of them. After some banter, they learn that the child's name is Brian. The men present their gifts and depart, only to return a few seconds later when they discover that they are at the wrong stable.

So begins *Monty Python's Life of Brian* (1979), arguably one of the greatest Jesus films of all time. An impressive achievement, especially considering the film isn't even about Jesus but rather about Brian, who was born at the same time, just down the street. From his adventures with the People's Front of Judea (not to be confused with the Judean People's Front), to his Latin grammar lesson learned at the business end of a centurion's sword, to his conversation with Pontius Pilate, Brian's antics and misfortunes have amused and offended viewers for decades. While the film may give the impression that its creators were ignorantly flippant and immature with the subject matter, a closer look reveals that its scenes are fueled by sophisticated engagement with questions related to the study of first-century, Roman-occupied Palestine.[1] As it turns out, we can learn quite a bit about Jesus by thinking about Brian. Like Jesus in the Gospel of Matthew, Brian's story begins with a visit from the Magi, who are here played by John Cleese, Graham Chapman, and Michael Palin. All of them are dressed in elaborate robes and wear large hats. John Cleese stands out from the other two because of his ornate jewelry—and also because he appears in blackface.

The notion that one of the Magi was Black is standard in many living room nativities and church events around the world. Cleese's painted face in *Life of Brian* is offensive, but not an anomaly. At the Epiphany Mass at Cologne Cathedral, children arrive dressed as the Magi, and as part of the service, they process around the Shrine of the Three Kings, many of them in blackface. The city of Alcoy in Eastern Spain has made headlines in recent years for its "Three Kings Parade," in which hundreds of teenagers in the city march through the streets with their faces painted black, their lips bright red. The image of the Black Magus first developed during the medieval period. It is rooted in the claim that the Magi came to Bethlehem from a few different locations. Already in the *Armenian*

---

1 In the summer of 2014, a conference was even held at King's College London to discuss the significance of this film for historical Jesus studies. The proceedings of this conference were later published in Joan Taylor, ed., *Jesus and Brian: Exploring the Historical Jesus and His Times via "Monty Python's Life of Brian"* (London: T&T Clark, 2015).

Gospel of the Infancy, the Magi are kings from Persia, India, and Arabia (*[Arm.] Gos. Inf.* 11.1). By the start of the fourteenth century, the idea that one of them came from Africa is standard currency in literature.[2]

Cord Whitaker observes that having one of the Magi come from Africa "allowed theologians to argue that the three magi represented the three parts of the known world—Europe, Asia, and Africa."[3] On the one hand, this converging of the world in Bethlehem could be understood positively, as a sort of "coming together," but Whitaker cautions against such a rosy interpretation. The presence of the European and Asian Magi alongside the African one gives readers an option of which Magus represents them. "The world is unified," Whitaker writes, "yet the reader who wishes to assume holiness does not have to associate with the black magus."[4] Artists began to include this imagery in their paintings in the early Renaissance, a development that Paul Kaplan argues was linked with the proliferation of the African slave trade.[5] Like other media discussed in this book, the tradition of the Black Magus is an integral part of the reception history of Matthew's story. Unfortunate and troubling, but integral nonetheless. It stands as a prime example of how even interpretations formulated with the best intentions can have disastrous consequences.

---

2 In John of Hildesheim's *History of the Three Kings*, for example, Gaspar is an Ethiopian.

3 Cord J. Whitaker highlights Hildesheim's work as an example, as well as Hilary of Poitiers (ca. 315–67), one of the earlier theologians to make this connection (*Black Metaphors: How Modern Racism Emerged from Medieval Race-Thinking* [Philadelphia: University of Pennsylvania Press, 2019], 104).

4 Whitaker, 106–7.

5 Paul H. D. Kaplan, *The Rise of the Black Magus in Western Art* (Ann Arbor, MI: UMI Research Press, 1985), 119. Readers interested in a broader overview of the Black Magus tradition, including links to relevant artwork, should consult Sarah E. Bond and Nyasha Junior, "The Story of the Black King among the Magi," *Hyperallergic*, January 6, 2020, https://hyperallergic.com/535881/the-story-of-the-black-king-among-the-magi/.

Our focus in this chapter is a collection of texts commonly called "patristic literature." Like their apocryphal counterparts, these authors interpreted the Magi in light of their own contexts and experiences and in service of their own rhetorical aims. They often produce interpretations that are quite different from what Matthew seemed to intend. And they provide further, valuable insight into how Matthew's story has been read, understood, and used in various theological contexts.

Whats, Whys, and Warnings

The word *patristic* comes from the Greek *patēr*, meaning "father." In much the same way that people in the United States speak of "the founding fathers," patristic authors are sometimes referred to as "fathers of the church." This designation reflects the profound influence that they had in shaping the beliefs and practices of early Christians, as well as the continued influence that many of their writings have exercised on doctrinal debates up to the present. Like all periods of history, the question of when the "patristic period" begins and ends is not agreed upon by all. In this chapter, I cast a wide net by including sources that span roughly five hundred years, from the early second century CE up until the late seventh century CE.

While this chapter follows the one on Christian apocrypha, it is important to remember that these two bodies of literature were written alongside each other, during the same span of time. As we shall see, evidence suggests that patristic authors knew of apocryphal texts and traditions about the Magi and, in some cases, even incorporated them into their own writings. Patristic texts, like apocrypha, vary from one another in many respects. Some are letters, some are sermons, and some are books. Some are meant to encourage, while others are meant to challenge and indict. All of them provide glimpses into how their authors thought as well as how and why theological concepts originated and changed over time.

One of the most important things that we can learn from this body of literature is how patristic authors were reading and interpreting texts like Matthew's Gospel. What details stood out to them? What questions did they have? How did they construct meaning from the stories that they read? These are the same sorts of questions that were asked of the apocryphal texts. But unlike those texts, whose narrative retellings of the Magi story are often not explicit in terms of what their authors were trying to accomplish, patristic authors generally write with the goal of conveying their thoughts to readers in a more direct way.

This is not to suggest that the meanings of these texts are necessarily clear to most modern readers. An imperfect analogy might be the difference between a parable and an instruction manual. Parables are stories that are meant to impart some type of lesson, but they are told in such a way that readers are responsible for thinking through the story and then drawing their own conclusions. It is both possible and expected that different readers will draw different lessons from the same parable. An instruction manual, by contrast, is not a document that is meant to inspire creative interpretation. Instruction manuals are meant to convey information in a way that is clear, thereby enabling readers to accomplish a task. Although, as anyone who has ended up with a palmful of random screws and parts can attest, instruction manuals do not always succeed in this. This could happen because of how a manual is written or because of how it is read. Some manuals are clear and easy to follow, while some are convoluted. Some are meant for laypeople, while others are written with trained experts in mind.

The same is true for patristic texts. Like all authors, patristic authors wrote using terms and concepts that were familiar to them and to their earliest readers. Just like instruction manuals, some of these texts are clearer and more effective than others, and all of them were written with different audiences in mind. Reading patristic texts today poses challenges similar to those posed by other ancient texts. We are not their target audience, and the concepts and methods of reading that they employ are often foreign, even nonsensical to modern readers. The question of what Matthew's story of the Magi meant to him and his earliest readers was not a high priority for these authors, at least not in the way that I have framed it here. They are far more interested in how the story informs spiritual and ethical reasoning and how it can be applied allegorically to various situations encountered in the world.[6] Our aim in this chapter is to understand not only how patristic authors thought about the Magi but how they used this story in the service of their own rhetorical and theological aims.

The Magi are popular subjects in the patristic period, and they appear in more texts than is prudent to discuss in a single chapter. In what follows, I focus on six texts: Ignatius of Antioch's *Letter to the Ephesians*, Justin Martyr's *Dialogue with Trypho the Jew*, Ephrem the Syrian's *Hymns on the Nativity*, John Chrysostom's *Homilies on Matthew*, the anonymous *Opus Imperfectum in Matthaeum*, and the *Life of the Virgin*, which is attributed to Maximus the Confessor.[7]

A brief but important disclaimer is needed before we start. Many patristic authors are overtly supersessionist in their views of

---

6 In introductions to patristic literature, this is often articulated as the "four senses of Scripture," which include literal, allegorical, tropological, and anagogical.

7 Timothy P. Hein discusses a different array of authors in his work on patristic reception of the Magi, including Justin, Irenaeus of Lyons, Tertullian, Clement of Alexandria, Origen, and Hippolytus ("The First Christian 'Magicians': Early Christian Afterlives of Matthew's Magi [Matt 2:1–12]" [PhD diss., University of Edinburgh, 2020]).

early Christianity and its relationship with Judaism. They view Judaism as deficient and believe it has been improved, replaced, or "superseded" by Christianity. Because these authors are writing in different contexts, to different audiences, and with different aims in mind, this view manifests in different ways. Supersessionism is not unique to the patristic period, and it is also not the creation of patristic authors. It is present in the apocryphal texts surveyed in the last chapter, and one can find plenty of supersessionist tendencies in New Testament writings. It persists in some Christian groups up to the present. But the story of the Magi seems particularly prone to supersessionist readings by patristic authors. My aim is not to champion what these authors wrote but to understand what they wrote and why.

Ignatius of Antioch's *Letter to the Ephesians*

In the second century CE, a philosopher named Celsus wrote a scathing critique of Christianity titled *The True Word* (*Alēthēs Logos*). He criticized some of the central tenets of many early Christians, and he pointed out what he saw as logical inconsistencies within early Christianity. Celsus claimed, for example, that Jesus's father was actually a Roman soldier named Pantera and that Mary's conception of Jesus was the consequence of a sexual assault.[8] He suggested that the story of the Magi affirms the legitimacy of astrology as a tool that could be used to tell the future or understand the present. Would this not pose a problem for early Christians who are attempting to maintain the superiority of their god and rituals? Is it

---

8 Like so many ancient authors, Celsus's work survives only in fragments. But it is possible to get a sense of what he wrote by looking at how his claims were challenged by early Christian authors. One of his staunchest critics—and, ironically, the best source for reconstructing his arguments—was a theologian named Origen. Writing in the third century in Alexandria, Egypt, Origen produced a book-length response to Celsus that is titled, appropriately, *Against Celsus*.

not problematic that the Magi use a "pagan" practice in their journey to Jerusalem and Bethlehem? Or, as Nicola Denzey Lewis puts it, "Since the Magi learned by means of astrology where Jesus had been born, did this mean astrology in itself was a valid type of foreknowledge, apart from prophecy?"[9] These are precisely the types of questions that Matthew invited by choosing the word *magoi* to describe his visitors. Concerns about the Magi and astrology did not originate with Celsus, however. Even before he wrote *The True Word*, similar concerns had been raised and addressed by others. One of the earliest was the early and influential Christian author Ignatius of Antioch (d. ca. 108 CE).

Much of what we know about Ignatius and his theology comes from seven of his letters, which are part of a special collection of early Christian texts commonly called the "Apostolic Fathers."[10] Ignatius alludes to the story of the Magi in his *Letter to the Ephesians*. Unlike the narrative retellings analyzed in the previous chapter, however, Ignatius's reference to the Magi is easy to miss if you aren't looking for it. The Magi aren't even mentioned, at least not directly. The overall tone of this letter is warm and encouraging. Ignatius claims to be writing it from the city of Smyrna (*Eph.* 21.1), and in it, he urges his readers to work together with their bishop (*Eph.* 4.1) and to be on the lookout for false teachers (*Eph.* 7.1) and false teachings (*Eph.* 9.1). Toward the end, he includes a short theological treatise

---

9 Nicola Denzey, "A New Star on the Horizon: Astral Christologies and Stellar Debates in Early Christian Discourse," in *Prayer, Magic, and the Stars in the Ancient and Late Antique World*, Magic in History, ed. Scott Noegel et al. (University Park: Pennsylvania State University Press, 2003), 211. Origen addresses Celsus's claim about astrology by first conceding the point that the Magi probably were astrologers (*Cels.* 1.58), but then he points out that this skill set only did so much for them. In order to understand what they had seen in the heavens, Origen writes, the Magi had to look to the Scriptures of Israel, specifically Balaam's oracle in Num 24:17. Denzey Lewis notes that Origen's goal is not to destroy astrology in favor of prophecy but rather to specify how the two are related (Denzey, "New Star," 216).

10 The Greek text of the Apostolic Fathers with accompanying English translation is available in Bart D. Ehrman, *The Apostolic Fathers*, 2 vols., Loeb Classical Library (Cambridge, MA: Harvard University Press, 2003).

on the birth of Jesus, and as part of this, he includes an extended reflection on the star. Because this portion seems to be written in verse, scholars today often refer to this part of the letter as the "Star Hymn."[11]

The Star Hymn itself is rightly classified as "eschatological," meaning it imagines the world in terms of the way that it exists now, but with an eye toward a cosmic transformation that has already begun and that will soon come to fruition. For Ignatius and so many other early Christian authors, this transformation was precipitated in some way by Jesus—whether by his birth, death, or some combination thereof—and it often involves a sort of ongoing battle between evil and good. In the hymn's preface, for example, Ignatius says that Mary's virginity as well as Jesus's birth and death all "eluded the ruler of this age" (*Eph.* 19.1).[12] But while these things were hidden from some, they were not hidden from all. The means by which they were revealed, according to Ignatius, was the star.

Here in the hymn, the star's brightness is its chief characteristic: "A star shone in heaven, brighter than all the stars, and its light was

---

11 Scholars of Ignatius generally agree that the Star Hymn is not Ignatius's own work but a pre-Ignatian formula. This has been argued most influentially by Reinhard Deichgräber (in *Gotteshymnus und Christushymnus in der frühen Christenheit: Untersuchungen zur Form, Sprache und Stil der früchristlichen Hymnen*, Studien zur Umwelt des Neuen Testaments 5 [Göttingen, Germany: Vandenhoeck & Ruprecht, 1967]). Shaily Shashikant Patel has argued that the hymn is Docetic and that Ignatius reappropriates and "recodes" it for his own proto-orthodox audience ("The 'Starhymn' of Ignatius' *Epistle to the Ephesians*: Re-appropriation as Polemic," in *Studia Patristica*, vol. 93, ed. Markus Vinzent [Leuven, Belgium: Peeters, 2017], 93–104). For the purposes of this analysis, I address it as part of his letter, but without necessarily concluding that he is originally responsible for it. In what follows, I employ the English translation in William R. Schoedel (in *Ignatius of Antioch: A Commentary on the Letters of Ignatius of Antioch* [Minneapolis: Fortress, 1985], 87) because of his attempt to preserve the poetic nature of these lines.

12 Language like this is commonplace in first- and second-century Christian texts, and it generally refers to some type of evil, supernatural figure (Satan, the devil, etc.). Paul refers to "the god of this age who has blinded the minds of the faithless" (2 Cor 4:4), and the author of the Gospel of John refers to "the ruler of this world" being expelled (John 12:31). The idea that Mary's virginity and Jesus's birth and death have "eluded" this ruler is found in other texts as well. In the second-century CE *Martyrdom and Ascension of Isaiah*, for example, Jesus descends through all of the various levels of heaven, through where "the prince of this world lives" (*Mart. Ascen. Isa.* 10.29), and then finally assumes the form of a human baby to avoid being recognized (*Mart. Ascen. Isa.* 11.1).

ineffable, and its novelty caused astonishment" (*Eph.* 19.2). The focus then shifts to how other heavenly bodies reacted to it: "All the other stars, together with sun and moon, became a chorus for the star, and it outshone them with its light; and there was perplexity as to whence came this novelty so unlike them" (*Eph.* 19.2). This opening scene differs from Matthew's account in terms of focus and detail, but it is also in step with how Matthew seems to understand the star and how it functions to indicate the rising of a new king. It is unclear whether the star in this hymn is drawing directly from Matthew's Gospel or from an oral tradition that involves the Magi and the star. It is also possible that its author did not understand it as referring to the Magi's star. Regardless of whether the Star Hymn was *originally* meant to refer to the story of the Magi, the fact that Ignatius prefaces it with a reference to the birth of Jesus suggests that it is one of his intended reference points.

The hymn's emphasis on the brightness of the star as well as all the other stars in its midst is reminiscent of the *Protevangelium of James*, written decades after Ignatius. In both texts, the other stars are outshined by the bright star, but the hymn takes things a step further. In their description of the other stars forming a chorus around the bright star and then being confounded by it, the author builds upon the metaphorical language that ties the star to Jesus and his kingship. The star still signifies the dawning of a new king (Jesus), but the other heavenly bodies that flock toward the star may signify the people for whom Jesus's kingship is a challenge: Herod, the Roman emperor, and so on. While the Star Hymn does not go as far as the *Revelation of the Magi* by saying that the star *actually* was Jesus, it does make this claim on a metaphorical level; the star points toward Jesus in Matthew, but here in the Star Hymn, it also represents him. Ignatius uses this correlation to address the "problem" of astrology and whether Jesus's birth was determined by the course of the stars. Shaily Patel notes that "by describing Jesus as *being* the star, as opposed to his birth being represented by the star, Ignatius places Jesus beyond astral determinism, as it is the heavenly bodies who pay obedience to him in 19:2."[13] Kings are subordinate to Jesus, but the same can also be said of astrology itself.

The remainder of the hymn strengthens and nuances this reading by suggesting that the Magi are among those whose power is "challenged" by Jesus's birth. Directly after the description of the bright star and the chorus around it, the author speaks of the dramatic and sweeping consequences of the new king's reign: "Thence was destroyed all magic [*mageia*], and every bond vanished; evil's intolerance was abolished, the old kingdom perished, God being revealed as human to bring newness of eternal life, and what had been prepared by God had its beginning; hence all things were disturbed because the destruction of death was being worked out" (*Eph.* 19.3). When read in concert with the story of the Magi, this author's reference to the destruction of "all magic" could be understood as a commentary on Matthew's visitors from the East. Just as the chorus of stars in the hymn are drawn to the bright star in their midst, so too are the Magi drawn westward by a celestial object that they understand as having some significance. And in Matthew, they are correct; the star *is* significant, and it leads them to a king, as they suspected it would. In other words, the power by which the Magi came to Jerusalem and then Bethlehem is no illusion. On this reading of Matthew in light of the Star Hymn, the power of the Magi—their *mageia*—is destroyed once they are in the presence of the new king.

---

13 Patel, "Starhymn," 103; Denzey Lewis argues similarly, "Jesus' advent, as the star itself, had canceled astral destiny, throwing the stars off their regular courses and into confusion; by extension, Roman astrologers were no longer correct in their predictions" ("New Star," 213).

Matthew does not seem concerned with the legitimacy of astrology, much less Jesus's relation to it, but Ignatius's use of the Star Hymn is evidence that these issues did exist for some early Christian authors. In my reading of this hymn, the power that leads the Magi to Jesus is understood as a "real" power, but it is also invalidated once they reach their destination. But the question of astrology, magic, and the Magi will continue to manifest itself in different and more explicit ways in later patristic sources.

Justin Martyr's *Dialogue with Trypho the Jew*

Justin Martyr (ca. 100–165) was a Christian apologist and philosopher. Foremost among his works are two "apologies" addressed to the Roman emperor Antonius Pius (86–161 CE) and the senate of Rome. These texts are meant to present the central tenets of Christianity as reasonable but also to convince readers that Christians in the first century CE were not a threat to Rome or Roman society.[14] Another of his more well-known writings, and the focus of this section, is his *Dialogue with Trypho the Jew*. As the name suggests, Justin styles this text as a retelling of his discussion with a Jewish interlocutor named Trypho.[15] Justin's aim in the *Dialogue* is to persuade his readers that Judaism finds its fulfillment in Christianity. Relatively speaking, the Magi are a small part of that endeavor, but they also play an important role in it.

One of Justin's chief methods of argumentation in the *Dialogue* involves lifting passages from the Septuagint (LXX) and then

---

14   One of the things that early Christians are accused of, according to Justin, is atheism (*1 Apol.* 6). Such an accusation probably resulted from the refusal by some early Christians to participate in certain aspects of Roman religious life. Other accusations include promiscuity and cannibalism (*1 Apol.* 26).

15   Whether this discussion actually happened is unclear, although for the purposes of this analysis, the question also is largely irrelevant.

trying to make a case that they are about Jesus. It is not altogether different from Matthew's fulfillment formulae. Justin uses the story of the Magi to make three such connections. Two of these are brief and occur in tandem. The first connection is to a portion of Balaam's oracle in LXX Numbers 24:17, which was discussed in chapter 4 as a potential backdrop for Matthew's story. Justin's version of this passage reads, "A star [*astron*] shall rise out of Jacob, and a leader from Israel" (*Dial.* 106).[16] The second connection is to LXX Zechariah 6:12. Again, Justin's version reads, "Behold the Man; the east [*anatolē*] is his name" (*Dial.* 106). "Therefore," Justin writes, "when a star arose in the heavens at the time of [Jesus's] nativity . . . the Magi from Arabia knew the fact from this sign, and came to worship him" (*Dial.* 106). By posing these connections, Justin frames Matthew's story of the Magi as having clear "biblical" roots, which is a position that Matthew does not seem to espouse, at least not explicitly. This view leads Justin to several unusual places elsewhere in the *Dialogue*.

The Magi first appear in the *Dialogue* in a string of questions related to the birth of Jesus. Justin and Trypho are discussing Isaiah 8:4, which Justin quotes: "Before he had known how to call father or mother, he received the power of Damascus and the spoils of Samaria in the presence of the king of Assyria" (*Dial.* 77). The Hebrew of this passage is different from Justin's Greek and reads as follows: "Before the child knows how to call 'My father' or 'My

---

16 Justin's version of Num 24:17 specifies that a "ruler [*hēgoumenos*]" will rise out of Israel, while the LXX indicates a "person [*anthropos*]." Differences like this are common in patristic texts. One explanation is that many of these authors are likely quoting or paraphrasing these texts from memory; the preoccupation with precision is one that will come much, much later. Another explanation, equally important, is that the words of biblical texts are not "stable" at this point in time; because of the process of hand copying, variant readings were quite common. English translations of Justin's *Dialogue* in this section are taken (with minor changes to modernize language and improve readability) from Thomas B. Falls, *Writings of Saint Justin Martyr*, Fathers of the Church 6 (Washington, DC: Catholic University of America Press, 1948).

mother,' the wealth of Damascus and the spoil of Samaria will be carried away by the king of Assyria" (Isa 8:4). In the Hebrew text, "the child" refers to one of Isaiah's sons, and in this context, the passage is an omen of impending doom that foreshadows the horrors of the Assyrian invasion of the northern kingdom of Israel in 721 BCE. But Justin doesn't read it this way. In the Greek version that he is citing (or paraphrasing), the child whose ability to speak precedes the arrival of the Assyrians becomes the *recipient* of "the power of Damascus and the spoils of Samaria." These, Justin says, are received "in the presence of the king of Assyria." Trypho insists that this child in Isaiah should be understood as King Hezekiah, but Justin argues instead that it refers to Jesus (*Dial.* 77). He uses the story of the Magi to make the connection.

Justin claims that the Magi's visit to Bethlehem fulfills this passage from Isaiah. "At the time of [Jesus's] birth," he writes, "the Magi came from Arabia and worshipped [Jesus], after they had met Herod, then king of your country, whom Scripture calls king of Assyria because of his wicked ungodliness" (*Dial.* 77). The story that he references is recognizable as Matthew's, but two details are different. First, Justin's version specifies a more precise point of origin for the Magi: Arabia (*Arrabias*) instead of "the East." One could easily make the case that Arabia is part of "the East," although we will see a bit later that this detail also plays conveniently into the bigger argument that Justin is trying to make. Second, Justin's retelling of the Magi story ends with a commentary connecting Herod the Great with the king of Assyria. Because the "scripture" that labels Herod as king of Assyria is the same passage that Justin and Trypho are arguing about, this connection is both contrived and circular. Justin only interprets it this way because he has already decided that the passage must refer to Jesus. On his read, then, Jesus is the one who receives "the power of Damascus and the spoils of

Samaria," and he does so in the presence of Herod, who Justin identifies as "the king of Assyria." The Magi are the ones who deliver these things to Jesus, but Justin argues that the Magi are also, in some way, delivered to Jesus.

Justin's longer version of the Magi story appears in *Dial.* 78 and begins as follows:

> At that time when the Magi from Arabia came to King Herod and said, "From the star which has appeared in the heavens we know that a king has been born in your country, and we have come to worship Him," he asked the elders of your people and learned from them that Christ was to be born in Bethlehem; for they replied that it was written in the Prophet, "And you, Bethlehem, in the land of Judah, are by no means least among the princes of Judah; for out of you shall come forth a ruler who shall shepherd my people." Now, these Magi from Arabia came to Bethlehem, worshipped the child, and presented to him gifts of gold, frankincense, and myrrh. After they had worshipped him in Bethlehem, they were admonished in a vision not to return to Herod.

Justin's story coincides in part with Matthew's, but the Magi's question in the *Dialogue* is drained of the political force that it had in Matthew. The Magi in the *Dialogue* are looking for a king, but Justin does not specify what sort of king. He only says that it is "a king born in [Herod's] country" (*Dial.* 78).

Another detail in Justin's version that differs from what we find in Matthew is the Magi's destination when they reach Bethlehem. In Matthew, they travel to a house, while in Justin's *Dialogue*, they travel to a cave (*Dial.* 78). The cave as a location of Jesus's birth appeared in the apocryphal texts analyzed in the previous chapter, from the *Protevangelium of James*, where it provides a convenient place outside the city for Jesus to be born, to the *Revelation of the Magi*, where it is the counterpart to the mythical Cave of Treasures in the land of Shir. This tradition is therefore not unique to Justin. It also probably does not originate with him. Justin notes that caves are also prominent in Mithraic rituals—both as symbols of Mithras's birthplace and as places where Mithraic priests are initiated—and that many like to draw comparisons between Jesus's birth in a cave and the caves of Mithraism (*Dial.* 70, 78).[17] It is unlikely that he would have invented a tradition that would have encouraged comparisons like these. But he is eager to make use of the detail of the cave as another touch point between Jesus and the LXX. Even before the Magi arrive on the scene, he proposes understanding the cave in connection with Isaiah 33:13–19, in which a righteous person is described as being "in the lofty cave of the strong rock" (*Dial.* 70).

The final theological "payoff" for Justin's interpretation of the Magi comes after they depart Bethlehem and return home by a different route. What Justin does with this and the material that follows should strike modern readers as odd, because the success of his reading requires a willingness to be flexible in terms of where things are actually located. Drawing from the story of Herod's slaughter of the children, Justin notes Matthew's citation of Jeremiah 31:15, which in his version reads, "A voice was heard in Ramah, weeping and great lamentation; Rachel weeping for her children, and refusing to be comforted for them, because they are not" (*Dial.* 78). In

---

17 Mithraism was a popular "mystery religion" in the Roman world. The deity Mithras likely had a Persian origin, and Mithraic temples (called *Mithraea*) are common discoveries in ancient Roman cities. There are many in the city of Rome, but they are also found across Europe, in North Africa, and in the Middle East.

Jeremiah, Ramah likely refers to a small city not far to the north of Jerusalem.[18] But Justin claims that Ramah should instead be understood as a synonym for Arabia, where he also says the Magi are from. The voice and the cries of mourning that are heard in Ramah emanate from Bethlehem where, according to Justin and Genesis 35:19, Rachel is allegedly buried. The story therefore comes full circle, as the consequences of the Magi's visit—the slaughter of children—are heard in the land that they came from originally.

Justin concludes this portion of the *Dialogue* by revisiting the Isaiah 8:4 connection that he introduced previously. This argument likewise requires the reader to entertain a certain degree of geographical flexibility. Building on his understanding that it is Jesus who receives "the power of Damascus and the spoils of Samaria," Justin says that before the Magi came to Jesus, they were held spiritually captive "as spoils" by a wicked demon who lives in Damascus, which is a city in the north, in Syria. For his purposes, however, Justin says that Damascus is in Arabia and that the demon who lives there should be understood as Samaria, which is a region that was located south of Damascus, between Judea and Galilee. By coming to Bethlehem with the goal of worshipping Jesus, the Magi "openly revolted against that power that had held them in spoils" and so were freed (*Dial.* 78). Justin understands the Magi as having a conversion experience, or at least as being liberated from the forces that previously enslaved them, which echoes what we see in the Star Hymn of Ignatius. In both texts, the Magi's coming to Jesus precipitates a destruction of some type of power, which for Justin is an enslavement to demonic forces.

---

18 References to Ramah in the Hebrew Bible generally seem to locate it in or nearby the modern city of Al-Ram (see, for example, Josh 18:25; Judg 4:5; 1 Sam 1:19).

The notion that Jesus was able to free the Magi from the source of their enslavement is employed by Justin as a polemic against his interlocutor and Jews more broadly. He presents Trypho's inability to understand his argument as evidence of his own spiritual blindness. "It would be to your advantage," Justin writes, "to learn what you do not understand from us Christians, who have received the grace of God, and not to exert every effort to defend your peculiar teachings and scorn those of God." He closes this section with a final reference to Isaiah: "This people draws near me, with their lips they glorify me, but their heart is far from me. . . . I will take away the wisdom [*sophian*] of their wise men [*sophōn*], and will bring to nought the understanding of their prudent men" (*Dial.* 78; Isa 29:13–14). While Justin does not go so far as to state that Trypho is enslaved by a demon, it takes little effort to gather that this is what he is implying. According to Justin, Trypho is not capable of understanding his own Scriptures and enjoying fellowship with his own god for the simple reason that he has not received grace. Justin's understanding of the Magi story is therefore meant to be instructive. The Magi came to Jesus to be liberated from the forces that kept them in captivity. Trypho and others, according to Justin, would do well to follow suit.

Ephrem the Syrian's *Hymns on the Nativity*

Ephrem the Syrian (ca. 306–373) was a Christian theologian and teacher who lived in Nisibis and Edessa, cities located in present-day Turkey. He wrote in Syriac, so his primary audience was different from those of Ignatius, Justin, and other authors surveyed in this chapter. In addition to being a praised orator and theologian, Ephrem was also a prolific writer. He penned a commentary on Tatian's *Diatessaron*, for example, as well as commentaries on several canonical works. Above all, Ephrem is known for his hymns. We don't know how many hymns Ephrem wrote, but more than four hundred survive today. In this section, our focus is on Ephrem's *Hymns on the Nativity*, in which he reflects on the incarnation and birth of Jesus. They feature Jesus, Mary, and of course, the Magi.[19]

When Ephrem speaks of the Magi's star, he describes it in rich, symbolic terms. Like both Ignatius and Justin, he emphasizes the star's unusual brightness. He compares it to the sun, but instead of saying that the star was *brighter* than the sun, he says that it is *greater* than the sun "in hidden power because of its symbol" (*Hymn Nat.* 6.7). The star in this account plays an active role in the Magi's quest, serving as both "announcer and guardian" (*Hymn Nat.* 24.5). It announced the birth of Jesus and led the Magi to Jerusalem, and yet its light dimmed when they reached the city so that Herod and his people wouldn't be able to see it. While everyone in Jerusalem seems to know that Bethlehem is where the Magi need to go, the star alone can lead them to the right location.

At a few points, Ephrem places the star in conversation with John the Baptist, another character who heralds the arrival of Jesus. The star and John work together to help people achieve a balance between Jesus's divine and human natures: "Whoever considered Him earthly—the star of light would convince him that He was heavenly. And whoever considered him spiritual—John would convince him that He was also bodily" (*Hymn Nat.* 6.9–11). Moreover, Ephrem suggests that this pairing reveals something about the nature of Jesus, namely that he was "a Word and a Light." John—"a voice"—testifies to the former, while the star—"a shining forth"— testifies to the latter (*Hymn Nat.* 24.23). These two are united in their eagerness to announce the arrival of Jesus, but they are also

---

19 English translations and numbering of Ephrem's *Hymns on the Nativity* in this section are taken from Kathleen McVey, *Ephrem the Syrian: Hymns*, Classics of Western Spirituality (New York: Paulist, 1989).

distinct in terms of the role they play in that process. Unlike John, whose job it is to announce to any who will listen, the star hides its light for a time to confound Herod and his people. "The glorious star of light was not like John," Ephrem writes, "for there was [a place] where it rose and made straight the way for the simple, but there was [a place] where it sank and made the path of the wolves go astray" (*Hymn Nat.* 24.25).

Ephrem describes the Magi as "dark ones" who are guided by the star "like blind men" and who "came and received a great light" (*Hymn Nat.* 6.8). In contrast to what we saw in the Syriac *Revelation of the Magi*, where the Magi are deeply pious, separatist worshippers of God, Ephrem casts them in terms more like those in Justin and Ignatius. The Magi are unenlightened people, described elsewhere as "deceivers" (*Hymn Nat.* 25.3) who then become enlightened after they are led blindly. While he does not frame this as a critique of astrology per se, it is tempting to make that connection, particularly in light of texts like the Star Hymn. Elsewhere, Ephrem portrays the Magi as idolatrous fire worshippers who come to Bethlehem to worship Jesus, the "true" fire: "The Magi used to worship [fire]— they worshipped You! They left it and worshipped its Lord; Fire they exchanged for fire" (*Hymn Nat.* 22.13).[20] He also takes the opportunity to articulate this exchange in eucharistic terms: "Instead of the foolish fire that eats its own body . . . the Magi worshipped the Fire Who gave His body to those who eat" (*Hymn Nat.* 22.14).

The first two gifts of the Magi are likewise framed as relics of their former lives that they offer to Jesus as an act of worship. The gold was what their "dead" images and idols were made of (*Hymn Nat.* 22.26; repeated in 22.29), and the incense was what they used

---

20 An allusion to the tradition that the Magi were Zoroastrians, who were known (among other things) for the use of fire in rituals (see, e.g., Strabo, *Geogr.* 15.15).

in their worship of demons (*Hymn Nat.* 22.27). The myrrh, by contrast, has no negative association here; it worships Jesus "on its own behalf" (*Hymn Nat.* 22.28). In another place, he understands the gifts in light of two tragedies of Jewish history: the Assyrian sack of the northern kingdom and the destruction of the temple in Jerusalem by the Babylonians. When the Magi come to Jesus in Bethlehem, he writes, it is an act of repentance and repayment: "Those who had seized our silver, brought gold. Those who had wounded our bodies, brought myrrh. Those who had burned our sanctuary offered frankincense to Your divinity" (*Hymn Nat.* 19.3).

Ephrem's lengthiest and most sustained commentary on the Magi is in Hymn 24. Here he depicts Jesus in Matthean terms, as heir to the Davidic throne and the last of the Davidic monarchs (*Hymn Nat.* 24.2). Ephrem portrays Herod and his scribes—who he understands as representing Jews more broadly—in a negative light. Herod is seen as a murderous tyrant, and those under him are "villains" and "wolves" (*Hymn Nat.* 24.6–7), ignorant (*Hymn Nat.* 24.11), blind, and "sons of darkness" (*Hymn Nat.* 24.12). The Magi, by contrast, are people of profound faith who believe what they have been told about the messiah: not only that the messiah has been born but that he will return at some point in the future. The scribes, by contrast, believe neither of these things (*Hymn Nat.* 24.11). In terms of their knowledge, the Magi and scribes are complementary. "The scribes," Ephrem writes, "read every day that a star would shine forth from Jacob," while "the Magi saw in actions the flash of that reading" (*Hymn Nat.* 24.4). Like other patristic authors, Ephrem understands the story of the Magi against a backdrop of various prophetic texts—Balaam's oracle in Numbers 24:17 in particular—but he also claims that the knowledge of the Magi is ultimately what completes the oracle. "The prophets announced [Jesus's] birth," he writes, "but did not specify His time. He sent the

Magi, and they came and declared His time" (*Hymn Nat.* 24.13, 20). In addition to the timing of the birth, the most crucial piece of information is its location, and this is finally supplied by the star, which led them to where Jesus was (*Hymn Nat.* 24.13).

The Magi in Ephrem's *Hymns on the Nativity* are a study in contrasts: the Magi versus Herod and the scribes, faith versus idolatry, and good versus evil. While the Magi in Ignatius and Justin Martyr undergo some type of transformation as a consequence of their journey, Ephrem views this transformation as a conversion; the Magi surrender their old ways of life and worship in exchange for new ones. In this, they are pitted against Herod and those who want to kill Jesus, not worship him, which is why the star hides itself from them. At least from Ephrem's perspective, all of this is meant for good. The star conceals its light when it reaches Jerusalem so that Herod and his people won't kill Jesus, but ironically, it only saves Jesus from this death in order to preserve him for the one that will come later: "[The star] kept the Lamb from the slaughter so that the day for the slaughter would come, that in Him the flock would be pardoned" (*Hymn Nat.* 24.25). It is tempting to read this as a claim that the star acts the way that it does in order to save Herod and the others from themselves, but it is important to remember that for Ephrem, Herod and the people are not part of the flock; they are wolves, not sheep. There is, therefore, plenty of unfortunate Judeophobic rhetoric in Ephrem's reading of the Magi story, and similar rhetoric will continue to thrive in subsequent authors.

John Chrysostom's *Homilies on Matthew*

John Chrysostom (ca. 347–407) was a fourth-century theologian who lived and taught in Antioch. In the final ten years of his life, he served as archbishop of Constantinople. Chrysostom had a considerable impact on the development of Christian theology and is one of the most productive patristic authors. Even today, Eastern Orthodox Christians use a liturgy that is attributed to him. The name *Chrysostom* is a nickname that he obtained posthumously, in the sixth century CE. Translated roughly as "gold mouth," the name reflects his reputation as an eloquent and compelling preacher. While Chrysostom was still living in Antioch, he wrote and delivered a series of ninety *Homilies on Matthew*. The Magi feature prominently in three of these (*Hom. Matt.* 6–8).[21]

Chrysostom begins his homilies on Matthew 2 with a few curt responses to what he sees as misunderstandings of the Magi. He dismisses out of hand the notion that the story legitimizes astrology in any way, and he also pushes back against the notion that the Magi arrive in search of an earthly king. They call Jesus the king of the Judeans, but really, they are searching for something else (*Hom. Matt.* 6.1). If their function is to validate Jesus's kingship, then Chrysostom argues that they take on an almost absurd character. Were we to understand the story in this way, then should we also understand that the Magi's job is to travel the world in search of kings to validate? Surely not. Something else draws them to Jesus, and understanding what that something else is begins with the star (*Hom. Matt.* 6.2).

From the outset, Chrysostom insists that the star should not be understood as an actual star, in part because this is a convenient way of avoiding the problem of astrology; if the star isn't an actual star, then astrology is not really a problem. But he also makes a convincing case that Matthew pushes back on the notion that the

---

21 English translations of Chrysostom's *Homilies on Matthew* in this section are taken (with minor changes to modernize language and improve readability) from George Prevost and M. B. Riddle's translation in *Nicene and Post-Nicene Fathers* 1 (vol. 10 of *A Select Library of Nicene and Post-Nicene Fathers of the Christian Church*, ed. Philip Schaff and Henry Wace [1886–89]).

Magi's star was a "normal" astronomical phenomenon. The star in Matthew, he argues, gives no indication that it is a normal star. Its movements are erratic, it appears and disappears without warning, and at one point in the story, it comes so low that it rests directly over Jesus's head. Chrysostom also wanders outside the boundaries of Matthew's narrative when he, like other patristic authors, notes the star's unusual brightness. The star is visible at midday, he says, and it appears to outshine even the sun (*Hom. Matt.* 6.3).

Like the *Armenian Gospel of the Infancy*, Chrysostom claims that the star appears long before the birth of Jesus so that the Magi can arrive on time (*Hom. Matt.* 7.3). The star was chosen as the most appropriate means to lead the Magi because, Chrysostom says, this was a sign that they would recognize and be able to understand (*Hom. Matt.* 6.4). The star also functions to teach them something new, for when they see it above the head of Jesus, they see this as an indication of his divinity. It is only with the convergence of these two—the star and Jesus—that the Magi understand what they are seeking (*Hom. Matt.* 7.4).

Chrysostom's portrait of the Magi in these homilies is thoroughly theological. He does not frame their interest in Jesus in terms of kingship and goes out of his way to downplay Matthew's portrait of Herod as a king. The only reason he has this label, Chrysostom argues, is so readers won't confuse him with his son, Herod Antipas, who was not a king but a tetrarch (*Hom. Matt.* 6.5). He understands the Magi explicitly as Persians (*Hom. Matt.* 6.3), and he calls them "barbarians [*barbaroi*]" (*Hom. Matt.* 7.3). Something changes in Bethlehem, however, for before they depart, they are commissioned to be "teachers to the land of the Persians" (*Hom. Matt.* 8.2).[22] They

---

22 This is reminiscent of the *Revelation of the Magi*, where they are instructed to return to Shir and tell everyone what they saw.

are transformed from "barbarians" to "forefathers of the church" (*Hom. Matt.* 7.5).

Even before this striking conversion, the Magi play an important function in Chrysostom's reading of the story. When they arrive in Jerusalem, they and the residents of the city become mutual benefactors of one another's knowledge. Herod and the people of Jerusalem learn through the Magi that their prophecies about the Messiah are being fulfilled, and the Magi learn from the people where the star actually points (*Hom. Matt.* 7.1). The star leads them to Jerusalem and then disappears in order to facilitate this exchange (*Hom. Matt.* 7.4).

The Magi in Chrysostom's *Homilies* therefore emerge as models for imitation in terms of their faith and their conversion. When they arrive in Bethlehem, Chrysostom says that they worship Jesus not because anything that they behold is particularly impressive but because they trust the revelation of the star and because God has enlightened their minds. When they are warned by an angel about going back to Jerusalem, they obey without hesitation (*Hom. Matt.* 8.1). In fact, they never question or wonder about why they are being called to travel; they simply go. Their "conversion" experience is likewise held up by Chrysostom as exemplary. "Let us then also follow the magi," he writes. "Let us separate ourselves from our barbarian customs, and distance ourselves from them, that we may see Christ" (*Hom. Matt.* 7.6). Like other patristic authors, Chrysostom pits the Magi against "the Jews" in supersessionist terms and encourages his readers to take a side: "Therefore also leave the Jewish people, the troubled city, the blood-thirsty tyrant, the pomp of the world, and hasten to Bethlehem, where is the house of the spiritual Bread" (*Hom. Matt.* 7.6).

Opus Imperfectum in Matthaeum

The *Opus Imperfectum in Matthaeum* is a lengthy patristic commentary on the Gospel of Matthew that was written in Latin in the fifth century CE. Its author is unknown, and its title—which translates as "An Unfinished Work on Matthew"—reflects the fact that it was never completed. The text has been attributed to various authors in the past, including John Chrysostom. This seems unlikely, however, because of the text's pervasive Arian theology and, more importantly, because Chrysostom wrote in Greek, not Latin.[23] The second chapter of the *Opus* is an extended theological reflection on the Magi that incorporates many of the themes and concepts that appear in the other literature surveyed in this chapter but with a few unique twists.

The author begins by connecting Jesus's birth in Bethlehem with a story from Genesis, in which the patriarch Jacob has a vision of a giant ladder that spans the void between the ground and the sky. Angels are going up and down the ladder, and Jacob hears the voice of his god uttering promises about land, offspring, and protection (Gen 28:10–15). When Jacob arises from his slumber, he remarks that this place where he has slept is none other than "the house of God" and the "gate of heaven." He builds a monument and christens the place *Bethel*, which in Hebrew means "House of God" (Gen 28:18–19). Perhaps drawn by the similarity of this name with *Bethlehem*, the author of the *Opus* says that Jesus's birth is the fulfillment of this story.[24] "The gate of heaven

---

23 Certain Arian bishops have also been proposed as candidates. If the text was complete at some point, then significant portions of it have since been lost. In its extant form, the final three chapters of Matthew are missing, and similar *lacunae* are present in the middle, from Matt 8:14–10:15 and from Matt 14–18.

24 Etymologically, *Bethel* and *Bethlehem* are only related because of the *beth-* prefix, which means "house." Beth-el translates as "house of god," but Bethlehem translates as "house of bread."

is Christ," he writes, "through whom one enters into the heavenly realms" (*Opus* 2.1).[25]

Like other patristic writers, the author of the *Opus* addresses the question of whether Matthew's story of the Magi might be used to promote astrology. He first attempts to problematize the notion that the course of one's life is determined by the stars, whether that is with reference to their position when you are born or the way that they move while you are alive. People choose the course of their lives, he says; the stars do not make these choices for them. He cites the Magi as evidence for this claim. Yes, they travel westward following a star, but this is a star that doesn't follow a normal course. What is more, they follow this star in search of a new life that is divorced from their old ones (*Opus* 2.2). He also speaks of the star as something that not only points toward Jesus but was fully obedient to him as well (*Opus* 2.9). In fact, when the star reappears to the Magi once they leave Jerusalem, it is this realization of the star's subservience to Jesus that causes them to rejoice (*Opus* 2.10).

The author of this text also follows other patristic authors by framing the story of Jesus's birth in overtly Judeophobic terms and by using the story of the Magi to enhance and bolster that reading. He argues that Matthew's genealogy, for example, was intended to show precisely when Jesus was to be born, because "God knew the treachery of the Jews" and wanted to give them no excuse for not believing and, finally, for having Jesus killed (*Opus* 2.1). But in contrast to "the Jews," who the author presents as both faithless and hostile toward their god, the Magi are cast as paragons of faithfulness. Commenting on their question regarding the whereabouts of the

---

25 All translations of the *Opus* in this section are taken from James A. Kellerman, *Incomplete Commentary on Matthew (Opus imperfectum)*, Ancient Christian Texts 1 (Downers Grove, IL: InterVarsity Academic, 2010).

king, the author suggests that this query alone is a revelation of the depth of their devotion. Their arrival, he continues, was "an exoneration of the Gentiles" and "an indictment of the Jews" (*Opus* 2.2).

The disappearance of the star when the Magi reach Jerusalem is employed in service of this same rhetoric. Had the star not vanished, the author claims, it would have led the Magi directly to Bethlehem. It disappears when they reach Jerusalem so that the Magi must enter the city and ask about the birth of Jesus. The author interprets the confusion caused by their arrival as further contributing to the dichotomy between the Magi and "the Jews." Both groups were told about the birth of the anointed one; the Magi were told through their vision of the star, while "the Jews" were told through their Scriptures. The former responded to this vision by traveling a great distance, while the latter "did not welcome [the Christ], even though he had been born in their own country" (*Opus* 2.9).

Like Justin Martyr, the author of the *Opus* connects the Magi's journey and their gift giving with Isaiah's reference to "the wealth of Damascus and the spoil of Samaria" (Isa 8:4). Justin claims the Magi were shackled by demonic forces before they came to Jesus and that by coming to Jesus, they were themselves the things that were handed over and thereby freed from their earlier bondage. The author of the *Opus*, by contrast, speaks of them as positive characters even before they come to Jerusalem and Bethlehem. In this text, the Magi are Persians who are praised for their wisdom. They are gentiles, but they are also exemplary gentiles. As an illustration, the author refers to stories like those in the Syriac *Revelation of the Magi*, which was discussed in the previous chapter. The Magi are keepers of an ancient mystery, and they are called Magi "because they glorified God in silence and unspoken voice" (*Opus* 2.2). For the author of the *Opus*, the "king of Assyria" in Isaiah 8:4 refers not to Herod (as Justin argued) but rather to the devil. When the Magi bestow their gifts on Jesus, the gifts themselves are the devil's possessions that Jesus takes for himself, thereby foreshadowing the power over the devil that he would exercise later in his life.

The *Opus*'s portrait of Herod is also more complicated than what we find in the other sources surveyed in this chapter. It is through this portrait that we start to see how the author of the *Opus* understands the story of the Magi—namely, as evidencing an ongoing cosmic battle between good and evil. Herod's confusion at the Magi's arrival is interpreted as evidence that he understood this new king as an "earthly king" (*Opus* 2.3). The author of the *Opus* indicates—in concert with our analysis of Herod's character in Matthew—that Herod was worried about this new king precisely because he was an Idumean by birth. This author takes an additional step and suggests that Herod's consternation is a manifestation of something darker, perhaps even demonic. When Herod summons his officials to inquire about the birthplace of the anointed one, it is not because Herod is curious. Rather, according to the *Opus*, it is because "the devil inside him" was doing research on Jesus. Herod's advisers are similarly construed as being on the side of wickedness. When they are asked where the anointed one is to be born, the author comments that they should have remained silent. By answering Herod's question honestly, his advisers became facilitators of an evil that would culminate in the slaughter of children (*Opus* 2.5).

Herod and the Magi also differ in terms of their understandings of what sort of king the anointed one would be. This contrast is highlighted when they reach Bethlehem and make their way to Jesus. Had the Magi been imagining Jesus as an "earthly king"—as Herod was—they would have anticipated finding him inside an ornate palace, dressed in fine clothes, his mother seated nearby, crowned. But this is not what they expect and not what they find. When they arrive in Bethlehem, the scene that they discover includes several elements borrowed from the Gospel of Luke. They come to "a dark and dirty inn, more suitable for animals than for people," and they find Jesus wrapped in filthy linens and resting in a feeding trough. Mary is nearby and dressed simply (*Opus* 2.11). None of this is particularly impressive, but the Magi nevertheless rejoice, believing the testimony of the star that had led them there. What they found in this scene, writes the author, was not an "earthly king" but a "heavenly king," and therefore they are content to worship and then depart home. If they had understood him to be an earthly ruler, then certainly they would have wished to stay with him in Bethlehem.

Further evidence that the Magi understand Jesus as a heavenly king is found in the quality and cost of their gifts. The author of the *Opus* sees their presentation of these gifts as contributing to the notion that the gentiles, and not Jews, were the first to worship him as such. He comes to this conclusion by connecting this scene with a passage from Isaiah: "All those from Sheba shall come. They shall bring gold and frankincense, and shall proclaim the praise of the Lord" (Isa 60:6–7). The Magi's gifts are also interpreted as signifying proper dispositions and behaviors for later readers. The gold symbolizes "the faithful who are perfect and wise," while the incense symbolizes prayer. The myrrh is connected with the death of Jesus but also represents "good works." Because "just as myrrh preserves the body of the deceased from decomposition, so the good works constantly preserve the crucified Christ in the memory of a person and preserve him in Christ." Understanding the gifts in this way encourages readers not only to pray but to act and give as well. "Weak is the prayer," the author writes, "that is not strengthened by the power of alms" (*Opus* 2.11).

The Magi's journey home by a different route is understood similarly as providing a model. By obeying the angel's instructions to not return to Jerusalem, the author of the *Opus* argues that the Magi again display their profound faith. They do not question why they are to return home in this way; they simply do it. But the *Opus* also frames this different route as indicative of a conversion experience and a warning. "Those who leave Herod behind and come to Christ with all their heart," the author writes, "will never return to Herod" (*Opus* 2.12). He then spells out what this means for his readers. "Whoever comes from the devil to God," he writes, "should never walk on that same path through which he came to the devil. . . . But if you return by the very same road, you walk again under the kingdom of Herod, and you will betray Christ" (*Opus* 2.12).

Maximus the Confessor's *Life of the Virgin*

The *Life of the Virgin* is a seventh-century text whose focus is on stories about the birth, life, and death of Mary. Although originally written in Greek, it survives today in an Old Georgian translation.[26] Extant copies of the text credit the great Eastern theologian Maximus the Confessor (ca. 580–662) as its author, although without access to the Greek version, it is difficult to judge this attribution with any certainty. Because of its highly narrative character, this text is frequently included alongside apocrypha like those discussed in chapter 5. I include it in the present chapter because regardless of whether Maximus is the text's author, it is styled as a patristic commentary on the life of Mary. The way that its author understands the story of the Magi is likewise similar to other patristic interpretations.

---

26 All English translations of the *Life of the Virgin* in this section are taken from Stephen J. Shoemaker, *The Life of the Virgin* (New Haven, CT: Yale University Press, 2012).

The first reference to the Magi in the *Life* is in passing—they are mentioned alongside shepherds from Luke (*Life* 24). A more extended account of their journey begins several chapters later, when they come from Persia to Jerusalem and Bethlehem (*Life* 36). In an effort to preempt any concerns about astrology, the author of the *Life* makes a point to specify that the star they followed was not actually a star but an angel appearing in the form of a star (*Life* 39), "a power sent from above that completely abolished the deception of astronomy and annihilated the darkness of such ignorance" (*Life* 36). This is evident not only in its sometimes erratic movements but also in its extreme brightness. It outshines the other stars and is also visible in the daytime, even eclipsing the light of the sun (*Life* 36, 38). Because their journey was long, the star appeared to the Magi long before the birth of Jesus so that they would be able to get a head start and arrive on time. As was the case in the *Revelation of the Magi*, the star in this text plays an active role in the Magi's journey, determining when they travel and when they rest (*Life* 36).

Like other patristic sources, the *Life* portrays the Magi as people who are shackled to evil powers and practices and who are therefore in need of some type of conversion. This author describes them as "pagans," as servants of "the demon guardians of the air," and as people who both observe the stars and sacrifice to them (*Life* 55). All of this changes, though, when they arrive in Bethlehem and make their way to the cave. When the Magi see Jesus, "they [are] filled with grace, sweetness, and light, and indescribable joy suffused their hearts" (*Life* 39). Because this text is a commentary on the life of Mary, its author also notes how she appears to the Magi, as "brilliant and exceedingly beautiful" and "the height of grace and glory" (*Life* 39). The sight of both her and Jesus compels the Magi not only to honor Jesus as a king but to worship him as a god

(*Life* 39). As was the case in Justin Martyr, John Chrysostom, and the *Opus Imperfectum*, the Magi in *Life of the Virgin* are held up as models for both conversion and generosity. "They offered [Jesus] visible gifts," the author writes, "and with them they offered themselves and their souls to the Lord" (*Life* 40).

The gifts of the Magi in this text are understood in a few ways that are in line with other patristic readings. First, they are understood as symbolizing what this author sees as the various dimensions of Jesus's life and identity but also how they are related to one another: "Gold, frankincense, and myrrh . . . as to a king and God and to the one who became incarnate for our sake and who was headed for death so that we will receive from him immortality" (*Life* 39). The gifts are also understood as symbolizing dispositions and practices that the author sees as positive. Gold is "a good and holy character," frankincense is "comprehension and spiritual insight," and myrrh is "mortification of the passions and bodily members" (*Life* 39). Readers cannot bring gold, frankincense, and myrrh to the infant Jesus, but they can still become like the Magi by cultivating these various dispositions and offering them in service to their god. Finally, the author of the *Life* understands the giving of gifts as evidence of the Magi's own conversion from their old "pagan" ways. As such, "they became the beginning of the conversion of the gentiles and precursors of their acceptance of service to Christ" (*Life* 40).

Herod in this text is a paragon of wickedness and is described by the author as both stupid and hungry for power (*Life* 38). The contrast between the Magi and "the Jews" more broadly is also stark. The author considers the Magi to be "pagans" before they see Jesus and his mother in the Bethlehem cave, but even before their arrival, they are cast in a far more positive light than their interlocutors. For example, the author of the *Life* argues that the star brings the Magi to Jerusalem and then disappears so that they will have to enter the city and ask about "he who has been born the king of the Jews" (*Life* 37). Their question is also a revelation to the city's inhabitants; without it, they wouldn't have known that a new king had been born because, presumably, they weren't paying attention. The author heightens this rhetoric when introducing Herod's advisers, whom the author refers to as "scribes and Pharisees" and "enemies" (*Life* 37). The critique becomes even sharper when the author describes the Magi as foreshadowing "the conversion of the gentiles" not only because of their worship of Jesus but because of their "rejection of the lies of the Jews" (*Life* 40).

Conclusions

Patristic authors evidence a persistent and ongoing fascination with Matthew's story of the Magi. One of the primary interests among the sources surveyed here is the star. Because it is what prompts the journey of the Magi in the first place, the star is an indispensable part of Matthew's story. Aside from acknowledging its existence, however, Matthew shows little interest in it. The star becomes an object of fascination because of concerns about astrology and the degree to which the story of the Magi seems to validate it as a source of knowledge. Patristic authors address these concerns in several ways. The Star Hymn in Ignatius's *Letter to the Ephesians* seems to suggest that the stars lose their ability to lead when the Magi come to Bethlehem. At the very least, the Magi lose their ability to find meaning in the stars. Others address this concern by stressing that the star wasn't *actually* a star or that if it was a star, then it is fully obedient to the divine will.

The transformation of the Magi from pagan idolaters into faithful followers of Jesus is likewise a popular theme among these authors. The Magi in Matthew can be understood as gentiles traveling a long distance to worship Jesus as a deity, but this reading is not necessary for understanding the story in Matthew, and it also isn't the most natural sense of the story in that context. The *Armenian Gospel of the Infancy* and the *Revelation of the Magi* both emphasize this "theological" reading of the Magi, although neither of these texts depicts the Magi arriving in Bethlehem as pagan idolaters. The patristic authors surveyed in this chapter, by contrast, see the Magi as needing and undergoing a spiritual transformation after they are led to Jesus. This is a theme among patristic texts more broadly, not just those surveyed here.[27] The Magi thus become examples and exemplars of conversion.

Judeophobic and supersessionist readings of the Magi story—those that would pit the Magi against "the Jews"—are painfully common in patristic literature. Like the theological reading of the Magi, the supersessionist interpretation is possible, although it seems quite detached from Matthew's broader aims in telling the story. Christian animosity toward Jews has a history that is long, unfortunate, and devastating. The rhetoric used to facilitate the murder of millions in the Shoah was energized by Hitler, but it did not originate with him. In fact, it was already quite antique when Martin Luther published *On the Jews and Their Lies* in 1543. Today, Judeophobic rhetoric has become so normalized and frequent in the pulpit and the political square that it is often not even considered newsworthy. It is tempting to explore whether supersessionist interpretations like those in this chapter generate the problem or merely reflect it. A case can probably be made that they do both. When reading these texts, we would do well to remember that interpretations have consequences and that this is true regardless of the purity of the intentions that undergird them.

---

27 Hein arrives at a similar conclusion in his study of the Magi in a different selection of patristic texts: "[Early Christian authors] nearly always explicitly 'convert' [the Magi], puncturing their 'magic' prowess and recasting their identity to accomplish each early Christian author's exegetical goal" ("First Christian 'Magicians,'" 2).

7

Buddhists, Watches, and Endings

ON OR AROUND EPIPHANY, MANY Christians around the world perform a curious ritual involving a piece of chalk, the door to their residence, and a cryptic series of numbers, letters, and symbols. The ritual begins with a short prayer, the contents of which will differ depending on context. The chalk is then used to inscribe the symbols over the door, a combination of the current year, crosses, and the letters C, M, and B. The symbols for the year 2022 would read as follows:

$$20 + C + M + B + 22$$

When ordered this way, the letters are meant as an abbreviation for the Latin petition *Christus mansionem benedicat*, "May Christ bless this house." You may have also noticed, however—here at the end of a book on the Magi—that they are also the first letters of the names Caspar, Melchior, and Balthasar.

This Epiphany ritual is popular among Roman Catholics, but one can find plenty of non-Catholic Christians "chalking the door" at the start of the new year. Like so many household rituals, the question of what people hope to accomplish by performing this one has a range of possible answers. From an outsider's perspective, the chalking ritual may well be understood as a sort of incantation or spell, the symbols functioning as magic to protect people in the house from anything bad that may be lurking outside. On this read, it is reminiscent of a scene in Exodus in which the enslaved Hebrews in Egypt paint the doorposts of their homes with blood so that their firstborn children might be spared from the tenth plague (Exod 12:22–23). Some who perform the ritual might understand it in this way, but I would venture that most do not.

The chalking of doors at Epiphany is best understood not as an incantation but as a tradition with no singular, fixed meaning. Individuals and families generally perform this ritual as a way of asking their god to watch over them and their house but also as an expression of hope in what the upcoming year might bring. For some, the chalk that remains over the door throughout the year is a persistent and visible expression of that hope. The Magi are present in this ritual to commemorate Epiphany, but they also may function as intercessory figures who aid the home's residents in their prayers for a safe and fruitful year. Or maybe they are present as a reminder of the importance of hospitality, of being open to those who might come to the door. Mary, Joseph, and Jesus welcomed the Magi, so it stands to reason that anyone who invokes their names should likewise practice radical hospitality toward strangers, especially those in need. Or at least one could hope that this would be the case.

The Magi's journey as literary characters begins in Matthew's Gospel, but even today it remains lively and ongoing. The chalking of doors is one visible sign of their continued influence, but one need not search for long before finding other examples. They appear in many well-loved Christmas and Epiphany hymns, of course, including "Sons of Men, Behold from Far" (Charles Wesley, 1739), "We Three Kings" (John H. Hopkins Jr., 1857), and "What Child Is This?" (William Chatterton Dix, 1865). They also show up on James Taylor's 1988 album *Never Die Young* in the song "Home by Another Way." Here their story appears in abbreviated form, and as the song's title suggests, the focus is on the different route that they took back to their own land. Matthew notes this detail as a shorthand way of saying that they did not go back through Jerusalem. But for Taylor, to "go home by another way" is to change one's mind about something, whether big or small, and to choose a path that is new, more fulfilling, or perhaps less dangerous.

In this final chapter, we look at a few ways that the Magi have been recast in more contemporary literary works. It is not possible to cover everything in such a short space, so I limit myself to four examples, all of which were written and published in the United States in the last 130 years. The first is a story by Henry van Dyke entitled *The Story of the Other Wise Man*, which follows the adventures of a forgotten Magus who travels to Bethlehem to see Jesus but arrives after everyone else has already left. The second is O. Henry's famous short story "The Gift of the Magi," which is distinct from others in this chapter because the Magi aren't characters in the story in the traditional sense. The third is a novel by Christopher Moore entitled *Lamb: The Gospel according to Biff, Christ's Childhood Pal*. In this book, Jesus has some questions about his identity, so he and his good friend Biff travel eastward to find the Magi and see whether they have any answers. I close by examining Barbara Brown Taylor's recent children's book, *Home by Another Way: A Christmas Story*, a more "traditional" retelling of the Magi story, but one that also reproduces several themes found also in apocryphal and patristic literature.

It may seem odd to examine more contemporary works of fiction alongside the Gospel of Matthew, Christian apocrypha, and patristic authors. What could modern pieces of fiction possibly teach us about the Magi? It is a mistake to assume that the reception of the Magi is something that takes place entirely in the past and that it is therefore something "complete" or "finished." Authors and readers today are not divorced from this process; they are an essential part of it. By looking at how more recent authors think about the Magi, and how they use them as characters in their stories, we can see with a greater clarity the enormous impact that these visitors continue to exercise on our collective imaginations.

The One Who Didn't Make It

Henry van Dyke (1852–1933) was a master of many trades. He was an ordained Presbyterian minister and a professor of English literature at Princeton University, and he served as the US ambassador to the Netherlands and Luxembourg under President Woodrow Wilson. Van Dyke was good friends with Mark Twain, and in 1910 was one of the officiants at his funeral. He was also a poet and hymn writer, and one of his more well-known pieces is the Christian hymn "Joyful, Joyful, We Adore Thee" (1907). In the late 1800s, van Dyke also wrote a short story about the Magi. Well, one of them, at least. *The Story of the Other Wise Man* is the tragic but heartwarming tale of Artaban, a fourth Magus who was mostly forgotten by the centuries.[1]

The story begins in the city of Ecbatana, whose ruins are thought to be in the modern city of Hamedan, in western Iran (15).

---

1 Page numbers in this section correspond with Henry van Dyke, *The Story of the Other Wise Man* (New York: Harper & Brothers, 1896). This story is widely available in various digital and print media. While he does not call him a *magos*, Herodotus references an adviser to King Xerxes whom he calls Artaban (*Hist.* 7.10–18).

Van Dyke describes Artaban as a Mede and as one of the Magi, which he understands explicitly as a class of priests and followers of Zoroaster "called the fire worshippers" (16–17). In the opening scene, Artaban welcomes his fellow Magi into an upper chamber of his home, where there is an altar and a flame. As they begin to chant to the deity Ahura Mazda, the flame dances and grows. When they finish their chanting, Artaban articulates the purpose of their ritual: "You have come tonight . . . at my call, as the faithful scholars of Zoroaster, to renew your worship and rekindle your faith in the God of Purity, even as this fire has been rekindled on the altar. We worship not the fire, but Him of whom it is the chosen symbol, because it is the purest of all created things. It speaks to us of one who is Light and Truth" (20). In this opening scene, van Dyke paints Zoroastrian rituals and philosophies in an apologetic hue; they are fire worshippers, but what they're *actually* worshipping isn't the fire but the god whom the fire symbolizes. The "religion" of the Magi is seen from the outset as compatible or at least congruent with the forms of Christianity and Judaism that he was familiar with, and this framing continues into the following scene.

Artaban begins to discuss the importance of astrology for the Magi, referring to it as "the highest form of learning" (21). The conversation shifts rather abruptly to talk of a coming "messianic" figure called "Sosiosh the Victorious," and Artaban's father, Abgarus, remarks, "In that day, [he] shall arise out of the number of the prophets in the east country. Around him shall shine a mighty brightness, and he shall make life everlasting, incorruptible, and immortal, and the dead shall rise again" (22–23). There is division among the Magi on how best to respond. One of them suggests that it is far better to focus on the here and now, on bolstering "the influence of the Magi in their own country," than to spend time waiting for the arrival of someone who may end up being "a stranger" (23).

Others agree, at which point Artaban produces two scrolls. One contains a record of Balaam's oracle from Numbers 24:17: "There shall come a star out of Jacob, and a sceptre shall rise out of Israel" (24). The reading is met with disapproval because how is it possible for this messianic figure to come out of a previously enslaved and exiled people? Artaban notes Daniel as an example of someone who was influential among the Magi, but to no end. Even Artaban's father, Abgarus, remains skeptical (25).

At this point, van Dyke begins to draw more heavily on the "traditional" version of the Magi story, as Artaban reveals that he has been coordinating with three others: Caspar, Melchior, and Balthazar. Echoing the new star theory of Johannes Kepler that was discussed in chapter 4, Artaban tells the group that he and these other Magi had witnessed the birth of a new star out of a planetary conjunction earlier that year and that they had calculated that it would happen again that night. Artaban says that when this happens, he will meet the other three in Babylon and that they will go on together to Jerusalem to see the new king (26). And he will not be going empty-handed. He tells the others that he had recently sold everything to purchase expensive gifts for this king: a sapphire, a ruby, and a pearl (27).

In other retellings of the Magi story, authors frequently pit the determined Magi against the indifferent people of Jerusalem. The scene involving the Magi and Herod doesn't occur in van Dyke's work, for reasons that will become clear in a moment. But van Dyke has effectively reproduced it in this initial episode involving the Magi in Ecbatana. Artaban and the Magi with whom he is coordinating are eager to welcome the new king, while the others in his circle are not. They are either more interested in maintaining the status quo or are simply not sure that any potential payoff from the journey would be worth the risk. Even at this early point in the story, a facet of van Dyke's understanding of Matthew comes into focus; the Magi are searching for something that should be of interest to everyone but isn't. The other Magi remain uninterested in joining him; some indicate that they are too busy, but all seem doubtful that Artaban's quest will lead to anyone or anything worthwhile. "No king will ever rise from the broken race of Israel," one remarks (27). But Artaban's determination persists, and when he sees the planets come together later that night, the new star shining in their midst, he sets out to meet the other Magi by himself (30–31).

When he arrives in Babylon, Artaban comes across a Jewish man lying in the road, sick and at the point of death. He stops to help him even though he knows that it will delay his journey (40–41).[2] Artaban tells the man where he is headed and what he is searching for, and the man tells Artaban that he should be heading to Bethlehem, not Jerusalem (44). They say their goodbyes, and Artaban continues. But when he reaches the rendezvous point, he finds a note from the other Magi indicating that they have gone on without him. Artaban is determined to make the journey, so he goes back to Babylon and trades his sapphire for supplies (47–48).

The streets of Bethlehem are silent when Artaban arrives, and he encounters a young woman singing to her baby. She tells him that the Magi had been in Bethlehem, but that they departed quickly, and that the family they were there to see had likewise left and gone to Egypt (54). The peaceful city is thrown into panic as Herod's soldiers arrive and begin carrying out their order to kill the young children. Artaban stands in the doorway of the house

---

2 He initially turns away from the man, van Dyke says, "consigning the body to that strange burial which the Magians deem most fitting—the funeral of the desert, from which the kites and vultures rise on dark wings, and the beasts of prey slink furtively away, leaving only a heap of white bones in the sand" (*Story of the Other*, 41). This echoes the burial rituals of the *magoi* described by Strabo in *Geogr.* 15.20 and discussed in chap. 3.

as if to block it, and when a soldier approaches and demands entry, he offers him a ruby—the second of his three gifts meant for the king—if he will leave this house alone and be on his way (58–59). The plan works, but while the woman is grateful, the encounter leaves Artaban feeling sad. In addition to having lied, he laments the loss of yet another gift. "I have spent for a man that which was meant for God," he says. "Shall I ever be worthy to see the face of the King?" (60).

Years pass quickly as Artaban travels throughout Egypt in search of the king. He marvels at the pyramids and talks with the rabbis in Alexandria (63–64). One of them helps him understand "the prophecies of Israel," and also that the king he is looking for "is not to be found in a palace, nor among the rich and powerful. . . . The light for which the world is waiting is a new light, the glory that shall rise out of patient and triumphant suffering" (65). The years continue to flash by, and Artaban searches for his king among the poor, the sick, and the injured. The quest that began with helping others—the man on the road and the woman and her child—now continues along those lines: "He fed the hungry, and clothed the naked, and healed the sick, and comforted the captive" (66–69).

Three more years pass, and Artaban finds himself in Jerusalem at Passover (74). He hears from a group of Parthian Jews that a man named Jesus of Nazareth is being executed outside the city for allegedly claiming to be the son of God and the king of the Jews (75). When Artaban hears this, he wonders whether this could be the same king that he traveled to Bethlehem to see, the one he's been searching for all these years. As he is making his way to the execution along with the crowd, he encounters a group of soldiers dragging a woman down the street with the intention of selling her into slavery. She recognizes Artaban as a Magus, and she runs to him and begs him to help her. "I also am a daughter of the true religion which is taught by the Magi," she says (76). He responds by taking the pearl from his cloak—the last of his gifts—and handing it to the woman as her ransom (79–80).

Although this is not made explicit in the story, Artaban's gift of the pearl is understood as coinciding with the death of Jesus. For as soon as the woman takes it from his hand, the sky darkens, and the ground starts to quake. A tile from a nearby roof falls and strikes Artaban in the head, knocking him unconscious (80–81). When the woman rushes to his aid, she hears a quiet voice in the distance but cannot make out what it is saying (82). Artaban hears it as well and responds, "Not so, my Lord! For when [did I see you hungry], and fed thee? Or thirsty, and gave thee drink? Or naked, and clothed thee? . . . Three-and-thirty years have I looked for thee; but I have never seen thy face, nor ministered to thee, my King" (82). The voice speaks again: "Verily I say unto thee, inasmuch as thou hast done unto one of the least of these my brethren, thou has done it unto me" (82). Artaban's face glows, and he breathes one last time. "His journey was ended," van Dyke writes. "His treasures were accepted. The other Wise Man had found the King" (85).

Unlike the other Magi, Artaban never sees Jesus in the flesh because he is late arriving to Bethlehem. But according to van Dyke, Artaban *does* see Jesus through his work with the poor. The last scene of the book draws from another passage in Matthew's Gospel, in which Jesus talks about the final judgment and the separation of "the sheep and the goats" (Matt 25:31–46). The sheep are rewarded because they have served their god by attending to those in need: the poor, the hungry, the naked. The goats, on the other hand, are punished because they chose to ignore such things. "Truly I tell you," Jesus says, "whatever you did not do for the least of these, you also didn't do for me" (Matt 25:45). Van Dyke's presentation of Artaban as a sort of model disciple is in keeping with other uses of the Magi tradition. But this story also follows Matthew in the way that it reframes readers' expectations for Jesus's kingship. This king is found not among the elites but among the marginalized.

Giving until the Gifts Don't Make Sense

William Sydney Porter (1862–1910) was an American author who is perhaps better known by his pseudonym, O. Henry. After being accused and found guilty of embezzlement in 1896, Porter spent a few years in prison. When he was released, he moved to New York City and spent the remainder of his life writing. In 1906, he published *The Four Million*, a collection of twenty-five short stories. The title reflects the population of New York City at the time of the book's publication, and according to the epigraph, it is a response to the claim "that there were only 'Four Hundred' people in New York City who were really worth noticing." To the contrary, Porter writes, "a wiser man has arisen—the census taker—and his larger estimate of human interest has been preferred in marking out the field of these little stories of the 'Four Million.'" Driven as he was by the notion that all people are worth noticing, it should come as no surprise that Porter's stories are known for featuring characters and situations that could easily be dismissed as mundane. One of the most well-known stories from *The Four Million*—"The Gift of the Magi"—is a case in point.[3]

The story begins with Della, who is in a state of despair. It is Christmas Eve, and she has been saving actual pennies for months to buy a Christmas gift for her husband, Jim. Despite her best efforts, she has succeeded in saving only $1.87. Although this converts to

---

3 Before appearing in *The Four Million*, this story was first published in the December 10, 1905, Sunday edition of the *New York World* newspaper. Page numbers in this section correspond with the version found in O. Henry, *The Four Million* (New York: Doubleday, 1906).

roughly $60 today, Della considers it a paltry amount, and she collapses on the couch and weeps (16). Times have been tough, particularly after Jim's income dropped by a third. Della wanted to buy him "something fine and rare and sterling—something just a little bit near to being worthy of the honour of being owned by Jim" (17–18). Here at the start, the narrator makes it a point to emphasize that this couple lives modestly, and certainly not beyond their means. They get by on $20 per week, and nearly half of that goes to rent (16–17).

The narrator also notes that Della and Jim take pride in only two of their possessions. One is Jim's gold pocket watch, an heirloom passed down to him from his grandfather. The other—an entirely different sort of possession—is Della's hair. Porter contrasts both treasures with the riches of ancient monarchs: "Had the queen of Sheba lived in the flat across the air shaft, Della would have let her hair hang out the window some day to dry just to depreciate Her Majesty's jewels and gifts. Had King Solomon been the janitor, with all his treasures piled up in the basement, Jim would have pulled out his watch every time he passed, just to see him pluck at his beard from envy" (18). As Della gazes at her beautiful, knee-length hair in the mirror, she has an idea: she will sell it, and then she will have enough money for an elegant, fitting gift for Jim (19).

She finds a buyer in no time. A few snips, and she walks away with $20, the equivalent of their weekly budget and around $650 today. No small amount, and surely enough for a Christmas gift. Della runs from store to store before she spots the perfect thing: a platinum watch chain, "simple and chaste in design," for Jim's watch. It was perfect, and for $21, she brings it home. Della then sets to work on what remains of her hair, "repairing the ravages made by generosity added to love" (20). As she waits for Jim to come home, Della is nervous about what he will think. She reminds herself, "What could I do with a dollar and eighty-seven cents?" (21).

Della hears Jim's footsteps outside, and she prays that he will still find her attractive (21). As Jim enters, the narrator describes him as "thin and very serious." His coat is shabby, and he doesn't even have gloves. Jim freezes when he sees Della, and his expression frightens her because it is both unexpected and difficult to interpret (21–22). She rushes to him to explain the situation, reassuring him that her hair will grow back (22). Jim is clearly in a state of shock, but he snaps out of it and embraces her (23). He produces a package from his pocket and assures Della that she will understand his demeanor if she would just open it. She does and weeps again when she sees what's inside: expensive hair combs that she had for some time admired through a shop window (23–24). Although Della has no use for these combs at the moment, she treasures them because she knows that her hair will grow back (24). She leaps up with excitement and gives the watch chain to Jim. She asks him for the watch so that she can see how they look together, but Jim responds by sitting on the couch, putting his hands back behind his head, and smiling—a posture that could suggest either helpless annoyance or deep satisfaction. He then reveals to Della that he got the money for her combs by selling his prized watch (25). The story ends with a reflection on the Magi that I quote here in full:

> The magi, as you know, were wise men—wonderfully wise men—who brought gifts to the Babe in the manger. They invented the art of giving Christmas presents. Being wise, their gifts were no doubt wise ones, possibly bearing the privilege of exchange in case of duplication. And here I have lamely related to you the uneventful chronicle of two

foolish children in a flat who most unwisely sacrificed for each other the greatest treasures of their house. But in the last word to the wise of these days let it be said that of all who give gifts these two were the wisest. Of all who give and receive gifts, such as they are wisest. Everywhere they are wisest. They are the magi. (25)

There are no stars in this story, and no journeys westward. There are no babies, no incense, and no kings. But there are gifts, and there are Magi, at least in a sense. Porter's understanding of the Magi is in line with patristic interpretations that stress the idea of conversion—namely, that the Magi travel to Bethlehem and give their whole selves along with their material gifts. And that process changes them. In this short story, Della and Jim give of themselves until their material gifts for each other no longer make sense. Jim receives a watch chain for a watch that he no longer owns, and Della receives combs for hair that she no longer has. And while Della's hair will grow back, the scene on Christmas Eve remains deeply and painfully ironic. The gifts that they have exchanged, while valuable in terms of their material cost, are worth little in terms of their practicality. The same is true for the actual gifts of the Magi, of course; infants don't have much use for gold, incense, or myrrh, and yet the whole point of these gifts for Matthew is that they are expensive. It is tempting to read this story of Della and Jim as a tragedy, yet as Porter specifies in the postscript, this would be a mistake. Both were foolish to have exchanged their most valuable possessions, but it is precisely this foolishness that reveals the depth of their commitment to each other and therefore makes them wise.

"The Greatest Story Never Told"

Christopher Moore is a comic fantasy author whose works are consistently hilarious and difficult to categorize. He writes about angels, demons, and vampires, and in 2002, he wrote a book about Jesus and the Magi. *Lamb: The Gospel according to Biff, Christ's Childhood Pal* is a best-selling novel that explores the enormous portion of Jesus's life—between his infancy and the start of his ministry—that the canonical Gospels hardly mention.[4] *Lamb* is in many ways a sort of modern infancy gospel, not altogether different from the *Protevangelium of James* or the *Gospel of Pseudo-Matthew*. The story is narrated from the perspective of Biff, Jesus's best friend and one of his earliest disciples.[5] At the start of the book, Biff is raised from the dead by an angel and then taken to the Hyatt Regency in St. Louis. There he is instructed to write about his experiences with Jesus when they were children. Approximately one-third of the book is about the time they spend with the Magi.

Throughout *Lamb*, Biff refers to Jesus as "Josh" or "Joshua," an homage to the Hebrew name *Yeshua*. Josh is curious, smart, and powerful. He can perform resurrections (7), cause his likeness to appear on crackers (19), and heal skin diseases (90–91). He is also aware that powers like these are not normal for children, and he has a keen sense that he is "the Messiah" and a divine being. But he doesn't quite understand how he is supposed to respond to these aspects of his identity. At the age of thirteen, Josh and Biff seek

---

4 Outside of the stories of Jesus's birth in Matthew and Luke, his childhood is not of interest to the Gospel writers. One exception is a short story in Luke about Jesus as a twelve-year-old. His parents go up to Jerusalem for Passover, and they leave him behind by accident as they are returning home. When they go back to look for him, they find him in the temple with the rabbis (Luke 2:41–51).

5 Biff's real name is Levi, son of Alphaeus (a disciple of Jesus mentioned in Mark 2:14). The nickname "Biff," he says, "comes from our slang word for a smack upside the head, something that my mother said I required at least daily from an early age" (Christopher Moore, *Lamb: The Gospel according to Biff, Christ's Childhood Pal* [New York: HarperCollins, 2003], 9). Page numbers in this section correspond with Moore's *Lamb*.

out Rabbi Hillel in Jerusalem to see what wisdom he might be able to bestow. If Josh is the Messiah, then what? After some back and forth, Hillel says to Josh, "Look, kid, your mother says that some very wise men came to Bethlehem to see you when you were born. They obviously knew something that no one else knew. Why don't you go see them? Ask them about being the Messiah" (97).

Josh and Biff start wandering around Jerusalem trying to determine whether anyone remembers the Magi, but they are unsuccessful. Mary does remember, however. "The one named Balthasar," she remarks, "the black one, he said he came from a village north of Antioch" (99). She goes on to describe him as "a rich, Ethiopian magician" (100). Mary says that the others—Gaspar and Melchior—were from farther east and had come to Jerusalem "by the Silk Road" (100). But if they can find Balthasar, Mary guesses, then he will know where the other two are. Josh and Biff soon embark on their journey. Unbeknown to them, they won't return home for twenty years.

Josh and Biff arrive in Antioch and discover that Balthasar is no longer there; he has moved to Kabul (131–34). Traveling eastward along the Silk Road, they finally make it to Balthasar's house, which is a fortress carved into the rock of a steep canyon (142). Balthasar doesn't recognize Josh "without the swaddling clothes," but he welcomes both him and Biff into his house. While leading them through the lavishly decorated halls, Balthasar recites the wisdom of Lao-Tzu, the sixth-century BCE Chinese philosopher whose teachings are the foundation of Taoism. As he speaks about his experiences in China and Egypt, Biff begins to suspect that Balthasar is much older than he appears and so asks what his secret is. Balthasar responds with a grin, "Magic" (150). Readers discover later that he is 260 years old (179) and that his secret to long life is that he has a demon—named "Catch"—imprisoned in his house. As long as Catch is on earth, Balthasar is immortal (181–83). When the demon escapes from its cell because of Biff's curiosity, Josh banishes it to hell. With the source of his life now gone, Balthasar dies ten days later. Before he takes his last breath, he points Jesus and Biff in the direction of China, toward Gaspar, the second of the Magi (195).

During his stay with Balthasar, Josh asks why he and the others came to Bethlehem to see him after he was born. Balthasar says that they did not set out together but their paths crossed while they were on their way, and when they discovered that they were all heading to the same place, they finished the journey together. Balthasar elsewhere refers to Josh as "child of the star" (153), which would indicate that he found some type of significance in the phenomenon that led them. But he also claims that the star was relatively insignificant and not what prompted them to travel to Jerusalem and Bethlehem. "It was only our means of navigation" (179), Balthasar claims. He and the other Magi all traveled for different reasons, each with a different hope about what they would find when they reached their destination. Balthasar believed—and in fact, continues to believe—that Josh has "power over evil and victory over death" and as such carries "the key to immortality" (179). In light of his story about the demon whose existence sustains his own, Balthasar's interest in Josh becomes clear. He wants to live forever but also be freed from his dependence on an evil power. Josh, he maintains, has the power to defeat the demon *and* guarantee that Balthasar will continue to live even in its absence. Only the first of these things ends up being true.

Josh and Biff travel to China after Balthasar's death. After a long journey, part of which involves trying to walk *around* the Great Wall of China, they arrive at Gaspar's home: a Buddhist monastery perched high up on a mountain. They gain entrance to the monastery after a three-day wait outside the front doors, a test by the monks to gauge their level of commitment. When they encounter Gaspar, he is deep in meditation, and his body is so still that they mistake him for a statue (208). His eyes snap open as they approach, and he asks, in Aramaic, "Is that you, Joshua?" (208). The following day, Biff and Josh begin learning meditation, Kung Fu, and the ways of the monks at Gaspar's monastery. Josh attains a state of enlightenment with remarkable speed and is then able to move about the monastery as a disembodied voice. Gaspar encourages him to return to bodily form by teaching him the ways of the bodhisattva, a being who becomes enlightened "but makes a decision that he will not evolve to nirvana until sentient beings have preceded him there" (230).[6] Josh hesitates when Gaspar describes this decision as "an act of self-love," but he comes around with the realization that to "love your neighbor as you love yourself" requires first that you love yourself. He rematerializes with the determination, "I will be a bodhisattva to my people" (230).

There are no demons involved in their visit to Gaspar's monastery, but there is a yeti (241–43). He lives somewhere on the mountain, and the monks leave food for him to eat. After an initial encounter with him, Josh and Biff visit this friendly creature on a regular basis (246). The yeti's unexpected death precipitates their departure from the monastery, as Gaspar insists that they have learned what they could learn (251). Before they leave, Biff confronts Gaspar and suggests that he isn't what he claims to be. "What enlightened being," he says, "travels halfway around the world following a star on the rumor that a Messiah has been

---

6 Broadly speaking, "nirvana" in Buddhist traditions is understood as liberation from the cycle of birth, death, and rebirth that is fueled by karma and characterized by suffering. Bodhisattvas are enlightened beings who are able to escape the cycle but opt to be reborn into it in order to help others become enlightened as well. Tenzin Gyatso, the fourteenth Dalai Lama, is considered by some Buddhists to be a bodhisattva.

born?" (252). Gaspar then explains why he came to Bethlehem in the first place. Balthasar was looking for immortality, but he and Melchior were searching for someone or something that would help them in their quest for enlightenment. While he and the others realized even in Bethlehem that Josh was different, all of them also realized that he wasn't what they were looking for, "not yet, anyway" (252). Gaspar explains that he found the yeti when he returned east and decided to build the monastery in part to care for him, hoping that in that process, perhaps he would attain enlightenment. But now that the yeti is dead, he fears all is lost. Josh explains, however, that the yeti taught compassion through the way that he lived and that Gaspar likewise embodied this through his care of the yeti (253). Moore does not say that Josh's words to Gaspar have helped him attain enlightenment, but as Biff and Josh depart, there is a sense that what Gaspar had hoped to find in Bethlehem had now found him.

Six years after arriving at Gaspar's monastery, when Josh is twenty-four, he and Biff depart in search of Melchior, who as it turns out is Gaspar's brother. Their destination is Tamil, in southern India. After several months of searching, they find him nestled into a cliff, sitting among seagulls, and looking out at the ocean. Josh starts to introduce himself when Melchior interrupts and says that he knows who Josh is and that he recognizes him from the time that he saw him when he was first born. "A man's self does not change," Melchior says. "Only his body. I see you grew out of the swaddling clothes" (285). They remain with Melchior for two years—far less time than they spent with Balthasar and Gaspar. Their visit is cut short when Josh's mother appears in a water stain in a temple of the Hindu god Vishnu. "Yeah, she does that," Josh remarks (298). But while they are with Melchior, he teaches Josh about "the Divine Spark" and also how to manipulate matter. Josh is a quick study, and before long, he can make entire bowls of rice out of only a few grains (292).

Moore's tale of Josh, Biff, and the Magi is as hilarious as it is profound. In the afterword, he writes about some of his motivations for writing the book as well as some of his sources of inspiration. Josh and Biff's journey to find the Magi draws from the hypothesis that the historical Jesus of Nazareth traveled east when he was young and that during his travels, he was inspired by Taoism, Buddhism, and Hinduism. This hypothesis was popular for a time in some circles, but today it carries little weight among most scholars of antiquity. But it is also not Moore's goal to paint an accurate portrait of Jesus as a historical figure. In addition to all the motivations and questions he outlines in the afterword, Moore's story is meant to explore the question of why the Magi *really* came to Bethlehem. The texts surveyed thus far have provided several answers to that question. In *Lamb*, they travel to Bethlehem not to give Josh something but in hopes that Josh will give *them* something that is lacking from their own knowledge or religious sensibilities. While their visit to Bethlehem wasn't what they had hoped, it is what ultimately inspired Josh and Biff to locate them. And that process did bear fruit, although not in the way that the Magi had originally intended.

Stars in Their Eyes

The focus of this final section is an illustrated children's book by Barbara Brown Taylor, an Episcopal priest, teacher, and prolific author whose works on preaching are standard readings in many mainline Protestant seminaries. Children's books like this are one of the ways that people learn the story of the Magi and its various interpretations. They appear under Christmas trees and in stockings and are read, enjoyed, and internalized by adults and children alike. Taylor's book on the Magi, *Home by Another Way: A Christmas Story*, was published in 2018.[7] As is the case with so many books that would dare tackle biblical subjects, it has been met with mixed reviews. Some readers praise it for its beautiful art and compelling narrative, while others criticize it for how the story deviates from Matthew. Taylor's work serves as the end point for this chapter because of how effectively it encapsulates so many of the themes that have emerged over the course of the preceding chapters.

The Magi are depicted throughout this book as exotic, religious sages from faraway lands. In all the illustrations, they are dressed colorfully, and all of them wear turbans and have long beards. One is old and gray, and the other two are younger. One of the younger ones has darker skin than the other two, a clear homage to the tradition of the Black Magus. Taylor introduces them as three "very wise men" who do not know one another. They are each situated in their own countries when suddenly, they have a vision of a star. Taylor emphasizes the star's brightness, and this brightness leads the Magi to wonder whether it is "real" or just in their imaginations (2).[8] As the story goes on, we discover that the truth about the star lies somewhere in between, but here at the start, the Magi understand it as a sign that beckons them to follow it. To explain why they follow the star so readily, Taylor constructs short backstories for them. "Each in his own country," she writes, "had tried books, tried magic, tried astrology" (4). One is described as a scholar who spends all his resources learning an unspecified ancient language. One is an ascetic who lives on "dried herbs boiled in water." The third has mastered the art of walking over hot coals. All the Magi are thus depicted

---

7 The book is richly illustrated, and not by the author. The illustrations generally complement the words on the page, however, and amplify some of what is said in the text of the story.

8 Page numbers in this section correspond with Barbara Brown Taylor, *Home by Another Way: A Christmas Story*, illustrated by Melanie Cataldo (Louisville, KY: Flyaway, 2018).

as searching for something, whether that be spiritual or intellectual enlightenment. But they aren't sure precisely what that something is; all they know is that it is missing (4).

This story also presents a familiar portrait of Herod as an evil and perhaps even demonic figure. When the Magi depart from their respective countries, they encounter one another on the road. They discover that their visions of the star are shared rather than individual. They also discover that all of them have interpreted this vision as meaning the same thing: that they should head to Jerusalem in search of a king (8). Attention shifts quickly to Herod. In the first illustration of Herod, he appears overweight and bored. Taylor describes him as "lumpy and rumpled," with "terrible breath" and skin that had "a funny orange color" (10). His guards are terrified of him and are trembling. In stark contrast with Matthew, in which it is Herod who seeks out the Magi, here it is the Magi who ask for an audience with the king. And this comes at no great difficulty, since "they looked rich" (10). The question that the Magi pose—"Do you know of any other kings in the area?"—is vague, but it succeeds in grabbing Herod's attention (11–13). It is here that readers begin to see that the star guiding the Magi isn't a normal star at all. For when Herod looks at the Magi, he sees its light twinkling in their eyes. Taylor describes his eyes as growing "perfectly round, like the eyes of a snake" (13). Herod does not even know what the star means at this point, and yet there is something about it that he almost instinctively desires for himself.

Herod's meeting with his advisers is characterized by some common Judeophobic tropes that frequently come packaged with stories about the Magi. Herod's advisers produce "reference books" that smell of mold, and they tell Herod that although the prophet Micah spoke of a new king for Israel, they didn't think that he had anything to worry about. The messages that this scene conveys are far from subtle. Herod's advisers are depicted as Jews whose books—presumably, their "Scriptures"—are moldy, and not from age but from disuse. What is more, even though these advisers are aware of Micah's "prophecy," they are either apathetic or lazy in terms of following up themselves. They suggest that sending the Magi to investigate instead would be better. This, Taylor writes, would also "save the king a little money" (15). The illustration that spans these pages (14–15) cements a clear dichotomy between the "good" Magi and the "not-so-good" king and his advisers. There is a doorway to the left, outside of which the Magi stand patiently in a well-lit space. Herod and his advisers, by contrast, crouch together in a poorly lit room, immersed in darkness.

Herod cleans himself up before returning to the Magi and sending them to Bethlehem. The Magi sense that something isn't quite right as they are leaving the place, but when they make it outside and are able to see the star again, they press on (16). The star leads them to Mary and Joseph's small and unassuming house. The couple is frightened at this unexpected band of visitors, but they enter and find Jesus. Their long journey is validated when they look at his face and see in his eye the light of the same star that led them there, and they kneel before his bed (20–23). They present their gifts with a hint of embarrassment. Had they known that they were going to visit a baby, perhaps they would have chosen differently. Maybe "goats milk, a warm blanket, something shiny to hang above his crib" (25). Mary hands Jesus to the Magi, and they pass him around in wonder. They then fall asleep before the sun sets, worn out from their journey (26).

When they awake the next morning, they are troubled to find that none of them can see the star that had led them from their countries (29). But they realize that just as the star's appearing was a sign that they should set out, the star's disappearing was an indication that they had found what they set out to find. Whatever was missing before the star appeared is missing no longer. As they plan their departure, they agree to take another route home because all of them had been warned in a dream to avoid going back to Jerusalem. The closing scene echoes those apocryphal traditions in which the Magi receive gifts back from Jesus and his family. Here they thank Mary for "the scent and weight and skin of a baby, . . . for this home and the love here, . . . [and] for a really great story" (32).

Taylor's book is by far the most "conventional" of the ones surveyed in this chapter. There are no Buddhist monks, no forgotten Magi, and no expensive hair combs or pocket watches. It presents itself not as a straightforward, objective retelling of Matthew's story but as an imaginative account inspired by the Magi in Matthew. The details that Taylor emphasizes, adds, and changes bring out several themes that we have seen elsewhere: the brightness and strangeness of the star, the Magi arriving from different locations, the reciprocity of gifts, and also the unfortunate Judeophobic rhetoric that seems to plague the Magi at nearly every stage of their reception. As has been the case with all the works analyzed here and in previous chapters, authorial intent and intentionality behind these details are difficult to gauge with any certainty. If nothing else, their presence in this children's book testifies to how widespread and pervasive they are in popular understandings of the Magi story.

Why They Still Fascinate

Now we come to the end of our exploration of the Magi and their story. We have discussed who they were—or, at least, who Matthew thought they were—and how they have been remembered at various points over the past two thousand years. We have seen them transformed into kings and priests, and we have watched their star morph from a slightly peculiar dot in the sky to Jesus himself. Their story has been used to inspire and encourage but also to foster division and hatred. My hope is that this book has encouraged you to think in new ways about the Magi and the people who have told and retold their story and that you have more questions now than you had when you started. The journey of the Magi through our imaginations is ongoing, and so too should be our quest to understand them. This leads to a final question: Why do they still fascinate?

There is obviously something about the Magi, but what is it? Why does this book exist? Why did you just read it? Why do we see such elaborate storytelling develop around these characters and find nothing remotely similar with, for example, the shepherds who visit Jesus in the Gospel of Luke? The story of the Magi in Matthew strikes a delicate balance between specificity and ambiguity, and these in turn give rise to curiosity and creativity. Matthew says that these visitors were led by a star, but the star in this story does not behave like a normal star. It appears and disappears and comes so low to the ground that it can mark the location of a single person. So what is it supposed to be? What *could* it have been? Does it matter? Matthew could have said that "people" came from the East, but instead, he said that Magi came from the East. There are a few ways to make sense of this choice, but none of them is certain. Perhaps Matthew's choice of this term is illustrative of a first-century fascination with the East and the people who lived there. Perhaps he has in mind a specific type of person. It is also possible that mystery is the goal and that the identity of these visitors is meant to keep readers guessing. If that is the case, then we can all agree that this goal has been accomplished many times over.

I would agree that the intrigue surrounding the Magi is one of the things that has kept these characters at the forefront of our collective imaginations. As they have moved from one era to the next, the relatively nonspecific nature of their identity in Matthew has allowed them to take on the characteristics, hopes, dreams, and ideologies of their readers. Sometimes, this has led to dangerous and violent places where they have been used to promote racial division and to foster Judeophobia. These unfortunate chapters are part of the Magi's story, and we would do well to pay attention to how and why these visitors from the East have been employed for unsavory purposes. While these chapters are part of their story, however, they are not the whole story. The Magi have also been held up as paragons of generosity and self-giving and as challenges to despotic rulers and unjust systems of power. For two thousand years, they have reminded readers that change is possible and that taking a different road home is sometimes the better option. They are, in short, complicated. They evade the categories that we select for them, and they resist our best attempts at tidy interpretations. Unlike the gifts they bear, the Magi cannot be packaged with a neat little bow. Just when we think that we have them deciphered, we find some new way of understanding them. And perhaps this is why they still fascinate. When we look at the Magi—and all the ways they have been understood, misunderstood, and appropriated—perhaps we behold a dynamic complexity that mirrors our own experiences of the world. Perhaps we see in the Magi the profound messiness of human existence and the mystery and beauty so frequently found in it.

Bibliography

Texts and Translations

Aland, Barbara, Kurt Aland, Johannes Karavidopoulos, Carlo M.
Martini, and Bruce M. Metzger, eds. *Novum Testamentum Graece*.
28th ed. Stuttgart, Germany: Deutsche Bibelgesellschaft, 2012.

Burke, Tony, ed. *New Testament Apocrypha: More Noncanonical
Scriptures*. Vol. 2. Grand Rapids, MI: Eerdmans, 2020.

Charlesworth, James H., ed. *The Old Testament Pseudepigrapha*.
2 vols. Garden City, NY: Doubleday, 1983–1985.

Chrysostom, *Homilies on Matthew*. Translated by George Prevost and
M. B. Riddle. In *A Select Library of Nicene and Post-Nicene Fathers
of the Christian Church*, vol. 10, ed. Philip Schaff and Henry Wace.
1886–89.

De Strycker, Émile. *La Forme la plus ancienne du Protévangile de Jacques.* Subsidia Hagiographica 33. Brussels: Société des Bollandistes, 1961.

Ehrman, Bart D. *The Apostolic Fathers.* 2 vols. Loeb Classical Library. Cambridge, MA: Harvard University Press, 2003.

Falls, Thomas B. *Writings of Saint Justin Martyr.* Fathers of the Church 6. Washington, DC: Catholic University of America Press, 1948.

Gijsel, Jan. *Libri de nativitate Mariae: Pseudo-Matthaei Evangelium, textus et commentarius.* Corpus Christianorum Series Apocryphorum 9. Turnhout, Belgium: Brepols, 1997.

Hawk, Brandon. *The Gospel of Pseudo-Matthew and the Nativity of Mary.* Early Christian Apocrypha 8. Eugene, OR: Cascade, 2019.

Henry, O. *The Four Million.* New York: Doubleday Page, 1906.

Hock, Ronald. *The Infancy Gospels of James and Thomas.* Scholars Bible 2. Santa Rosa, CA: Polebridge, 1995.

Kellerman, James A. *Incomplete Commentary on Matthew (Opus imperfectum).* Ancient Christian Texts 1. Downers Grove, IL: InterVarsity Academic, 2010.

Landau, Brent. *The Revelation of the Magi: The Lost Tale of the Wise Men's Journey to Bethlehem.* New York: HarperOne, 2010.

McVey, Kathleen E. *Ephrem the Syrian: Hymns.* Classics of Western Spirituality. New York: Paulist, 1989.

Moore, Christopher. *Lamb: The Gospel according to Biff, Christ's Childhood Pal.* New York: HarperCollins, 2003.

Shakespeare, William. *Hamlet, Prince of Denmark.* Edited by Philip Edwards. Cambridge: Cambridge University Press, 1985.

Shoemaker, Stephen J. *The Life of the Virgin.* New Haven, CT: Yale University Press, 2012.

Taylor, Barbara Brown. *Home by Another Way: A Christmas Story.* Illustrated by Melanie Cataldo. Louisville, KY: Flyaway, 2018.

Terian, Abraham. *The Armenian Gospel of the Infancy.* Oxford: Oxford University Press, 2008.

Tischendorf, Constantin von, ed. *Evangelia Apocrypha, adhibitis plurimus codicibus Graecis et Latinis maximam partem nunc primum consultis atque ineditorum copia insignibus.* 2nd ed. Leipzig, Germany: Mendelssohn, 1876.

van Dyke, Henry. *The Story of the Other Wise Man.* New York: Harper & Brothers, 1896.

Vuong, Lily. *The Protevangelium of James.* Early Christian Apocrypha 7. Eugene, OR: Cascade, 2019.

Studies and Other Works Cited

Ahmadi, Amir. "The *Magoi* and *Daimones* in Column VI of the Derveni Papyrus." *Numen* 61 (2014): 484–508.

Barthel, Peter, and George van Kooten, eds. *The Star of Bethlehem and the Magi: Interdisciplinary Perspectives from Experts on the Ancient Near East, the Greco-Roman World, and Modern Astronomy.* Leiden: Brill, 2015.

Betegh, Gábor. *The Derveni Papyrus: Cosmology, Theology and Interpretation.* Cambridge: Cambridge University Press, 2004.

Bond, Sarah E., and Nyasha Junior. "The Story of the Black King among the Magi." *Hyperallergic*, January 6, 2020. https://hyperallergic.com/535881/the-story-of-the-black-king-among -the-magi/.

Bremmer, Jan N. *Greek Religion and Culture, the Bible and the Ancient Near East.* Jerusalem Studies in Religion and Culture 8. Leiden: Brill, 2008.

Brown, Raymond E. *The Birth of the Messiah: A Commentary on the Infancy Narratives in the Gospels of Matthew and Luke.* Anchor Bible Reference Library. New York: Doubleday, 1993.

Burke, Tony. *Secret Scriptures Revealed: A New Introduction to the Christian Apocrypha.* Grand Rapids, MI: Eerdmans, 2013.

Burnett, D. Clint. *Studying the New Testament through Inscriptions: An Introduction.* Peabody, MA: Hendrickson, 2020.

Carlson, Stephen C. "The Accommodations of Joseph and Mary in Bethlehem: Κατάλυμα in Luke 2.7." *New Testament Studies* 56, no. 3 (2010): 326–342.

Cartlidge, David R., and J. Keith Elliott. *Art and the Christian Apocrypha.* London: Routledge, 2001.

Caspar, Max. *Kepler.* Translated and edited by C. Doris Hellman. New York: Dover, 1959.

Charlesworth, James H. "Who Claimed Herod Was 'the Christ'?" *Eretz-Israel: Archaeological, Historical and Geographical Studies* 31 (2015): 29–39.

Clarke, W. K. Lowther. *Divine Humanity: Doctrinal Essays on New Testament Problems.* London: Society for Promoting Christian Knowledge, 1936.

Cohen, Shaye J. D. *The Beginnings of Jewishness: Boundaries, Varieties, Uncertainties.* Berkeley: University of California Press, 1999.

Davies, W. D., and D. C. Allison. *Matthew 1–7.* International Critical Commentary. London: T&T Clark, 2004.

Deichgräber, Reinhard. *Gotteshymnus und Christushymnus in der frühen Christenheit: Untersuchungen zur Form, Sprache und Stil der frühchristlichen Hymnen.* Studien zur Umwelt des Neuen Testaments 5. Göttingen, Germany: Vandenhoeck & Ruprecht, 1967.

de Jong, Albert. *Traditions of the Magi: Zoroastrianism in Greek and Latin Literature.* Religions in the Graeco-Roman World 133. Leiden: Brill, 1997.

Denzey, Nicola. "A New Star on the Horizon: Astral Christologies and Stellar Debates in Early Christian Discourse." In *Prayer, Magic, and the Stars in the Ancient and Late Antique World,*

Magic in History, edited by Scott Noegel et al., 207–221. University Park: Pennsylvania State University Press, 2003.

Eco, Umberto. *Semiotics and the Philosophy of Language*. Advances in Semiotics. Bloomington: Indiana University Press, 1984.

Floss, Heinrich Joseph. *Dreikönigenbuch: Die Übertragung der hh. Dreikönige von Mailand nach Köln*. Cologne, Germany: DuMont-Schauberg, 1864.

Gilbert, Adrian G. *Magi: The Quest for a Secret Tradition*. London: Bloomsbury, 1996.

Gradel, Ittai. *Emperor Worship and Roman Religion*. Oxford: Clarendon, 2002.

Haelewyck, Jean-Claude. "Le nombre des Rois Mages: Les hésitations de la tradition syriaque." In *Les (Rois) Mages*, edited by Jean-Marc Vercruysse, 25–37. Paris: Artois Presses Université, 2011.

Hagner, Donald A. *Matthew 1–13*. Dallas: Word Books, 1993.

Haines-Eitzen, Kim. *Guardians of Letters: Literacy, Power, and the Transmitters of Early Christian Literature*. Oxford: Oxford University Press, 2000.

Harrington, Daniel. *The Gospel of Matthew*. Sacra Pagina 1. Collegeville, MN: Liturgical, 2007.

Harris, William V. *Ancient Literacy*. Cambridge, MA: Harvard University Press, 1989.

Hawk, Brandon. *Apocrypha for Beginners: A Guide to Understanding and Exploring Scriptures beyond the Bible*. Emeryville, CA: Rockridge, 2021.

Hein, Timothy P. "The First Christian 'Magicians': Early Christian Afterlives of Matthew's Magi (Matt 2:1–12)." PhD diss., University of Edinburgh, 2020.

Horsley, Richard A. *The Liberation of Christmas: The Infancy Narratives in Social Context*. Eugene, OR: Wipf & Stock, 2006.

Hurlbut, Jesse Lyman. *Hurlbut's Life of Christ for Young and Old: A Complete Life of Christ Written in Simple Language, Based on the Gospel Narrative*. Philadelphia: John C. Winston, 1915.

Jensen, Robin Margaret. *Understanding Early Christian Art*. London: Routledge, 2000.

Judaken, Jonathan. Introduction to "Rethinking Anti-Semitism." *American Historical Review* 123, no. 4 (October 2018): 1122–1138.

Kaplan, Paul H. D. *The Rise of the Black Magus in Western Art*. Ann Arbor, MI: UMI Research, 1985.

Keener, Craig. *The Gospel of Matthew: A Socio-rhetorical Commentary*. Grand Rapids, MI: Eerdmans, 2009.

Kelber, Werner. "Jesus and Tradition: Words in Time, Words in Space." In *Imprints, Voiceprints, and Footprints of Memory: Collected Essays of Werner Kelber*, 103–132. Resources for Biblical Study 74. Atlanta: Society of Biblical Literature, 2013.

Kepler, Johannes. *De Stella Nova in Pede Serpentarii*. Prague: Paul Sessius, 1606.

Kirschbaum, Engelbert. "Der Prophet Balaam und die Anbetung der Weisen." *Römische Quartalschrift für christliche Altertumskunde und Kirchengeschichte* 49, no. 3/4 (1954): 129–171.

Kronk, Gary W. *Cometography: A Catalog of Comets*. Vol. 1, *Ancient–1799*. Cambridge: Cambridge University Press, 1999.

Landau, Brent. "Under the Influence (of the Magi): Did Hallucinogens Play a Role in the Inspired Composition of the Pseudepigraphic *Revelation of the Magi?*" In *Fakes, Forgeries, and Fictions: Writing Ancient and Modern Apocrypha: Proceedings from the 2015 York University Christian Apocrypha Symposium*, edited by Tony Burke, 79–94. Eugene, OR: Cascade, 2017.

Law, Timothy Michael. *When God Spoke Greek: The Septuagint and the Making of the Christian Bible*. Oxford: Oxford University Press, 2013.

Longenecker, Dwight. *Mystery of the Magi: The Quest to Identify the Three Wise Men*. Washington, DC: Regnery, 2017.

Luz, Ulrich. *Matthew 1–7: A Commentary on Matthew 1–7*. Hermeneia. Translated by James E. Crouch. Minneapolis: Fortress, 2007.

Mann, C. S. "Epiphany—Wise Men or Charlatans?" *Theology* 61, no. 462 (1958): 495–500.

Mason, Steve. "Jews, Judaeans, Judaizing, Judaism: Problems of Categorization in Ancient History." *Journal for the Study of Judaism* 38, nos. 4–5 (2007): 457–512.

Matthews, Shelly. *The Acts of the Apostles: An Introduction and Study Guide: Taming the Tongues of Fire*. T&T Clark Study Guides to the New Testament. London: T&T Clark, 2017.

McLay, Timothy R. *The OG and Th Versions of Daniel*. Society of Biblical Literature Septuagint and Cognate Studies Series 43. Atlanta: Scholars, 1996.

———. "The Old Greek Translation of Daniel IV–VI and the Formation of the Book of Daniel." *Vetus Testamentum* 55, no. 3 (2005): 304–323.

Metzger, Bruce M. "Names for the Nameless in the New Testament: A Study in the Growth of Christian Tradition." In *Kyriakon: Festschrift Johannes Quasten*, edited by Patrick Granfield and Josef A. Jungmann, 79–99. Münster, Germany: Aschendorff, 1970.

Metzger, Bruce M., and Bart D. Ehrman. *The Text of the New Testament: Its Transmission, Corruption, and Restoration*. 4th ed. Oxford: Oxford University Press, 2005.

Meyers, Eric M., and Mark A. Chancey. *Alexander to Constantine: Archaeology and the Land of the Bible*. Anchor Yale Bible Reference Library 3. New Haven, CT: Yale University Press, 2012.

Molnar, Michael R. *The Star of Bethlehem: The Legacy of the Magi*. New Brunswick, NJ: Rutgers University Press, 1999.

Nongbri, Brent. *Before Religion: A History of a Modern Concept.* New Haven, CT: Yale University Press, 2013.

Novenson, Matthew V. *The Grammar of Messianism: An Ancient Jewish Political Idiom and Its Users.* New York: Oxford University Press, 2017.

Pandey, Nandini B. *The Poetics of Power in Augustan Rome: Latin Poetic Responses to Early Imperial Iconography.* Cambridge: Cambridge University Press, 2018.

Patel, Shaily Shashikant. "Magical Practices and Discourses of Magic in Early Christian Traditions: Jesus, Peter, and Paul." PhD diss., University of North Carolina at Chapel Hill, 2017.

———. "The 'Starhymn' of Ignatius' *Epistle to the Ephesians*: Reappropriation as Polemic." In *Studia Patristica*, edited by Markus Vinzent, vol. 93, 93–104. Leuven, Belgium: Peeters, 2017.

Powell, Mark Allan. *Chasing the Eastern Star: Adventures in Biblical Reader-Response Criticism.* Louisville, KY: Westminster John Knox, 2001.

Ramsey, John T., and A. Lewis Licht. *The Comet of 44 B.C. and Caesar's Funeral Games.* American Philological Association American Classical Studies 39. Atlanta: Scholars, 1997.

Reinhartz, Adele. "The Vanishing Jews of Antiquity." In *Marginalia Ioudaios Forum*, edited by Timothy Michael Law and Charles Halton, 5–10. Los Angeles: Marginalia Review of Books, 2014.

Rose, Jenny. *Zoroastrianism: A Guide for the Perplexed.* London: Continuum, 2011.

Schaefer, Bradley E. "Confluences of Astronomical Spectacles." *Archaeoastronomy* 11 (1989): 91–99.

———. "A Critical Look at the History of Interpreting the Star of Bethlehem in Scientific Literature and Biblical Studies." In *The Star of Bethlehem and the Magi: Interdisciplinary Perspectives from Experts on the Ancient Near East, the Greco-Roman World, and Modern Astronomy*, edited by Peter Barthel and George van Kooten, 85–102. Leiden: Brill, 2015.

Schäfer, Peter. *Judeophobia: Attitudes toward the Jews in the Ancient World*. Cambridge, MA: Harvard University Press, 1997.

Schoedel, William R. *Ignatius of Antioch: A Commentary on the Letters of Ignatius of Antioch*. Hermeneia. Minneapolis: Fortress, 1985.

Taylor, Joan, ed. *Jesus and Brian: Exploring the Historical Jesus and His Times via "Monty Python's Life of Brian."* London: T&T Clark, 2015.

Trexler, Richard C. *The Journey of the Magi: Meanings in History of a Christian Story*. Princeton, NJ: Princeton University Press, 1997.

Tuckerman, Bryant. *Planetary, Lunar, and Solar Positions 601 B.C. to A.D. 1 at Five-Day and Ten-Day Intervals*. Philadelphia: American Philosophical Society, 1962.

Tyson, Joseph B. *Marcion and Luke-Acts: A Defining Struggle*. Columbia: University of South Carolina Press, 2006.

Vanden Eykel, Eric M. *"But Their Faces Were All Looking Up": Author and Reader in the "Protevangelium of James."* Reception of Jesus in the First Three Centuries 1. London: T&T Clark, 2016.

Vermes, Géza. *The True Herod*. London: T&T Clark, 2014.

Vuong, Lily. *Gender and Purity in the Protevangelium of James*. Wissenschaftliche Untersuchungen Zum Neuen Testament 2. Tübingen, Germany: Mohr Siebeck, 2013.

Walsh, Robyn Faith. *The Origins of Early Christian Literature: Contextualizing the New Testament within Greco-Roman Literary Culture*. Cambridge: Cambridge University Press, 2021.

Whitaker, Cord J. *Black Metaphors: How Modern Racism Emerged from Medieval Race-Thinking*. Philadelphia: University of Pennsylvania Press, 2019.

Witakowski, Witold. "The Magi in Ethiopic Tradition." *Aethiopica* 2 (1999): 69–89.

——. "The Magi in Syrian Tradition." In *Malphono w-Rabo d-Malphone: Studies in Honor of Sebastian P. Brock*, edited by George A. Kiraz, 809–843. Piscataway, NJ: Gorgias, 2008.

Index

215

Caesar Augustus, 78, 93–95
Caesarea Maritima, 77, 99n51
canonization process, 109–10
Catacomb of Priscilla, 37–40, 68; Greek
    Chapel, 38–39; Severa, 39
Cave of Treasures, 134–39
Celsus, 149–50
Chaldeans, 51, 53n23, 59, 63
Christ. *See* anointed one
Christian apocrypha, 108–13
Chronicle of Zuqnin, 133n23
Chrysostom, John, 148, 164–68, 175
Cologne, Germany, 105–7, 144
Constantine, 106–7
cultural encyclopedia, 11–14, 41, 48, 53
Cyrus the Great, 54–58, 62, 82, 128

Daniel: book of, 41, 47–53; character, 47,
    49–53, 59, 63, 121, 184
David (king), xvi, 71–73, 75n11, 76–77,
    80, 82–85, 95, 98, 100, 129, 163
Derveni papyrus, 62, 62n34
Diatessaron, 2, 160
Didache, 111
Dreikönigenschrein, 105–7, 144

Elymas. *See* Bar-Jesus
Ephrem the Syrian, 148, 160–64
Epiphany (holiday), 69, 106, 144, 179–81
Eucharist, 162
Eunus, 59
Eve, 6

frankincense. *See* incense
Frederick Barbarossa, 105, 107
fulfillment formulae, 9, 12, 49n18, 74,
    90, 99, 155

Garden of Eden, 128, 130, 135, 137
Gelasian Decree, 111n4
gematria, 72–73
Giotto di Bondone, 87–88
gold, xvi, 34, 97–101, 122–24, 129–30,
    157, 162–63, 172, 175, 191
Gospel of Pseudo-Matthew, 113, 119–24,
    141
Greek Chapel. *See* Catacomb of Priscilla

Halley's Comet, 87–88
Helena, 106–7
Henry, O., 188–91
Herod Antipas, 77, 166
Herod Archelaus, 64n38, 75, 77
Herodotus, 42, 54–55, 57, 59, 61, 64, 98,
    100, 182n1
Herod the Great, xvi, xxi, 3–5, 29,
    33–34, 39n6, 69, 74–75, 77–82,
    84–86, 88, 92, 95–96, 99n51,
    103, 107, 115–17, 120–21,
    126–32, 135, 139, 141, 152,
    156–58, 161–64, 166–67,
    170–71, 173, 175–76, 184–85,
    199–200
Hippocrates, 40–41, 97–98
Hurlbut, Jesse Lyman, 1–6, 14–15

Idumea/Idumean(s), 29, 78–79, 171
Ignatius of Antioch, 117n12, 148–54,
    159–62, 164, 176
incense, xvi, 34, 34n18, 97–101, 122,
    127, 129, 130, 157, 162–63, 172,
    175, 191
Infancy Gospel of Thomas, 110
Irish infancy traditions, 113n6